Corporate Management in a Knowledge-Based Economy

Corporate Management in a Knowledge-Based Economy

Edited by

Gianfranco Zanda

First published 2012 by
PALGRAVE MACMILLAN

Palgrave Macmillan in the UK is an imprint of Macmillan Publishers Limited, registered in England, company number 785998, of Houndmills, Basingstoke, Hampshire RG21 6XS.

Palgrave Macmillan in the US is a division of St Martin's Press LLC, 175 Fifth Avenue, New York, NY 10010.

Palgrave Macmillan is the global academic imprint of the above companies and has companies and representatives throughout the world.

Palgrave® and Macmillan® are registered trademarks in the United States, the United Kingdom, Europe and other countries.

ISBN 978-0-230-29425-7

This book is printed on paper suitable for recycling and made from fully managed and sustained forest sources. Logging, pulping and manufacturing processes are expected to conform to the environmental regulations of the country of origin.

A catalogue record for this book is available from the British Library.

A catalog record for this book is available from the Library of Congress.

10 9 8 7 6 5 4 3 2 1
21 20 19 18 17 16 15 14 13 12

Printed and bound in the United States of America

Contents

Tables and Figures   ix

Notes on Contributors   xi

1   **Company Management: Its Historical
    Evolution**   1
    Gianfranco Zanda
    1.1   Foreword   1
    1.2   Aims and outline of the present work   3

2   **The Period in which Power Is Associated
    with Land Ownership**   8
    Daniela Coluccia
    2.1   The organization of production and consumption
          before feudalism: from the Greek city-state to the
          late Roman period   8
    2.2   The socio-economic system of European peoples
          in the first phase of feudalism
          (8th century to the 10th/11th century)   17
    2.3   The socio-economic system of European peoples in
          the second phase of feudalism (11th century to the
          second half of the 15th century)   21
    2.4   Mercantile capitalism: the European socio-economic
          system from the second half of the 15th century to
          the second half of the 18th century   26

3   **The First Industrial Revolution (c1760–c1870)**   41
    Daniela Coluccia
    3.1   The application of the scientific method to economic,
          social and political problems   41
    3.2   The long, complex and systematic process called
          'the Industrial Revolution'   43
    3.3   The main catalysts of the process   46

4   **The Second Industrial Revolution
    (late 1800s and early 1900s)**   52
    Daniela Coluccia
    4.1   Introduction   52
    4.2   The use of electricity and increase in productivity   53

v

4.3 Technological progress, economic discontinuity, oligopoly and high profitability   54

4.4 The institutionalization of research and development within companies   55

4.5 The growing use of capital. The beginning of mass production and mass consumption and the appearance of large corporations   57

4.6 The development of studies and practices in the field of management   58

5 **The 'Managerial Revolution': The Origin and Growth of Managerial Capitalism (from the 1930s to the End of the 1970s)**   65

Gianfranco Zanda

5.1 The first two decades of the 20th century and the Great War   65

5.2 From the Great War to the Great Economic Crisis   67

5.3 The 'managerial revolution'   71

5.4 The power of non-owner managers in the large corporations   77

5.5 The growing interest of scholars and managers in the decision-making process and human resources management   81

5.6 Managerial motivation and the goals of the corporation: theoretical outlines   89

5.7 The relationship between profitability and increase in company size   95

5.8 The relationship between objectives of social responsibility and rate of profitability and company size development   97

5.9 The 'utility function' of professional managers of dominant large corporations from the 1930s to the appearance of 'financial shareholding managerial capitalism'   98

6 **The Appearance and Establishment of 'Financial Shareholding Managerial Capitalism'**   111

Gianfranco Zanda

6.1 Preliminary remarks   111

6.2 Internal and external crises of economic systems and the fall in profits   113

6.3 The reaffirmation of the principle of the
maximization of profit and of the value of the
company. The return to 'investor capitalism'   119
6.4 Shareholding managerial capitalism based on the
'financialization' of business: some remarks   124
6.5 The problem of irresponsible corporations   126
6.6 The main provisions to adopt   129
6.7 The predominance of the financial economy
over the real economy. Irresponsible behaviour
of global finance and its impact on the recent
economic and financial crisis   135

7 **The Efficient-market Hypothesis (EMH) and
Financial Crisis**   155
Gianluca Oricchio
7.1 Originate-to-distribute and originate-and-hold:
the challenge to the efficient-market
hypothesis begins   155
7.2 Two recent crises and the efficient-market
hypothesis: lessons learnt   158
7.3 The efficient-market hypothesis and accounting
behaviour   160

8 **Control of Intangible Resources and Corporate
Management**   169
Gianfranco Zanda
8.1 Preliminary remarks   169
8.2 The new scientific and technological knowledge   170
8.3 The use of the multimedia network and market
changes   171
8.4 The relationship between the market, the
industrial system and innovative services.
The arrival of the 'light' company based on access
to Internet services and outsourcing   173
8.5 New services in the field of culture and the
development of the 'experience' industry   175
8.6 Changes in marketing in the emerging sectors
of the modern economy   178
8.7 Intangible resources and knowledge as the
strategic factor of corporate management   181

9 Ethical Foundations of Corporate Social
   Responsibility. The Contribution of Christian Social
   Thought   189
   Helen Alford
   9.1 The problematic link between ethics and CSR,
        and what the Christian social tradition can
        offer to help   189
   9.2 The idea of the human being as both individual
        and person   194
   9.3 The idea of society as a common good with both
        foundational and excellent dimensions   202
   9.4 CSR and the personalist approach: can the latter
        give the former a more solid ethical footing?   207

10 Patterns of Management and Their Influence on Business
    Behaviour   212
    Silvia Solimene
    10.1 Preliminary remarks   212
    10.2 Organizational entropy and leadership models   215
    10.3 The traditional approach to leadership   219
    10.4 Towards new management models   224
    10.5 Effective models of management: basic assumptions   225
    10.6 Research, recruiting, training, personnel development
          and their influence on the company system   229
    10.7 Final considerations   232

11 Summary and Closing Remarks   237
    Gianfranco Zanda

Bibliography   245

Index   258

Tables and Figures

Tables

7.1 Cumulative losses and cumulative capital increases of main
    international quoted credit institutions in billions of euros
    (2009)   159
7.2 Four different 'situations'   167
9.1 The individual–person duality   198

Figures

5.1 Rate of growth and rate of profitability   97
5.2 Rate of growth and rate of profitability (modified)   100
7.1 Credit spreads before the financial crisis   156
7.2 Credit spreads during the financial crisis   157
7.3 Credit Treasury high level business model   158
7.4 Hard-to-value assets (2009)   160
7.5 The smaller the earnings volatility, other conditions being
    equal, the higher the price of shares   163
7.6 The higher the earnings volatility, other conditions being
    equal, the lower the price of shares   164
7.7 Linear relation between share price variation and future
    earning variation, other conditions being equal, in a
    simplified framework   165
7.8 Future earnings increments that are considered to be
    permanent have a linear impact on share price; future
    earnings increments that are not considered permanent
    have less impact on share price   166
7.9 Future earnings negative variations that are considered
    to be permanent have a linear impact on share price;
    future earnings negative variation that are not considered
    permanent have less impact on share price   166

7.10   The theoretical relation vs. the empirical relation between the level of future earnings variations and the impact on market capitalization   167

10.1   Effective and efficient company behaviour   218

Notes on Contributors

Gianfranco Zanda has held senior corporate management positions at several global institutions for more than 40 years. He is Full Professor of Corporate Management at Sapienza University of Rome. He has written several books on corporate management, human capital, business valuation and advanced accounting.

Helen Alford is Dean of the Faculty of Social Sciences at the Pontifical University of Saint Thomas (the 'Angelicum') and Director of the Masters programme in Management and Corporate Social Responsibility there. She is co-author, with Michael Naughton, of *Managing as If Faith Mattered* (UNDP 2001) and directs a multi-centre, multi-year research project on 'Ethics and Corporate Social Responsibility'.

Gianluca Oricchio has held senior capital and risk management positions at several global financial institutions for more than 20 years. He has been Head of ACPM at Capitalia Banking Group and Head of Group Credit Treasury at Unicredit Group. Mr Oricchio has written several books on financial markets, corporate finance and risk management. He is Professor of Finance and Capital Markets at CBM University of Rome.

Daniela Coluccia, PhD, is an assistant professor of Accounting and Mergers and Acquisitions at Sapienza University of Rome. She has written several books and papers on intangible assets, accounting and corporate finance.

Silvia Solimene, PhD, is an assistant professor of Accounting at Sapienza Univerity of Rome. She has written several books and papers on organizational behaviour and corporate management.

1
Company Management: Its Historical Evolution

Gianfranco Zanda

1.1 Foreword

An economic system is the organization that societies, in a particular time and place, have developed to solve common problems regarding the production and consumption of goods and services in order to satisfy their needs. This organization, naturally, gives rise to social relationships that are more or less close and stable.

The organization of production and consumption has taken different forms according to the period in history and the geographical location concerned. Gradually, as organizations become stronger and more incisive, the social relationships between the forces of production and consumption stabilize, to create situations in which they become 'institutionalized'. However, this is always a temporary, relative stability, since social relationships of production and consumption and the organization in which they are expressed change slowly but progressively. These changes take place in relation to a complex system of phenomena that are connected to the evolution of the needs, aspirations and will of people. In a particular human context, the factors that tend towards the development of uniformity in behaviour and lifestyle finally create new social institutions. The changes in these institutions and their duration are closely linked to their capacity to satisfy people's developing needs and to the extent that they are considered preeminent. Needs are a deciding factor in bringing about change in the organization of the social relationships of production and consumption and the creation of new forms of behaviour, new institutions and new economic systems.

Economic systems, in the course of history, have revolved around two fundamental institutions: a) firms; and b) the political system which

1

influences the objectives, values and organization of society as a whole and therefore also the behaviour of firms, which have the responsibility of finding solutions to economic problems.

It is known that the firm is a socio-economic institution that has the function of producing goods and services in order to meet the needs of people. The firm consists of a system of people (organization), coordinated goods (capital or assets) and a system of functions (operational activities and management).[1] Therefore, the firm is a coordinated entity of complementary elements: that is, it is an organized combination of factors of production, which, in terms of the traditions of classical economics, can be classified as land, capital and labour. The firm is further qualified by the characteristics of continuity and independence, in the sense that it is destined to continue in time and to operate in spite of the mobility of the factors of production.[2] In other words, with time, the people change and are replaced, as are goods and management, but the entity continues to exist, on condition that it satisfies the requirements of a lasting economic and financial equilibrium.[3] The combination of these factors, and above all the relationship between the factors of production in terms of cooperation and power, have changed in the course of history, resulting in various configurations of firms. However the firm has remained the instrument through which production and consumption, for the satisfaction of human needs, have been organized.[4]

The second institution that influences economic systems is the ruling political system. It establishes the values and the basic strategies of society as a whole and affects the organization of production and consumption as well as the behaviour of firms. The political system is a reflection of the nucleus that holds power and that consequently strongly influences, with varying degrees of stability, who holds positions of power within society and in firms. It decides who defines the social relationships of production and consumption and who decides what firms can and must do and what things they cannot do. It also decides who determines the procedures by which the particular interests of firms must be integrated with and tempered by the wider interests of the community and the expectations of the various internal groups that have an interest in the conduct and results of firms. But political systems are also pervaded by change. They experience renewal and modifications that can be slow or sudden and unexpected. This produces important consequences for social and economic relationships and for the structure and operation of firms.

The question of power in society and in firms has been analysed from various points of view by historians and scholars of politics, economics, sociology and ethics. All have underlined the historical dynamism and evolution of institutions. Some scholars have found that the owners of the factors of production, land, capital and labour, have aspired, at various times in history, to enlarge their 'room for manoeuvre', expanding their sphere of influence in society and to the system of production. They have also pointed out that power is exercised by those who control the most important (strategic) factors of production of the moment. They have also shown that a change in the importance of a production factor with time causes a shift in power from that factor to another. Finally, they have predicted that, given the changing importance of factors of production, future shifts of power in society and in firms may occur. In summary, in the course of history, everything seems to be in movement. It is therefore very important to interpret such movement and explain in a rational and convincing way what circumstances and phenomena cause change and foresee the meaning and tendency of its future evolution.

In order to understand the causes that have conferred power on different factors of production, it is indispensable to study the question by observing and interpreting the historical facts with the help of adequate bibliographical support. As J. A. Schumpeter[5] explains, it is not possible to adequately understand the economic factors of any period without a good command of the historical facts and without a valid supporting historical guide.

1.2   Aims and outline of the present work

This work will consider the following phenomena:

a)   the exercise of power in society and in firms by landowners. The analysis will be limited to the illustration of the following fundamental aspects and moments:

- the organization of production and consumption in the period preceding the onset of feudalism;
- the European socio-economic system in the first phase of feudalism from the 8th century until the year 1000. In this period, production is effectively developed in rural areas, with the labour of the family satisfying the needs of the family itself. The activity is organized on the estates of the great landlords and on the *mansi servili*. At this time the life of cities tends to decline;
- the socio-economic system in Europe in the second phase of feudalism that lasted until about 1450. In this period, the creation of wealth is still strongly based on agriculture, but a series of conditions

favour the production of a surplus from the lands and estates of land-lords. This surplus leads to exchange between the country and the villages and cities. Cities establish themselves as centres of culture, manufactured production and commercial activity based on money;
- the European socio-economic system based on mercantile capitalism, which lasts until well into the second half of the 18th century. In this period, both local and international commerce are developed. The capitalist merchant and the banker both belong to this period. The market emerges from the shadows of feudalism. Merchants achieve positions of power within the community. Land now becomes abundant as a result of the discovery of new geographical areas and land as a factor of production slowly declines. This is the period in which city-states and modern states are established. There is a massive increase in prices due to the coining of imported metal, especially silver. In this period the belief that the wealth of individuals, firms and the State can be developed by the accumulation of money starts to spread. Merchants in search of privileges and monopolies make use of anonymous limited companies;

b)   the First Industrial Revolution. This coincides with the use of steam in industrial machines and with the development and application of new technologies to production processes. However, technology means the investment of capital and so, very soon, capital (in its various technical and financial forms) begins to assert its superiority and the land factor begins to decline. Power, in society as a whole and in firms, tends to pass from large landowners to industrial capitalists;

c)   the Second Industrial Revolution. This takes place between the final decades of the 19th century and the first decades of the 20th century with the use of electrical power. It is now possible to use more advanced technologies systematically in the various sectors of industry. Research and development becomes institutionalized within enterprises which also become larger, together with markets. These conditions result in the emergence of mass production and mass consumption;

d)   scientific impact on the activity of managers of enterprises and the 'managerial revolution'. This complex phenomenon began to progressively take root, especially in the United States of America in the first half of the 20th century. Technological progress, market dynamism, considerable competition and the development of organizations composed of highly qualified specialists created demand for a scientifically qualified and professional executive. Managerial know-how became the strategic factor of production of large firms. On the other hand, capital by this time tended to be readily available and not all the savings produced could be automatically reinvested in some form of production. Also, land even became abundant because in more advanced countries, agricultural earnings represented a modest percentage of total income. A direct consequence of these developments was the creation of the conditions for the onset of managerial capitalism, in which, very often, the management of enterprises was exclusively in the hands of executives whose relationship with the company was not through capital invested but by a work contract;

e)   'financial shareholding managerial capitalism'. Between the mid-1960s and the end of the 1980s, there was a considerable fall in profits due to the development of a system of political and social conditions. This stimulated the establishment of the theory of the maximization of profits and of the value of corporate stock in the management of enterprises, above all in the USA, Great Britain, Germany and France. There was an 'awakening' of owners (especially institutional investors) and strong conditioning of the activity of the professional manager. It is according to this background that so-called 'financial shareholding managerial capitalism' originated, accompanied by a series of important economic and social phenomena. In particular, it became an absolute necessity for large corporations to apply the principle of the maximization of profit and the economic value of firms from a short-term point of view. In addition, the focus on financial issues in company management tended to prevail over the production of goods and services, that is, the real economy. Operations were increasingly characterized by speculative intention instead of typically entrepreneurial behaviour. From the beginning of the 1990s a new kind of enterprise, the so-called irresponsible corporation, made its appearance on the economic scene. These companies pursued their objective of the maximization of profits and share value unrelentingly, without taking into consideration the values, interests or aspirations of the other stakeholders;

f)   the need to control intangible assets to manage enterprises effectively. In the last two decades of the 20th century, management skills have become strategic, together with new types of knowledge in the fields of telecommunications, information technology, microelectronics, artificial materials, robotics and biotechnologies, which will probably have an important impact on the exercise of power in society and in corporations. Markets have become global and have transformed into a multimedia network. The market and the production of cultural goods and services have developed rapidly. The power of management appears to be increasingly linked to the possibility to control of production of, and access to, this new knowledge.[6]

This work aims to analyse the phenomena that, in the course of time, have conferred power in the management of organizations to different factors of production (land, capital, labour, knowledge). Therefore the factors that have contributed to the birth and evolution of the various economic systems will be studied: from the economy based on the power of landowners, to industrial capitalism, to managerial capitalism and finally the present financial shareholding managerial capitalism. In particular, the utility function (preference function) of those who have held power in the management of enterprises in each period of history will be analysed.

Special attention will be given to the theory of the behaviour of companies within the framework of managerial capitalism (between 1930 and 1970). This topic is still in need of further investigation.

Our intention is also to understand the aims and operation of financial shareholding managerial capitalism, which established itself between the end of the 1960s and the beginning of the 1980s. Therefore it is necessary to analyse the behaviour of large corporations. This examination will also identify the links between the arrival of financial shareholding managerial capitalism and the appearance of the large, irresponsible corporation characterized by a culture that is not inspired by high ethical principles. This culture does not allow managers to consider interests and values of stakeholders different from those of the shareholders with the controlling interest. Our research will also extend to the irresponsible behaviour of the global financial system and to the relationships with the present economic and financial crisis. Suggestions will be made on how to deal with the various problems considered.

Finally, another fundamental aim of our work is to analyse the impact of the knowledge revolution and the birth of intellectual capitalism on the behaviour of large corporations. We will examine the influence of the knowledge revolution on the 'utility function' of managers, in order to see how far profit will continue to be the driving force of the economic system and to what extent and in what ways entrepreneurial behaviour will be inspired by ethics and social responsibility. This subject will be discussed in more detail in the following pages in order to identify the principles which should guide modern enterprises and to outline the patterns of management which can simultaneousiy satisfy the interests of companies and the needs of those who work inside organizations. Also, we will examine whether the financial shareholding managerial capitalism system is moving towards its decline as a direct result of 'intellectual capitalism', which seems to be oriented towards producing a new cultural, economic and social order.

Notes

1. Onida (1971), pp. 3–4; Zanda (2006, Chapter 2).
2. Viganò (1997), pp. 1–32.
3. The principle of the continuity of the corporate system in the presence of variations in both the environment as well as in production factors is particularly emphasized by Onida (1971), pp. 4–5 and 39–54.
4. '[. . .] Whatever the political system that the country has adopted, whatever the manner in which the tasks are distributed between the State and the private sector concerning the production of goods and services, whatever the degree of collabouration between them in the management of social services, the organizational instrument through which production is realized, is the "firm". Whether the State produces, whether the private sector produces, whether they both produce together, the instrument utilized is always the same; this instrument is the "firm", which is an organization center for the systematic production of goods and services' (Capaldo 2008, p. 18).
5. Schumpeter (1954), Chapter 1.
6. Laghi (2001), pp. 7–66.

2
The Period in which Power Is Associated with Land Ownership

Daniela Coluccia

2.1 The organization of production and consumption before feudalism: from the Greek city-state to the late Roman period

In economies in which agricultural wealth has an impact of over 95 per cent of available internal production, it is natural that the land is the dominant factor in the production combination and in consumption. Land – at least up to the onset of mercantile capitalism – was undoubtedly the scarcest production factor, and the most difficult to obtain, increase or replace. It was, in short, the strategic production factor and therefore it was given a very high utility rating.[1]

The economic systems of the period made use of relatively small quantities of capital. Labour was abundant, easy to find and cheap, because at least some work could be done by slaves. For these reasons, the ownership of land permitted the exercise of considerable power in firms and in society as a whole. It was very important to be able to control land or alternatively capital or labour. The availability of land facilitated control of the other factors of production as well as offering the opportunity to reach the top of the social and political hierarchy and consequently to exercise authority. The availability of capital or the ability to control a large labour force did not offer any of these possibilities. In essence, not to possess land meant being in the lower social ranks or on the margins of society. A passage from Homer illustrates this point: 'Ulysses visits Hades. He meets the ghost of Achilles and asks how things were for him among the dead. The reply is extremely bitter: rather than be lord of all the dead, says Achilles, I would prefer to be a *thete* [serf or menial] . . . For Achilles, therefore, the most humble social condition was not that of a slave but that of a *thete* without land [. . .]; the *thetes* were free men.

The swineherd, Eumeo, was a slave but he had a more secure position because he was connected to an *oikos*, a princely household.'[2]

The dawn of the Aegean-European civilization took place in Crete and in that which A. J. Evans (1851–1941) defines as the Minoan civilization. This was the cradle of the Mycenaean civilization that flourished in about 1500 BC in Argolis (Peloponnesia).[3] The Minoan civilization (which is a little later than the Egyptian-Memphis and the Mesapotamian-Sumerian civilizations) is based, in the opinion of Melis,[4] on an agricultural and pastoral way of life. In fact, the economic activity of Crete was substantially based on agriculture and on the breeding of livestock, even if activities such as metallurgy and shipbuilding began to appear. Step by step, a craft industry for the manufacture of tools also developed and, with time, agricultural production began to be the source of export. But even at the highest point of its splendour, Crete was a civilization in which work activities and power in society and in firms were strongly linked to land.

If we consider ancient Greek civilization from the prehistoric period to the beginning of the Christian era, it must be admitted that at its base there was an economic system that 'developed passing from the eminently pastoral stage of the third and second millennia BC to the agricultural-pastoral stage of the Homeric era, to the agricultural-manufacturing-commercial stage of the 6th–5th centuries, to arrive at the apex under Alexander the Great and then begin its slow, and later, fast decline'.[5] However, even in its period of maximum splendour, agriculture and the ownership of land were pre-eminent in the sphere of production and socio-economic relationships.[6] The Greeks, in general, recognized private ownership of land and did everything to regulate and protect this right, with the aim of preventing its concentration. Small landowners directly cultivated their smallholdings while large landowners used slaves and the free labour of dependent personnel. The crop-sharing system was widespread, as was the long-term rent contract 'especially for the territories belonging to the sovereign or the temples, with rents in kind or in money and with improvement clauses'.[7] The technical capital used in agriculture was not very important and the related productivity of labour improved only with daily experience. Furthermore, agriculture supplied the raw material for the production of consumer goods in rural areas and for the manufacturing activity that was carried out in the cities. Complementing agricultural activity was that of mining to extract silver, copper and zinc (for brass), lead and iron.

In the Greek world, manufacturing was slowly developed over the course of the centuries. This included metallurgy, arms, textile products, ceramics and perfumes. Before 1000 BC, economic activity was – with some exceptions – characterized by subsistence production. It was, in other words, agriculture for personal use on a domestic basis, which had very little to do with markets. Later, production became organized in craft industries such as handicrafts, which became increasingly specialized, established in cities and often employed considerable numbers of labourers (primarily slaves) in workshops, construction sites and mines. Thus firms similar to present-day small manufacturing companies were born.

'The colonization of the 8th century [BC], the introduction of money in the 7th century and the progress made in agriculture and manufacturing in the 6th century, created the pre-conditions for more intense commercial activity. Development of this activity went hand in hand with the enlarging sphere of cultural and political influence of Greek cities.'[8] Money only replaced barter[9] to a small extent. Even at its socio-economic height, the Greek world continued to be characterized by the pre-eminence of agriculture and a relatively low use of capital among the factors of manufacturing production. The State regulated manufacturing and commerce. Weights and measures were standardized, prices and contracts were controlled and customs duty was imposed on imported and exported goods, while particular limits were also placed on the circulation of goods in internal markets.

Civil life was organized in the city-state and gave rise to a variety of associations – alliances to satisfy the need for defence and economic collaboration. These leagues of Greek cities could be considered almost as supra-regional economic and political entities. Of great importance between the 8th and the 6th centuries BC was the expansion in the Mediterranean with the establishment of flourishing colonies in Africa, Asia and southern Italy. This favoured the increase of commercial relations and the accumulation of wealth. Internal markets developed, as did international commerce. This stimulated the art of trading and the construction techniques of merchant vessels and warships[10] and allowed the Greek city-states and their colonies to control the maritime routes that had previously been under the dominance of Phoenician navigators and merchants, at least until the death of Alexander the Great (322 BC).

The Greek world seemed to place its full trust in hedonism and private property, which drove progress and ensured development and the adequate functioning of the economy. In the opinion of Aristotle, the institution of private property generated happiness, self-esteem and allowed people to satisfy their need for freedom.[11]

Other Greek ideals in the field of economics concerned the moral superiority of agricultural labour and the necessity of philosophers (through their thought) and politicians (through laws) to intervene to create an economic order that responded to the standards of justice, truth and rationality. In the view of these ideals, freedom – it would seem – does not produce a morally desirable and satisfying economic order. Economics is included in the area of ethics. Judgments on slavery, on loans attracting interest, the reconciliation of public and private interests, on the relationship between the price of goods and their utility are inspired by and conform to the morals and the ethical and political aims of the most important citizens, who hold power and guide the life of the State. Naturally these norms, because they reflected the political and moral values of those who formulated them, were clearly destined to change in the course of time.[12]

The intense struggle to achieve wealth and power in Greek society, it has been said, was tempered by philosophers and statesmen who established the rules for living together (social morals) and tended to neutralize the limitless appetites of individuals that led to social degradation. The greater the number of philosophers and politicians who were capable of guiding the behaviour of individuals towards what is good for the whole community, through good personal example, the faster the State could take the path to socio-economic progress.

With the Roman conquest of Greece, from the economic point of view[13] it could be said that Rome inherited the following:

- an ample, essentially unified economic and commercial community, concentrated on the Mediterranean that also had practical relations with non-coastal countries of Asia and Africa;
- a sound knowledge of maritime and land routes in these areas; a large, explored and tested market;
- an economic system mainly based on agriculture, but already oriented towards commerce and manufacture;
- an economic territory in which both an economic system based on money and on the first forms of credit are present as well as a number of operators who had begun to acquire awareness of the risks connected to production and to commercial transactions. This system is certainly not a capitalist system, but it was an economic order that contained some interesting seeds that would in future characterize entrepreneurial systems based on capital and on production for exchange in the market.[14]

Now we must briefly describe the economic system that characterized the rise and then the decadence of Rome.

Rome succeeded in unifying the Mediterranean from the economic and political points of view, also as a result of what had already been done in these fields by the Etruscans and by the Greek city-states and Greek colonies (800–600 BC) in Italy, in the Orient and in Africa. The Etruscans, starting from the 8th century BC, integrated their cities and their agriculture into the system of trade with neighbouring populations and, more generally, in the Mediterranean area.

The economic and political union of the Mediterranean was already clearly visible under Emperor Augustus and was completed in the first two centuries of the Christian era. In essence, it could be said that this union was completed by the time of the death of Marcus Aurelius (180 AD).

Regarding the unification of the Mediterranean area, between the 8th and 4th centuries BC, Rome adapted to the supremacy of the Carthaginians in the west and of the Greeks in the east. Then, after the peninsular era (concentrated especially in Italy), the Mediterranean era began, based on the principles of the open sea and freedom of trade:[15]

> [. . .] in three centuries, from the 3rd to 1st century BC, regional divisions were merged into a compact unit; for three centuries, from the 1st to 3rd centuries AD, Rome strengthened and conserved the unity it had achieved with great effort and then in the following two centuries (4th and 5th AD), it made every attempt to oppose the destruction of its most admirable achievement: the political and economic unification of the Mediterranean market.[16]

If we consider the period from the end of the Punic Wars (146 BC) to the full establishment of Christianity (the 4th century of the Christian era), the economic ideals of the Romans could be summarized as follows:[17]

- the nobles, in particular those that were oriented towards a political career, aspired to owning land and they did not start any activity that was not agricultural or not closely connected to agriculture because they thought it was not convenient. Included in this category were senators who made up the class of the *optimates*, and those that controlled the State and magistrates' positions, thanks to the role they played and their ownership of immense landed estates in all the locations of the Empire;
- only a small minority of citizens that held executive office in society occupied themselves with manufacture and merchandise. But these citizens were not considered role models to be emulated and for a

long time they lived in a situation of moral inferiority compared to the nobles of senatorial rank. This small minority of citizens included the knights (*equites*), who had the possibility to enrich themselves by becoming judges and especially through business activities. They were, in fact, entrepreneurs, merchants, contractors, speculators, arms suppliers, and so on;

- the plebs, for a long period of time, clung to the ideals of the nobles and disdained the work of industry and commerce as well as any kind of manual work; later on, because of the opportunities offered by the economic life of the times, they began to understand that work was a fundamental means of satisfying their needs and achieving improvement in status, wealth and power;
- finally, there was the class of slaves for whom work was their entire life.[18] For them, work was the means by which to obtain (in exchange for loyalty and productive service to the slave owner) or buy their freedom.[19] They were the ones, together with a section of the plebs, that played an important role in the progress of operative technologies, largely because many of them were educated and were experts in various arts and professions;
- nobles, knights and plebs all aspired to a life of pleasure and relaxation, even if the plebs, in reality, could not put such an idea of life into practice. Knights and plebs constituted the *populares* party that tried to oppose the power of the *optimates*.

From the point of view of the economic activity and the social structure of the times, the following should be noted. Agricultural activity was always decidedly pre-eminent and was surrounded by an aura of superiority and therefore respectability.[20] Manufacturing gained a foothold with time, but it did not reach the point of creating a system of industrial production that utilized capital to any considerable extent. Work in the city and in the country was in part free and in part servile. Free labour was concentrated in the class of independent farm owners in the country and craftsmen in the city. Menial labour in the city and in the country was carried out in the largest firms. Both farmers and poor citizens, who were kept in a state of freedom and available for military service, constantly requested provisions that cancelled their debts and redistributed land.[21]

Trade was facilitated and stimulated in the whole of the Empire because of the admirable construction of a system of roads that united Europe, Asia and Africa to Rome. On these roads, 'the imperial administration organized a specially reserved postal service that was able to transport people and dispatches at a speed of eight kilometers an hour'.[22] Maritime commerce prospered because of the existence of known and trusted maritime routes, a constantly improving system of commerce and careful military vigilance on the seas.

The goods produced by Rome and Italy were not sufficient to satisfy the standard of living of Romans, especially on account of the grandiose investments in public works, luxurious buildings and public exhibitions and the high costs of assisting the large masses of poor that lived in Rome with the distribution of cereals.[23] It was therefore necessary to have massive imports from the provinces (France, Britain, Greece, Asia Minor, Egypt, Romania, Spain, and others) to satisfy the needs of Rome. The balance of payments was in equilibrium or even in Rome's favour but only because of the taxes imposed, the spoils of war and the earnings of the knights.[24] This situation proved to be enormously negative when it was no longer possible for Romans to continue to count on a predatory economy based on political dominance rather than on free trade, because new forces began to appear on the outskirts of the Empire and these forces revealed that the Italian peninsula had significant deficits in its balance of payments.

At the beginning of the Empire, Roman society was organized, as we have seen, according to the following hierarchy: the imperial family; the senatorial class; the class of knights (the equestrian class); the middle class and the plebs; the slaves.[25]

The size of each social class varied, naturally, from kingdom to kingdom and between the city and the country. Free workers were independent from the imperial family, the senatorial class and the knights, all of whom made use of slave labour to carry out their activities.

The peak of Rome's expansion arrived with the end of the rule of Marcus Aurelius (180 AD). At this point, a phase of defence of the conquests began, to ward off external forces that were exerting pressure on the borders of the empire. During this phase there began a gradual decline that became acute in the 3rd century and finished with the total dissolution of the political and economic unity of the Empire in the following century.[26]

The causes of the slow but unrelenting crisis of the Empire were numerous and systematic. They can be summarized as follows:[27]

a)   starting from the 3rd century AD, a profound political crisis decisively undermined the authority of the central power and its capacity to coordinate and unify the Empire. As a direct consequence, the political and economic peculiarities of the provinces developed and the initiatives and the resistance movements of certain non-Mediterranean populations – known as '*barbari*' [barbarians] – were encouraged by the crisis. The rule of the State passed successively to many leaders who governed for brief periods of time. Diocletian (284–305) and Constantine (306–337) both made every effort to avert the end of the Empire: they faced up to the weakening of political unity and the stability of government by introducing necessary fiscal measures for the survival of the central power (in spite of the fact that an important tax evasion movement had developed), and by reorganizing the army, the administration and transport.[28] They both attempted to develop religious unity: Diocletian by persecuting Christians (starting from the Edict of Nicomedia in 308 AD) and Constantine, by conceding religious freedom to Christians (313 AD) and later by making Christianity the official religion.[29] The efforts of the two great emperors (to whom the Emperor Theodosius, who ruled at the end of the 4th century, must also be added), only served to delay the process of decline of the Empire. The inadequacy of the central political power was probably also a result of the incapacity to generate social change to involve the best citizens in the process of government. The noble class was too individualistic and selfish and in favour of a predatory form of government with regard to the subjects of Rome and the provinces. Social mobility upwards or downwards between social classes was blocked and very repressive fiscal and administrative measures (such as the obligatory and hereditary nature of certain professions, the prohibition of abandoning the city to seek refuge in the country) made the social structure rigid and generated a good deal of resentment. To all this must be added the creation of professional colleges and the spread of Christian ideas according to which: 1) men of privilege by divine law and men destined to obey do not exist. People are all equal; 2) all work, including manual work, has equal dignity within the social organization; 3) the blind search for riches is in conflict with gaining eternal life and is contrary to a peaceful and just human society: therefore just prices, just interests and just salaries exist; the laws of men must introduce these concepts into the economic world.[30] The political inability to coordinate and unify the Empire was probably also linked to the total dependence of Rome on its provinces: the balance of trade was decidedly in the red. The problem was further aggravated both because Rome was not a centre of technological development and because the fiscal system no longer succeeded in securing the revenue that was indispensable for the maintenance of the army and the public administration;[31]

b)   also in the 3rd century, the demographic crisis, which had begun to make its effects felt in the 1st century BC, deepened. There was depopulation of cities,[32] regression of industry and commerce, the progressive reduction of cultivated land and the isolation of the country from the city. Since the wars fought were less numerous and there were fewer spoils of war available, the number of slaves diminished[33] and therefore attempts were made to use the free plebs and introduce particular measures such as the declaration of the obligatory and hereditary nature of certain professions;[34]

c) the political and demographic crises that were covered in points a) and b) had direct repercussions on the economy: uncultivated land increased, agricultural production decreased; the economic organization changed; manufacture and commerce contracted; money increasingly lost value; the number of city markets was reduced; people migrated to the country, thereby restoring the self-sufficient rural economy that tends to be closed,[35] to the disadvantage of the city economy. The escape to the country was also driven by the desire not to succumb to the exorbitant requests for taxes. The unified market broke down and was divided into a number of independent areas that tended to self-sufficiency and non-specialized production. The appearance of these local autarchies and the increase in the ruralization of the economy were the undeniable signs of feudalism. Or better, they represented the 'preparation for the Middle Ages'.[36]

Half-way through the 5th century AD, the process described above was practically completed, in spite of the fact that West and East continued to communicate. The final dissolution of the Empire and the end of communications between West and East are connected both to the action of the barbarians, who formally split the Empire, as well as to the creation by the Arabs of 'a political and religious barrier between the two basins of the Mediterranean, the eastern and the western'.[37] The barbarian kingdoms, up to the end of the 8th century, were unable to make improvements to the socio-economic system of the Mediterranean. The Arab expansion had considerable influence, both good and bad. Both these influences did not substantially modify the socio-economic system of the European peoples, which tended to be based on agriculture and on the ownership of land for personal use, also because the commercial relationships between the Christian and Muslim worlds had become more difficult and rather rare.[38]

In the period in which the western Roman Empire fell, the ancient world ceased to exist and the Roman-barbarian kingdoms gained importance. However, the production factor on which power in society and in enterprises centred was undoubtedly the ownership of land, which was more difficult to find and was therefore the strategic element. Here is an example of the importance of the land factor. At the end of this period the eastern Empire was reorganized by Heraclius (610–641 AD), also in order to ward off external attacks by the Persians. Heraclius divided the territory into administrative constituencies called '*temi*' and at the head of each he placed a military commander. Soldiers and settler/farmers were permanently posted to each constituency and free and full ownership of the land was conferred on them, as land was considered a highly desirable good and endowed with almost sacred properties.[39]

2.2 The socio-economic system of European peoples in the first phase of feudalism (8th century to the 10th/11th century)

The signs of change, which characterized the breakdown of the ancient world, constituted the humus on which a new mentality that gave birth to the medieval world developed.

Medieval civilization was the result of the fusion of three elements: Christianity, Roman culture and the Germanic tradition. It was the Germanic tradition in particular that contributed the phenomenon of the protection of small farmers by large landowners, and gave positive merit to the tie of 'personal loyalty' between individuals having different degrees of power in society.

Interpreted in positive terms – and not limiting the matter to a simple comparison and search for unequivocal indicators of discontinuity with regard to past epochs and epochs that followed – the Middle Ages appear, from some points of view, to be singular and innovative. This is true in the field of culture (considerable development in the study of philosophy and the creation of large universities starting from the 12th century), of art (the appearance of the Roman and Gothic styles), of institutions (the development of the conditions for the development of national monarchies) and of religion (a period of indisputable faith and of misleading superstitions).[40]

Traditional historians divide the Middle Ages into the Early Middle Ages (the period that goes from about 6th century up to 11th century) and the Late Middle Ages (that goes up to the 15th century).[41]

The Early Middle Ages begin with the process of degradation of Europe which came about under barbarian rulers (especially in the 5th–7th centuries). Between the second half of the 8th century and the first half of the 9th century, there was a limited political and cultural resurgence in central-western Europe by the Carolingian Franks who presented themselves as the true heirs of the Romans, especially because of their privileged relationship with the Roman church.[42] In the years from 850 to 1000/1100, the breakdown of the Carolingian Empire occurred and the result was feudal anarchy. Also in this period there were attempts made to reunite the regions of central-western Europe under the influence of two powers: that of the Pope and that of the Emperor.

Feudalism is based on the *commendatio* of the late Roman period. In order to receive physical protection as well as protection against the exorbitant demands of the public authorities in terms of tax or military service, an individual placed himself under the protection of a powerful person (*potens*) to whom he conceded his personal property (if he had any) and/or service and payment in kind. This pact had no official value and was frowned upon by States. Normally, the powerful party was a large landowner and those who entrusted themselves to his protection were small landowners, who, thereafter, became employees or tenants.

In the main Roman-barbarian kingdoms, the protection mechanism between a *potens* and the person protected took various forms depending on the practices and customs of the ruling conquerors. As is well known, in the kingdom of the Longobards, the authority of the king was exercised, with the purpose of controlling the territory, through dukes (within the various dukedoms) who were military leaders. The sovereign also had the services of the *gastaldi*, who were officials who carried out administrative and judiciary functions.

The methods of acquiring land – this pre-eminent instrument of production and social power – were variable: ranging from wars to confiscation, from expropriation to redistribution.

In the Early Middle Ages, the property held with full title of ownership by the king, the dukes (and by the persons faithful to them), by the monasteries and dioceses were called *allodiali* property. The property that was held as a title of concession of variable duration was usually designated by the title of *beneficium*, to underline the services rendered to the authority granting the concession.

In Gaul, under the Merovingian kings (between 500 and 750), the king bound to himself certain *potentes* who were faithful to him, in order to control the territory.[43] These *potentes* declared themselves the king's men. To them, the king granted the benefit of vast areas of land for a time, normally for the lifetime of the beneficiary. This is how the feudal relationship between lord and vassal[44] was born. The Carolingian kings used this mechanism as an important instrument of political and military expansion (from 750 to the first years of 800). The Frankish kings and emperors also delegated to the *comites* (companions in military expeditions) administrative, judicial and fiscal powers.[45]

This system extended to the Italian regions when, in 774, they were conquered by the Franks. In the central regions, this Germanic system was modified, especially because institutionalization (in other words the officialization between sovereign and subjects of the co-opting to power) did not take place on the basis of a *fidelitas* of a military kind; furthermore, often, in these regions the concession (of the *beneficium*) did not regard land taken from the royal treasury as recompense for services rendered to the sovereign. Charles the Great, between 700 and 800, though attempting to combat the forces that aimed at weakening central power, divided the Empire into counties and marquisates and legalized the patchwork of political particular interests that had formed with time.[46] This gave rise to a system of recognized political units, each centered on a villa, a castle, a monastery or a city (especially in the case of a *beneficium* granted to bishops). Those granted the *beneficium* governed the feud and, in turn, were controlled by a supreme authority. In other words, a 'State of feuds' was created which was then coordinated first, by the king, and later, by the emperor.[47] Feuds progressively tended towards self-sufficiency. Commerce inside and between feuds tended to decline. The movement of people was also limited. The coordinating effort of the sovereign was reduced with time and the feudal landlords worked to make the *beneficium* hereditary as they wished to detach themselves more and more from the central power. Though the king recognized the hereditary transfer of the *beneficium*, from 900 all effort was made to limit the granting of the *beneficium* solely to ecclesiastic dignitaries who, for obvious reasons, could not pass it on as an inheritance. The papal authority, on the other hand, did everything to increase its area of influence and have more room for manoeuvre. This was done with the help of the feudal landlords who, having obtained the right to pass on their *beneficium* as inheritance, had become a force that eroded the central power. Finally, in the 11th century, the 'Church even became the organizer of the struggle against the Empire, because of the famous question of investitures';[48] all of which contributed to create a permanent climate of conflict and instability and to increase particular socio-economic interests. Starting from the year 1000, the feudal system entered a profound crisis. The way out of this crisis, following battles and re-grouping among feuds, was to be the constitution of various regional states at first, and then national states, and the establishment of autonomy by cities.

Between the 6th and the 11th centuries, economic activity was concentrated on agriculture. The life of cities disappeared, as did the market. Money ceased to be the measure of value of trade. The fundamental centres of the economic system became the castles, the large villas, the monasteries and, on rare occasions, the seats of bishops. Around these was organized the economic system based on the *curtis*.[49] These were agricultural firms that tended to be self-sufficient and characterized by a dual system of production: a) *pars dominica*, or the lord's reserve of land, which was the land managed directly by the lord; and b) *pars massaricia*, the land, divided into distinct smallholdings that were assigned to individual farmers. Each portion of land constituted a manse.

A feud generally consisted of a number of manses. There was no specialization in production and each manse tended to subsistence farming and self-sufficiency. At times, a feud was composed of more than one *curtis*, each with its dual system of organization: *pars dominica* and *pars massaricia*.[50] The farmers cultivated the land of the *pars massaricia* in their own interest, but made payments in kind to the lord and at times also in cash and they were also obliged to work for a certain number of days each year (*corvées*), both on the land of the *pars dominica* as well as providing services in the castle, such as cleaning, cooking, building walls, taking care of the animals, and so on. Productive activity took the form of an exchange of services between the two parts – *dominica* and *massaricia*. But it also involved the part of the so-called commune of the *curtes* and in relation to which the farming families had the advantage of certain prerogatives: the right to pasture for livestock in woods and on the uncultivated land of the lord, the right to collect wood and the right to hunt and fish.[51] Weekly markets were held near the castle walls and the mansion of the lord, where the farmers from different *curtes* participated and where, by means of barter, the few consumer goods in surplus were exchanged. Annual fairs were also usually held next to the castle walls, attended by local farmers and travelling merchants. These events included participants from other feuds.

Naturally, all the land used by the lord as well as that of the manses remained the property of the lord. In rare cases, property of limited size belonging to free peasants existed; however, these peasant farmers were also obliged to contribute to the life of the castle, through payments of various kinds, in exchange for protection.[52]

At the end of the millennium, Europe had a closed rural economy within the *curtes*. It was divided up, quite poor and tormented by wars, violence, the arbitrary decisions of the powerful and the exploitation of menial labour. The economic organization had to provide food, housing and defence. The prevailing cultural environment consisted of selfish, ignorant lords, who were hostile to change and unable to manage the economy for the common good. The other components of society were a multitude of illiterate peasant farmers tormented by hunger and fear. There was no technological progress and even agricultural productivity languished.[53] The populations of north and central Europe and those of the north of Italy were rather backward, while the areas under Arab-Byzantine influence appeared more evolved from both a cultural and economic point of view.

2.3   The socio-economic system of European peoples in the second phase of feudalism (11th century to the second half of the 15th century)

At the beginning of the second millennium, various factors operating together systematically combined to trigger change in the development of European feudalism.

The invasions and plundering by the barbarian populations ceased and social disorder and political anarchy became less severe.[54] The return to public order reduced the risk to life and economic activity. Confidence, innovation, enterprise and human contact were renewed, together with the opportunity to plan a new and more productive system of economic activity. There was an increase in population growth.[55] In preceding centuries, especially because of the high death rate as a result of war, disease and famine, for many years the demographic balance was negative and a great shortage of labour resulted. As the labourers available were permanently tied to the lords of the land, they were, in reality, prevented from finding other alternatives. The rise in population led to a spectacular increase in the amount of cultivated land but only after the intensive work of deforestation, land reclamation and adaptation to agriculture.[56] The increase in the volume of production favoured both peasant farmers and feudal lords. However, the expansion in arable land required equipment and labour and the creation of new villages as well as the enlargement of existing ones. All these activities needed new investments of capital that the feudal lord had to provide and so money from agricultural income was used for agricultural improvement and development. It also stimulated growth in craft and manufacturing activities, especially in the small towns and cities.

At the dawn of the new millennium, there was important progress in agricultural techniques and especially in the equipment needed to cultivate the land: there was a new generation of harrows, mouldboards and ploughs.[57] There were other innovations in metallurgy and the construction of new machines that were capable of increasing productivity, not only in the cultivation of the land, but also in transforming agricultural products and in other new types of manufacturing.[58] But what is even more important to underline is that the technological progress generated an increase in agricultural productivity. By 1300 the harvest was three or four times what was sown.[59] This state of affairs broke the self-sufficiency cycle of the peasant farmers and of the feudal lords and surpluses brought into play an increasingly convenient exchange of goods. Technological progress, as has been said, also generated an increase in productivity in the manufacturing sector. In the past, the energy applied in agricultural and manufacturing production was almost entirely based on the strength of human labour, and extensive use was made of slavery, which, among other things, was very cheap. Human energy was supplemented by rudimentary equipment that represented a primitive form of capital. A boost to the creation of energy came later with the use of animals: oxen, horses, donkeys and mules. Wind energy was also harvested, using sails on boats. It was not until the Middle Ages that windmills and especially watermills came into use. Both of these were used in the High Middle Ages exclusively to grind wheat. However, around the year 1000, watermills began to be usefully employed in many other sectors of economic activity: in sawmills, and in the production of iron, beer, paper and the weaving of cloth, for example.[60] It could be said that the adoption of the watermill (especially in its overshot version, where the water falls from a height to move a wheel) was the fundamental condition for the development of manufacturing for several centuries of the new millennium.[61] In the period between the 11th and 15th centuries, the machine tool manufacturing sector was almost non-existent. 'The reason for this was the fact that the tools used in production were few and rather simple and consequently they were usually made by the same craftsmen that had to use them. The only truly complex machines of the time were the watermill and the windmill.'[62]

The centre of the economy was no longer only the countryside (feudal lands and peasant allotments), but also the village and the city. The social system became more complex and full of contrasts.[63] A lively exchange of services developed between the city and the country.[64] The population of the cities grew larger than that of the country, as urban centres attracted a large mass of people because they looked forward to a new life and especially the alluring economic opportunities in both commerce and manufacturing. In the city the level of culture and education rose and, above all, there were huge improvements in technological applications in the field of production. In the cities, a new, more complex social structure emerged composed of craftsmen, professionals of all types (notaries, doctors and so on), as well as merchant entrepreneurs. So, the transition was made from a rural feudal society to a middle-class urban society with a social structure that had emancipated itself from the country and had poured into small towns and cities with the expectation of achieving economic, social and cultural progress through engaging in commerce, manufacture and becoming sensitive to the arts and to science.[65]

Before long capital started to accumulate, not only as income from land but also as earnings derived from commerce and manufacture. Development was facilitated by the use of money and by the gradual growth in the presence of banks and the availability of credit.[66] Medieval cities became administrative, commercial and manufacturing centres, but, above all, they developed into politically independent organisms that were capable of defending their independence and administering themselves in relation to their needs and their aspirations. However, these cities remained anchored to the underlying countryside that still represented the fundamental sector of the economic system.

The driving force behind the development of Europe in the first three centuries of the new millennium were the Italian cities of the centre-north, the maritime republics, Genoa, Pisa and Venice, and many cities in Flanders, England, France and Germany. Also, some cities of the south of Italy, at least until the end of 1200, were centres that drove the economy. Being located at the centre of the Mediterranean, they were successful in commercial mediation between the West and the East.[67]

The activities of all these cities, aimed at profit by means of trade and manufacturing, coexisted with the permanent obsessive need of the aristocracy to increase their ownership of landed property. Both the needs of the cities and those of the aristocrats were often tied to the desire for adventure and to religion, as in the case of the recurring military expeditions in the East (the Crusades) in the first three centuries of the new millennium.[68]

The main character in the economic life of the cities (and of the economic system in general) tended to be the merchant, who united and coordinated the functions of trader, manufacturer and sometimes also of banker and entrepreneur, and who founded practical initiatives. The merchant took the risks, financed projects (with fixed and working capital) and organized economic activity.[69] In many cases he was a merchant entrepreneur who loved adventure and went in search of the challenges offered by the times – an individual not always guided by conscious calculations of convenience based on a rational methodology and on accounting, commercial and banking techniques.

Until the middle of the 14th century, the activity of the merchant entrepreneur was substantially opportunistic. It was based mainly on speculation; it did not have the basis of a sound behavioural strategy and, above all, was not supported by careful evaluation of business and environmental risks; as well, adequate management methodology and techniques were not always available to put to use. What would today be called management capacity was still lacking. In other words, there was no rational and professional system of planning, organization and control of the operations of firms.

Therefore, it was no surprise when, starting from 1341, a series of economic and financial crises led to the closure of many Florentine banking companies that had played the role of financial intermediaries on a European scale. This happened above all because the clientele had lost faith in the economic soundness and in the intention of these banks to honour their commitments.

> The crisis of the 1340s marked a turning point in the way to manage large international trading transactions. It highlighted, once and for all, the limits of exploitation of the opportunities offered by trade and by international finance based more on speculation than on an exact evaluation of the mechanisms of medieval economics [. . .]. A pause for thought was necessary to re-define objectives, map out geographical areas of intervention, and orient activities towards greater specialization. This is what happened starting from the second half of the 14th century, to the benefit of the still distant diffusion of capitalism, using the techniques and the new mentality which, thanks to the activity of the merchant bankers, had begun to mature in the heart of a Europe, still characterized by an economy that relied on the ownership of land.[70]

With time, the management of firms became more professional and relied on increasingly informed decision-making. Management was increasingly based on the study of the external environment, more rational systems of organization and on more careful, effective and centralized management control. To demonstrate this, it is useful to remember the following:

- the large merchant bankers dominated the national and international scene in the 15th and 16th centuries by entering into relationships, business transactions and friendships with sovereigns, princes and ecclesiastical bodies at every level. They succeeded in introducing themselves in this way into the circles of political and economic power of states and cities. 'This was the case of the great Genoese families behind the Spanish Crown, of the Chigi of Rome, the Borromeo of Milan but especially of the Medici in Florence'.[71] Therefore control of the environment increased, profits grew and the accumulation of capital for investment became widespread;

- the group of companies was introduced into the organization of operational activities: the creation of a holding dominated by the merchant and the institution (abroad or in other cities of the same nation that the headquarters belonged to) of autonomously controlled operative branches, at the head of which was placed a person that the merchant appointed. Very often this person did not belong to the merchant's family but was always someone able to carry out the activities of running the branch professionally. The branches (national or international) often had a peculiar specialization: some carried out banking activities, others commercial activities and others manufacturing. The companies forming the group sometimes had 'limited responsibility' in respect of the amount of capital conferred.[72] In the headquarters and in the branches of the group there were professionals who dedicated their working capacity practically full-time to carrying out management functions. The fact that the managers were not relatives of the merchant tended to go against the feudal commitment of the *beneficium* that was granted on the basis of family connections, and managers were now chosen on the criteria of competence. Management control became more systematic and balanced and permitted the coordination of the whole group of companies, which could be continuously guided in a unified manner towards the profit objectives desired by the merchant.

***

To return to the examination of the evolution of the socio-economic system in the second phase of feudalism, it must be pointed out that in Europe, starting from the mid-14th century – also in relation to the decrease in population as a result of the bubonic plague that, between 1348 and 1351, caused the death of a third of the population of Europe – the average income of the population increased. The development in commerce and manufacturing was also accompanied by a marked improvement in agriculture that saw an increase in investment from landowners and the new entrepreneurs, with the main objective of spreading irrigation, rural construction and the breeding of livestock.[73]

Social tensions, in the second half of the 14th century, became intense in the manufacturing sector, and in the country between landowners and peasant farmers. But compared to the previous period, the end of the Middle Ages saw an important evolution of the economic system which was stimulated by technological progress, the rebirth of the market and by the new mentality of the merchant entrepreneur. All of this converged to bring about the 'commercial revolution'. It should also be emphasized that in spite of determined attempts at limiting the power of landowners, agriculture (and the land factor) continued to be the foundation of European society during this period.[74] However, it could also be said that the long decline of the supremacy of land ownership was beginning.

2.4   Mercantile capitalism: the European socio-economic system from the second half of the 15th century to the second half of the 18th century

In this phase in history, the capitalist merchants increasingly took centre stage in the economic direction of firms in Europe. They financed production and trade, planned, organized and controlled productive activity, bore the risk and professionally managed firms.[75] This did not mean that the 'commercial revolution' excluded the owners of land (or agriculture) from production and from the system of power in society. Rather, in some states such as Italy, Spain and Portugal, the power of land was reinforced. In the whole of Europe, land, as a source of employment and income as well as prestige and power over the community, still maintained its pre-eminence for many years after the start of the industrial revolution of the end of the 1700s.

The period from the mid-1400s to the mid-1700s is marked by important upheavals and bitter military conflicts. This period can be subdivided into three parts:

1) *From 1400 to 1550*: a period in which there were wars between the French and the Spanish. There was also the invasion of Charles VIII, king of France (September 1494) and the resulting cruel conflicts on Italian soil, which concluded with the treaty of Cateau-Cambresis (1559). This treaty marked the beginning of the Hapsburg domination in Italy. Also during this period, Venice fought strenuously to retain commercial supremacy towards the East.

2) *From 1550 to 1600*: a period of peace and socio-economic development in almost all of Europe. In Italy, agriculture, manufacturing and

commerce achieved enviable progress. Northern Italy and also Venice, Florence and Genoa were at the forefront in the production and export of manufactured goods: wool, silk, soap, paper, arms and armory as well as an array of metallurgical products. The people of Genoa acquired a reputation for being excellent financiers, on a par with Antwerp and Amsterdam.[76] Spain emerged as a nation-state capable of colonizing much of the New World. It made use of silver from the Americas to improve its production and commercial capacity. Portugal, which had been so successful in the preceding fifty years, began its inexorable decline. France developed economically and began to demonstrate aspirations to hegemony in Europe. England began to make progress in the fields of manufacturing and technology. Central and South America became a source of minerals and plantations. The Middle East and Africa both became less important for trade with Europe while trade with Asia grew.

3) *From 1600 to the beginning of the second half of the 1700s*: a period in which those nations that would be at the forefront of industrial and commercial progress in future centuries and those that would be less evolved began to be differentiated in the global economy. The backward states continued for a long period of time to be at the service of the conservative values of a class of landowners that were not in line with technological progress or industrial activity, had no vocation for international trade and, above all, were deprived of an education and a mentality adequate for managing manufacturing and commercial firms.

In Italy in the third period there were signs of involution in production and trade. The crisis became obvious in 1619. The English and Dutch navies were increasingly active in the Mediterranean and supplanted Italian merchants. Italian exports collapsed and the balance of trade became negative. Manufacturing production and trade entered a deep recession. The causes of the great crisis are manifold, but they could be summarized as follows: inadequate technological progress; less efficient manufacturing processes compared to those of the competing foreign countries; less attractive quality of the products sold in international markets;[77] relatively high cost of the products sold; higher labour cost compared to that of competing countries, progressive development of intrusive corporate regulation; relatively high fiscal pressure; shifting of trade from the Mediterranean to the Atlantic and to continental Asia; fall in exports also due to the difficulty of some foreign countries in continuing to import Italian products;[78] the lack of a maritime fleet capable of managing transatlantic trade; and the presence of a class of 'feudal entrepreneurs' that still relied mainly on agriculture and lacked the capacity to manage an economic and social system oriented to industry and international trade. In short, the loss of competitiveness of its manufactured products in markets and of the stability of foreign demand for agricultural products forced the Italian economy to return to an economic system concentrated on agriculture.[79] This economic involution caused profound change in society. Merchants and industrialists lost importance and the large landowners became even more powerful. The Church tended to maintain the landed status quo and was opposed to progressive change.[80]

Spain and Portugal during this period – in spite of having pursued their trading and imperial vocation overseas and having done everything possible to create a unified and coordinated political order under an absolute monarch – were also to experience a process of socio-economic involution. In fact, well into the 1600s, they returned to the system in which the power of land, managed by aristocrats (old and new), was reinforced and in which manufacturing and trade were weakened. Spain and Portugal engaged actively in the competition for the conquest of overseas regions (land already discovered and new land); the adventure of colonial expansion was carried out directly and was financed by sovereigns: conquests were made in their name and under their control.[81] Naturally, the economic advantages of such undertakings spread beyond the sovereign to the aristocratic class and to those members of the merchant class that were closely connected to them. But colonial expansion, especially for Spain, had more territorial than commercial aims.[82]

From the 1600s, the Dutch republic began to be successful as a world power and was in direct conflict with Spain and Portugal, from whom it took bases in the East and in South America. The Dutch formed an Empire on a world level, whose main territories were in North and South America, Southeast Asia, South Africa and India.

England made its appearance on the ocean routes in the 1600s, initially in search of trade (expansion of a mainly commercial nature) and then with colonization of epoch-making dimensions that brought it into conflict with the Dutch in the 17th century and with France in the 18th century. The English middle classes acquired increasing power and, after a civil war, forged a political compromise with its sovereign. This laid the ground for international dominance and the enrichment of both the State and of merchants.

The colonial expansion of the Dutch and England, contrary to what had happened in Spain and Portugal, was not engaged in directly by the State, but by private mercantile companies recognized by the State, which gave them great privileges, among which, and of primary importance, was the granting of trade monopolies over certain geographical areas. Probably, because of this fact, in the opinion of Fanfani,[83] the expansion of the Dutch republic and of England was mainly commercial (and territorial expansion was only of secondary importance), while that of Spain (and to a lesser extent that of Portugal) had a mainly territorial and only secondly a commercial aim. The chief commercial companies were created at the beginning of the 1600s. In England, among the companies formed were the West India Company (1597), the East India Company (1600) and the Hudson Bay Company (1670). In France, the most important of the companies founded at that time were the East Indies Company (1604) and the New France Company (1604). The Dutch founded the East Indies Company (1602) and the West Indies Company (1621). Other similar companies were formed in Sweden, Denmark, Austria and Russia. Initially, many of these were trading corporations and only later were transformed into joint-stock companies. Some of them had the formal purpose of commercial trade and not the conquest of territories, others had a mixed purpose[84] and at times they engaged in piracy.[85]

During this period, France was at first weakened by religious wars and, in the 1600s, by conflicts opposing the hegemony of the Hapsburg dynasty in Spain and Austria. However, it recovered during the second half of the 1600s and at the end of the century it was well placed for the great commercial leap that it was to make in the 18th century.[86]

The Ottoman Empire declined during the 1600s. Following an initial period of expansion in the Mediterranean in the first millennium of the Christian era,[87] the Muslim peoples settled in Asia Minor in the first decades of the 1300s. In the second half of the century they conquered much territory in Europe at the expense of the Bulgarians, Serbs and Hungarians. In 1453 they conquered Constantinople. Their more efficient military capacity and the weakness of their adversaries permitted rapid consolidation of their power in the Mediterranean.[88]

For European countries, the Balkan-Asian-African Levant progressively lost importance, because the latest geographical discoveries increasingly rendered its position, as a bridge between the Mediterranean and the East, of less strategic interest. This contributed to provoking the crisis in the Ottoman Empire and in a number of ways its socio-economic position passed through a period of involution.

From the above, the following conclusions can be drawn: in the 1600s and the first half of the 1700s a new hierarchy of nations was established in terms of wealth, power and a new order of social classes. The countries that stood out particularly were England, the Dutch republic and France, all of which took part in overseas expansion with great determination and foresight and contributed to the creation of a new social context in which the market economy could develop and in which the main players were no longer landowners but merchants, bankers and entrepreneurs.[89] On the other hand, countries such as Italy, with its flourishing manufacturing and commercial cities, Spain and Portugal and the Turkish (Ottoman) Empire all began to decline. These states all experienced a clear involution, with manufacture and trade contracting to within national or, sometimes, even regional borders.

It is important to underline that the more developed nations aimed at dominating manufacturing activity, the conquest of commercial opportunities and the development of a world-view which gave importance to wealth and enrichment. This process, which could be called mercantile capitalism, was encouraged by sovereigns, who, though inspired by theories of absolutism that placed them above the law and society,[90] encouraged the merchant entrepreneurs and made alliances with them and with the broader middle class. Economic development progressively accelerated because of the increase in the use of capital in the combination of production factors and the corresponding growth in the size of firms, as well as in physical and technical productivity, which prepared the way for the industrial revolution (industrial capitalism). With the change in the economic geography of Europe and of the world, the fabric of social structures also changed:

> Where the economy remained or prevalently returned to being agricultural, in those places the ancient landed aristocracy and the old merchants (that had moved up into the nobility that they had imitated), assisted the sovereign in the government of the country. Where the economy evolved towards the commercial-industrial forms, there the government disdained the collaboration of the noble owners of land, encouraged the efforts of the middle classes or, as in the case of Holland and England, the government itself became the expression of middle-class interests.[91]

Finally, it should be remembered that in economics, during the period being discussed, the theory of mercantilism (or of mercantile capitalism) gained wide acceptance; it emphasized the following principles: centralized government by the monarch (the State); satisfaction of the individualistic ideal, in particular, of the merchant class; protection of the economy of the country against foreigners, because of the need to serve the interests of the State and satisfy the ideals and needs of individuals.

In the period between the 16th and the 18th centuries – it has been argued – the process that brought about the constitution of nation-states was established and in the majority of countries came to fruition. Nation-states, at the end of this period, were the result of a compromise between the aristocracy, the owners of land, and the merchant class that had emerged in politics, society and the economy. States and monarchs aspired to power; they needed wealth and money, not only to live in luxury and to provide for internal security, but especially to finance the wars that absorbed the greater part of their revenue. Conflicts, conquests, plundering and other even less savoury activities such as slave trading were all part of the order of things. Therefore, the financial resources required forced the State and the sovereign to find help from, procure the collaboration of and reach agreements with merchants and bankers.

Mercantilism was therefore stimulated by the situation described above. Prejudices against commerce that were typical of the past were no longer tenable; interest charged on loans (formerly condemned as usury), as well as the relentless pursuit of profit, were now acceptable.[92] In time, commercial activity and making profit actually became respectable, not least because a certain pillar of society gradually became reconciled to business activity: 'Religious faith was accommodated to economic circumstance and need'.[93] Adequate moral and economic justification were also found for the right price and the right salary as well as for the excessive exploitation of workers in the then-prevalent family firms, many of which operated on behalf of the merchants.[94]

Secondly, the State and the monarchs managed the economic system with the aim of making the country powerful, rich and in possession of strong reserves of money. The merchants acted together and were decisive, directly or indirectly, in achieving these goals. In exchange, they won privileges of all kinds. It is important to remember that typical merchants, above all, valued monopoly. They loathed competition and did everything possible so that the State intervened in the economic system in a way that allowed them to realize their ambitions. The merchants encouraged the entry into the market of large joint-stock companies and great commercial companies. These companies were granted commercial monopolies for specific products or particular foreign territories.

Finally, the theory according to which both the State and individuals had the strategic objective of accumulating gold and silver came into being. The wealth of nations and of individuals depended – according to the ideas that were then prevalent[95] – on their capacity to increase monetary reserves. Economic policy was therefore aimed at improving and making both the balance of trade and the balance of payments positive.[96] The growth in national power was linked, in essence, almost perfectly to the balance of payments surplus. With the aim of achieving these economic goals, the export of gold and silver was forbidden; trade in currency and exchange rates were controlled by government officials; prohibitions and duties were introduced and imposed on the import of foreign goods; the export of manufactured goods was facilitated. The idea also became widespread that anything that brought profit and advantage to one person could also be profitable for another person or for the whole community. The conviction that the wealth of the country was based on that of the individual merchant and producer gained wide currency:[97]

> Mercantilism did not signal the arrival of a true and proper science of political economics. Rather, it gave rise to a number of particular measures aimed at achieving a net flow of precious metals and of an adequate volume of monetary circulation. This is what would be done in France at the time of Colbert, by means of various provisions intended to increase export of manufactured goods and prevent the import of foreign goods. This is also what was followed in England in an equally tenacious manner both with a series of rigid prohibitions on the import of cereals as well as a strongly protectionist regime (introduced at the time of Cromwell) in favor of the shipyards and of the national maritime transportation system. But it was the private trading companies (formed at the beginning of the 1600s and destined to be in the front line of colonial expansion) that constituted the most tangible expression of mercantilism.[98]

The principles underlying the intervention of the State in economics, monopoly and the accumulation of monetary wealth were soon to be overturned and considered almost blasphemy. Industrial capitalism, with its new set of values, was about to take its place in history. On the other hand, this new system made use – though subject to much criticism – of an institution which had been engaged in competitive struggle since the beginning of the 1600s: the large joint-stock company. This institution, would, for good or evil, be the main player in the economy for centuries to come.

In conclusion, it must be pointed out that at the middle of the 18th century, precisely at the moment at which in nearly all the most developed nations in Europe the inexorable decline in the power of land ownership had gathered pace, the 'physiocratic movement' was born, with the aim of revitalizing the agricultural system and the power of landowners connected to it. In France, in spite of remarkable development in commerce and industry, the agricultural system

> had continued to conserve its supremacy and its great influence over political power. The court of Versailles, from Louis XIV to Louis XVI, was dominated by the landed aristocracy, whose members were often prominent in socio-economic life also because of their culture, intelligence and clarity regarding the strategic objectives to pursue.[99]

The physiocrats – among whom were Quesnay, Turgot and du Pont de Nemours – reaffirmed the supremacy of land and were opposed to both the mercantile movement and the industrial capitalism that had come to be regarded as unnatural and potentially dangerous. But these ideas soon vanished. The physiocratic movement had the effect of bringing the importance of the agricultural system alive again for a brief while:

> For the importance of the agricultural system this was the final 'swan song'. In the last three decades of the 1700s, in fact, the first industrial revolution arrogantly made its presence felt. It announced the birth of industrial capitalism based on technology and on manufacturing activity.[100]

Notes

1. Galbraith (1967), p. 56.
2. Finley (2008), p. 88. On p. 143, he states that in the 'ancient world', the majority of people lived essentially on the products of the land and that 'the ancient [world] considered the land the source of all their goods, material and moral'.
3. A. J. Evans was a British archaeologist who excavated the palace of Knossos on Crete and developed the concept of Minoan civilization. Evans – also making a chronological comparison with Egyptian civilization – distinguishes the following periods of the Minoan civilization: 1) Ancient Minoan Period (3400–2100 BC), corresponding to the period from the I to the XI Egyptian Dynasty; 2) Middle Minoan Period (2100–1580 BC), which corresponds to the Egyptian period that ends with the XVIII Dynasty; 3) Recent Minoan Period (1580–1200 BC), which coincides with the end of the XIX Egyptian Dynasty (Melis 1948).
4. Melis (1948), pp. 9ff.
5. Fanfani (1961), pp. 52–3.

6. Galbraith (1987), pp. 18ff.
7. Fanfani (1961), p. 43.
8. Fanfani (1961), p. 46.
9. Fanfani (1961), p. 49.
10. Fanfani (1961), p. 44.
11. Aristotle (1953), *Opere*, vol. IX.
12. Fanfani (1961), pp. 41–2.
13. Leaving aside the enormous contribution that the Greeks made to Rome and to the whole of humanity in the fields of philosophy, art, literature and culture in general.
14. On this point illustrated see Fanfani (1961), p. 54ff.
15. Generally, freedom of trade was supported by rigorous military supervision of the seas; this vigilance at times turned into conflict.
16. Fanfani (1961), p. 46.
17. Fanfani (1961), pp. 68–72.
18. In Rome, 'the slave trade is public and is carried out in various places: in the Forum or also in workshops. The rules are clear: it is necessary to sell the goods, evaluate the quality, negotiate, as in any market. Often in the market different categories of slaves are sold depending on the days: one day for those that are "strong" for heavy work, the day after is that of the "trades", that is, bakers, cooks, dancers, masseurs, and so on. The following day is for the sale of young boys and girls, ideal for the home and banquets. Then there is the day, or the sector of the deformed, dwarfs, giants, slaves with physical defects [. . .]. The slave market is well regulated: a merchant has to pay an "import–export duty" and also a tax on sales. These merchants are generally looked down upon by Romans and often come from the east' (Angela 2007, p. 158).
19. Slaves were remunerated with a subsistence food supply from their owners. In imperial times, a daily wage was paid to them and this at times allowed them to patiently save up and achieve freedom. The Romans' slaves – as seen previously – came mainly from the spoils of war or were bought in the various markets. The purchase price varied considerably according to the capacity of the slaves. Slaves were often highly qualified and were employed both in cultural positions (as librarians, scribes, readers, teachers, etc.) and in professional activities (engineers, doctors, etc.). The power of the owner over the slave was greater than in the Greek world. But this absolute authority was also gradually mitigated also because of the spread of the influence of Greek customs, whereby a slave that was mistreated was allowed to flee to a temple and be assigned to another owner (Lessico Universale Italiano 1978, p. 265).
20. Cato the Elder, in *De re rustica* – quoted by Fanfani (1961), p. 69 – wrote on the moral supremacy of land: 'When the ancients wanted to praise a good citizen, they called him a good farmer. In fact, it is among the farming classes that the best citizens and the most courageous soldiers are born. Their income is honourable, secure and not miserable. Those who dedicate themselves to agriculture are not capable of wrongdoing.'
21. Finley (2008), pp. 113–14.
22. Fanfani (1961), p. 77.
23. In the opinion of Carcopino (1947), p. 275, quoted by Fanfani (1961), p. 79, the proletarians that were fed at the expense of the State in Rome numbered about 150,000.

24. Fanfani (1961), pp. 73–4 and 82.
25. Carcopino (1947), pp. 106–09, quoted by Fanfani (1961), p. 80.
26. On this point see Brown (1971), Jones (1974–1981), Mazzarino (1959).
27. Delogu (2001).
28. Diocletian in particular, established imperial absolutism. He exalted the divine nature of the emperor, introduced the imperial tetrarchy, but keeping the supreme authority for himself. He reformed the structure of the empire by dividing it into 12 dioceses and each diocese into provinces. With regard to Flavius Valerius Constantinus, it must be remembered that he was the sole Emperor in 324 AD. He transferred the capital to Constantinople (ancient Byzantium). Constantine continued the absolutism of Diocletian, but he introduced the dynastic system of succession. He reorganized the hierarchy of the bureaucratic apparatus. He reformed the monetary system by basing it on *solidus aureus* (4.48 grams) and putting the copper *denarius* in second place. With the Edict of Milan of 313 he gave official recognition to Christianity. With the Oriental Edict (324) he urged his subjects to become Christians; there were never demonstrations of intolerance towards paganism. He devoted himself to resolve the Donatist controversy (developed by Donato, Bishop of Carthage, which intended to subordinate the efficacy of the Sacraments to the coherence of the person who administers them) and also to the spread of Arianism. In order to find a solution to these problems, he convened the Council of Nicaea in May 325.
29. The 4th and 5th centuries are the most pervasive phase for Christianity, which begins to develop an *Imperium Romanum Christianum* image. The expansion of Christianity was accompanied by the acquisition by Christians of greater influence in the life of the State and the obtaining of rights, special fiscal benefits, ordinary and extraordinary tax exemption, etc. On this point, see Gaudemet (1979).
30. Galbraith (1987), pp. 20ff.
31. Finley (2008), p. 131.
32. Between 400 AD and 600 AD, Rome's population fell from 450,000 to 20,000 or perhaps 30,000 inhabitants. Vauchez (2001), p. xi.
33. Mazzarino (1959), pp. 147ff.
34. Fanfani (1961), p. 101.
35. Fanfani (1961), pp. 96–7.
36. The statement is from Lot (1927), p. 62, quoted by Fanfani (1961), pp. 96, 104–5.
37. Fanfani (1961), p. 106.
38. In the opinion of Pirenne (1973), p. 143 – quoted by Fanfani (1961), p. 143 – the break in Mediterranean unity by Islam 'is the most important fact that happened in European history after the Punic wars. It marks the end of the ancient tradition. It marks the beginning of the Middle Ages in the moment in which Europe is on the point of becoming Byzantine'.
39. Lessico Universale Italiano (1971), p. 170.
40. 'The Middle Ages is not the age of gold that some romantics have wished to imagine, but, it is neither, in spite of its shortcomings and repugnant aspects, the obscurantist and gloomy period the humanists and illuminists wished to describe [. . .]. Certainly, the "bad" Middle Ages existed: the lords oppressed the peasants, the Church was intolerant and placed independent

spirits (those called heretics) under the rigor of the Inquisition which practised torture [. . .]. Famines were frequent and the poor were numerous.
Furthermore, there was fear, an irrational fear for example of the sea, of the
forest, of the devil [. . .]. Yet there was also the "good" Middle Ages, present
also in our times in the wonder felt, especially by the young, concerning
knights, castles, cathedrals, Romanic and Gothic art, colours (of stained
glass, for example) and feasts [. . .]. And then, the Middle Ages is the moment
when Europe was born' (Le Goff 2007a, pp. 12–13).

41. The term Middle Ages derives from the label attached 'by humanist philolo-
gists in the mid 15th century. They defined the period between antiquity
and their time as the "age in the middle". [The] Middle Ages was the non-
ancient period between those two ages. This division was established in
historiography only in the 16th and in the 17th centuries' (Fuhrmann 2004,
p. 2).

42. 'The Catholicism of the Franks made it possible to establish good relations
with the spiritual leaders of the Catholic Church. The successor of Peter, in
theory, was a subject of the Roman emperor, who continued to reside in
Byzantium, and could count on him to be defended from his enemies: from
the Longobards, for example, fierce barbarians [. . .] who entered Italy in 568
[. . .]. The emperor was far away; furthermore, he spoke and prayed in Greek,
according to a liturgy that, with time, had become increasingly extraneous
to the Latin Church. For all these reasons, popes very soon recognized the
usefulness of having a protector who was nearer and familiar, and as the
only true candidate to this role was the king of the Franks, in the Lateran
they began to proclaim that Franks were the new elect' (Barbero 2006,
pp. 18–19).

43. The *beneficium* of late-Roman culture will be denominated by the Germanic
term *feudum*.

44. In essence, it was a *fidelitas* of a military nature.

45. 'The counts, dukes or marquises that the Carolingian kings placed in the
government of the political and administrative districts, with the tasks of
policing and judicial coordination, were military leaders [. . .]. But in this
way, the power of the king officially accentuated and sanctioned the political meaning that the possession of land had tended to have for a long time
and transformed a fluid custom of lordly government of the farming population into a rigorous system' (Tabacco 1974, pp. 86 and 92, quoted by Manca
1995, p. 13).

46. Fanfani (1961), pp. 150–1.

47. Fanfani (1961), p. 152.

48. Fanfani (1961), p. 155.

49. 'The *curtis* is a complex organization [. . .]. It consists of two main parts: a
pars dominica or lord's domain, managed directly by the owner for his exclusive benefit; a *pars massaricia*, split up into a certain number of lands called
mansi or *tenures*, managed by agent farmers for their own benefit and for the
benefit of the landowner. Incorporated in the organization of the *curtis*, the
mansi had productive and fiscal functions: they provided food and shelter
for the families of the farmers; they gave the landowner a compulsory share
of products and of labor (*corvées*) necessary to improve the property, which
in practice represented his revenue' (Manca 1995, pp. 17–18).

50. Manca (1995), pp. 57–8.
51. Manca (1995), p. 56.
52. 'Free men and slaves, of various origin, converge towards a common condition of semi-freedom that imposes duties but also recognizes rights. This condition is called servitude. The servant is a born farmer, to whom it is forbidden, in the first place, to leave the land without the consent of the *dominus*, but at the same time the *dominus* is forbidden to leave him without land' (Manca 1995, p. 19).
53. Duby (1962), p. 42, quoted by Manca (1995), p. 28.
54. Bloch (1949).
55. According to Cipolla (1980), p. 171, quoted by Manca (1995), p. 32, from the middle of the 10th century to the middle of the 14th century, the population of France, Germany and the British Isles probably tripled, while that of Italy doubled. On this point, see also Fanfani (1961), p. 213.
56. The expansion of tillage and cultivation stopped at the end of 1200.
57. Manca (1995), pp. 59–71.
58. Manca (1995), pp. 72–92. This phenomenon is also defined as 'the Middle Ages Industrial Revolution'.
59. Duby (1962), p. 33, quoted by Manca (1995), p. 40.
60. 'Starting from the 10th century, a profound transformation took place in the economic structure of the rural world. Strengthened by their power command – which was called the "ban" – supported by some judicial powers whose development was then favored by the lack of states, the lords, or at least a large number of them, succeeded in obtaining some monopolies to their advantage: the monopoly of bakery, oil press, pig or bull, the sale of wine or beer (at least during some months), the supply of horses for corn husking in those places where this practice was in use, and finally, the most ancient and, without doubt, the most widespread, the monopoly of the watermill' (Bloch 2004, p. 97).
61. On this point see the work of Cipolla (2003), pp. 16ff. In Cipolla's opinion (p. 17), the productivity of watermills was extraordinary: 'it seemed that a mill of modest size carried out, in a day, the work that otherwise would require more than forty men.'
62. Fanfani (1961), p. 291.
63. Le Goff (2007b), pp. 11–12.
64. Pirenne (1927), p. 70, quoted by Manca (1995), p. 46.
65. Le Goff writes (referring to the thoughts of Jacques Rossiand): 'The citizen is in most cases a fresh immigrant, a farmer of yesterday. He must fit himself into the city and to succeed in his acculturation. It is rare that, as the German proverb says, the city air makes people free; but it offers everyone a set of opportunities [. . .]. The city is also a social center. Above all it is an economic center. Its heart is the market. The citizen learns that he is dependent on the market [. . .]. The citizen becomes aware of the variety and change [. . .]. The dominant mentality is the mercantile mentality, that of profit [. . .]. Here one learns to know the value of work and of time, but above all the perpetual mutations: the incessant movement of prices, the continuous transformations of status and conditions [. . .]. In the city the places of socializing are numerous [. . .], generally the citizen benefits from all the resources of integration in which the city is rich' (Le Goff 2007b, pp. 19–21).

66. On this point see Cipolla (2003), pp. 21–8 and Manca (1995), pp. 46ff.
67. Cipolla (2003), pp. 21ff.
68. Galbraith (1967), p. 51. He affirms: 'These perquisites of land ownership [. . .] gave a strong and even controlling direction to history. For two centuries, until about two hundred years before the discovery of America, it helped inspire the recurrent military campaigns to the East which were called crusades [. . .]. Jerusalem had been under Islam for 450 years; its redemption had not previously been considered of breathtaking urgency. The younger sons of the Frankish nobility, like the hungry peasants who followed Peter the Hermit, wanted land. Beneath the mantled cross beat hearts soundly attuned to the value of real estate. Baldwin, younger brother of Godfrey of Bouillon, found himself faced on the way to the Holy City with the drastic decision as to whether to continue with the redeeming armies or take up an attractive piece of property at Edessa. He unhesitatingly opted for the latter and, only on the death of his brother, did he leave his fief to become the first king of Jerusalem.' On the economic effects of the Crusades see Fanfani (1961), pp. 234ff.
69. Manca (1995), pp. 82ff. and 119ff.
70. Manca (1995), pp. 27–8.
71. Manca (1995), p. 36.
72. Manca (1995), p. 38.
73. Fanfani (1961), pp. 268ff.
74. Fanfani (1961) pp. 49–55 and Manca (1995), pp. 53ff., 129ff. and 145ff.
75. On the evolution of accounting theory between the 14th century and the advent of the first Industrial Revolution, see Catturi (1989), pp. 94ff.
76. Cipolla (2003), pp. 63–9.
77. Cipolla (2003), pp. 71–2.
78. Cipolla (2003), p. 71.
79. The productive reconversion affected both the North and the South. But the North conserved groups of manufacturers that re-emerged and flourished again later, when the conditions showed clear signals of being favourable.
80. Giordano Bruno in 1600, Tommaso Campanella in 1559 and Galileo Galilei in 1633 were placed under the Inquisition and suffered tragic consequences, fatal for the first, who was burnt at the stake.
81. Fanfani (1961), p. 417.
82. In 1580, the King of Spain, a member of the Hapsburg dynasty, governed an empire of worldwide dimensions. The defeat of the Invincible Armada in 1588 is the signal of the arrival of the decline phase. From the end of the 16th century the quantity of gold and silver acquired in America declined. The trade of great Spanish cities reduced drastically, the State balance became negative, the sovereign of Spain was no longer able to obtain credit, the population diminished, the currency lost value. There was a slump. In addition, Austria, an ally of Spain, since it was also governed by the Habsburgs, slowed down and fell behind in the race towards industrial capitalism.
83. Fanfani (1961), p. 418.
84. At times, the State granted not only the monopoly of the trade with certain zones, but also the right to the military defence and administration of the colonial settlements.
85. On this point, see the ample treatment of Fanfani (1961), p. 552ff. On the activities of the Dutch East Indies Company, see Crouzet (1953–56), Vol. IV.

86. Cipolla (2003), pp. 547ff.
87. Mohammed, with his organized troops, first conquered Mecca, destroying the idols of Kaaba, and later extended his power to the whole of Arabia. Later, the caliphs occupied Syria and Egypt (639 AD) to the detriment of the Byzantines, and Mesopotamia and Persia to the detriment of the Persians. The expansion continued towards the east (Turkestan, the region of the Indus) and towards the west (North Africa, Tunisia, Algeria and Morocco). In 711, the Arabs crossed the Straits of Gibraltar and entered Spain, where they defeated the Visigoths and founded a kingdom that lasted 800 years. They also passed into France, but a Frankish general, Charles the Hammer, defeated them at Poitiers in 732; this marked their final abandonment of France. In the 9th century, the Arabs succeeded in conquering the large Mediterranean islands. It can be said that, in the middle of 9th century, the Arabs held an important position in comparison to the Christian world in terms of the extent of lands governed and also in terms of economic and cultural development.
88. Fanfani (1961), pp. 409–11.
89. 'It was countries like England and Holland, where the most favorable political and institutional conditions existed and the Flemish and Hanseatic cities, which grew in a regime of self-government, that supplied the necessary humus for the acclimatization of the still weak plant of capitalism, and gathered the most abundant fruits deriving from the discovery of the New World and the alternative route to the Indies, opened by Vasco de Gama with the circumnavigation of Africa. Because of the lack of these requirements, Spain, which had opened the way to America, then suffered an irreversible decline. The succession of events that brought Spain to becoming the major power in the world during the course of the XVI century and then rapidly plunging it into an inexorable crisis shows, in an emblematic way, how the spirit of individual initiative and the existence of certain civil and cultural elements mattered for the progress of capitalism much more than dominion over a great number of lands and subjects' (Castronovo 2007, p. 8).
90. The thesis regarding the necessity of an absolutist State found in Thomas Hobbes its strongest supporter (*Leviathan: or the Matter, Form and Power of a Common Wealth, Ecclesiastical and Civil*, 1651). The reasoning of Hobbes was openly opposed by John Locke (*Two Treatises of Government*, 1690).
91. Fanfani (1961), pp. 406–7.
92. 'Having as their objective the strengthening of absolutism, the sovereigns and their counselors came to the conclusion that they would have to leave aside certain religious scruples and make use of the instruments offered by commercial and financial capitalism both to enrich the State (considered in this context, a personal patrimony of the sovereign), as well as for the accumulation of growing quantities of money to be used for the reinforcement of their army or as an antidote to famines' (Castronovo 2007, p. 19).
93. Galbraith (1987), p. 37.
94. Regarding the system of cottage industry, Galbraith (1987) writes (p. 37): 'Forgotten, at least by many, is the terrible exploitation forced on men and women by the threat of starvation and thus on children by their parents. Nor is management by the head of a family always at a high level of

efficiency or intelligence. More of those who have described or endorsed the homely romance of household industry over the centuries should have personally experienced its rigors when it was the sole source of income.'

95. On this point see Machiavelli (1969), in *Opere*, pp. 215ff. For Machiavelli, the problem in question related to how to preserve and increase the wealth of the prince, which consisted, above all, of gold and silver.

96. Deyon (1969).

97. de Montchrestien (1616), quoted by Denis (1965), pp. 125–26, maintains that 'the merchants are indispensable to the state because their desire for profit, in work and in industry, decidedly influences the public good. Therefore, they must be allowed to make profits. Naturally, they must be national merchants, because foreign merchants are like pumps that extract the substance from our people'.

98. Castronovo (2007), pp. 19–20.

99. Laghi (2001), p. 26.

100. Laghi (2001), p. 28.

3
The First Industrial Revolution (c1760–c1870)

Daniela Coluccia

3.1 The application of the scientific method to economic, social and political problems

It is common knowledge that the 18th century is defined as the 'century of enlightenment', as the period of the application of the scientific method to economic, social and political problems and to the development of advanced technologies affecting agriculture, commerce and industry. It is the period in which the 'capitalist spirit' expressed itself, first in England and to a lesser extent in France and the Netherlands. With the stimulus of profit, it pushed men to adopt behaviour guided by rational criteria to pursue objectives that were often very risky.[1]

The 18th century is also the century of the three 'revolutions': a) the American Revolution; b) the French Revolution; c) the First Industrial Revolution.

The mercantile policies adopted by the leading nations in trade had, for a long time, led to a series of colonial conquests by means of military action in which looting and the indiscriminate exploitation of indigenous peoples were not unheard of. In the second half of the 18th century, the importation of gold (and silver) from the Americas intensified. Profit was obtained from the production of sugar and the use of the labour of American slaves and slaves forcibly transferred from Africa. The profits from colonial production and trade were very important and the large companies, particularly English and French, came into violent conflict.

North America, which had an agricultural system that was primarily based on slavery in the South and on an agricultural – commercial – manufacturing system in the North, made considerable economic progress. As an English colony, it relied on the principle of exclusiveness: England had the monopoly in the purchase and sale of goods. From

1763, the English colonies began to protest against the taxes imposed by the home country. In 1774, England placed the colonies of the North under a military regime. On 4 July 1776, the Congress of the colonies voted for the Declaration of Independence. A war broke out that lasted six years and which the colonists fought with the help of France, Spain and Holland. All of this led to much desired independence, along with the influence of the ideals of the equality of men, the right to life, liberty and self-government and the pursuit of happiness. The independence of the North American colonies opened the way for other liberation movements, some of which had a positive outcome: for example, Argentina 1816, Colombia 1819, Mexico, 1821.

Besides the intercontinental colonial conflicts, important social unrest began to take place in France in the 18th century. As is well known, an ideological battle developed between the aristocracy and the middle class and this resulted in the Revolution of 1789. In the France of the early 1700s, the nobility (of sword and gown) held most of the land, enjoyed disproportionate incomes and, above all, held political power. The king chose his advisers from among the nobles. The middle classes were practically excluded from parliamentary positions and the most important positions in the administration, the army, the clergy and the judiciary. However, the middle classes aspired to enter politics and hold power. The upper middle class, composed of merchants, bankers and manufacturers, grew in wealth and dominated the world of business. Their wealth was also connected to the development of colonial trade with the Americas and with the East. Craftsmen operating in the city, domestic workers, the united craftsmen working in manufacturing organized under the control of the merchants, lived a poor existence. A great mass of peasant farmers lived a similar existence. Almost one tenth of the population lived in poverty and had to beg; but about 50 per cent of the population was in no condition to help the indigent.[2] During the 18th century, there were protests and revolts by the poor. These were promptly neutralized. However scientists and philosophers developed and spread innovative ideas that created an explosive ferment which contributed to social unrest. Great scientific progress was made, especially in chemistry, in mechanical engineering and in mathematics. Philosophical speculation called for knowledge to progress on the basis of evidence and reason. Natural laws were investigated as were the rights of people and natural ethics, and light was shed on how to frame discourses on political power, the organization of the State, laws, freedom, democracy, social interest, the social contract, ownership and its limits, and on progress in a broad sense, including economic progress.[3] These ideas soon spread throughout the whole of Europe and were codified in France in the *Encyclopédie* written between 1751 and 1772; they came to be seen as the cultural driver that pushed the French middle classes against the monarch and the privileges of the aristocracy.[4] The middle classes developed the protest with a strategy that tended to unify – or better to reconcile – the aspirations of the upper middle classes (merchants, bankers, businessmen and manufacturing entrepreneurs) with the needs of the lower middle classes, the peasant farmers and paid workers. As is well known, the revolutionary movements of 1789 overthrew the monarchy, dismantled many of their privileges, and abolished some monopolies and certain privileges of the trading companies. In reality, it was the aspirations of the upper middle classes that were mainly satisfied as they gained access to the highest parliamentary positions, the judiciary, the army and the administration. Those associated with them in the protest and in the revolution against the old regime – the peasant farmers, employed workers, small craftsmen and small merchants – were all disappointed. After attaining victory, the triumphant upper middle classes would look on the interests and expectations of their former allies with suspicion.[5]

The later 18th century (especially the last 30 years) ushered in the First Industrial Revolution, which caused profound social, political and economic changes.

This took place first in England and then in France, the Netherlands, North America and gradually in other nations. Even in England, this was not a process that began and ended with a rapid transformation or even a violent change in the economic and social system due to the will of individuals or a social class. Rather it was a process that had begun a long time before and had been set off by a series of factors that influenced each other and together embedded themselves in the economic and social systems.[6] With regard to England, these changes, which had already begun by 1500 and become established in the final years of the 17th century, accelerated after 1760 and were brought to a peak in the third decade of the 19th century.[7]

3.2 The long, complex and systematic process called 'the Industrial Revolution'

The Industrial Revolution can be regarded as a long, complex and systematic process that brought about the shift from small-scale manufacturing, from cottage industry (independent or coordinated by a merchant) and from firms owned by merchant entrepreneurs with paid workers, who used manual labour in production, to factories directed by capitalist entrepreneurs who also carried the risks of large-scale investment.

These factories were organized production units that employed paid workers. They made significant use of fixed and circulating capital and, in particular, of machines driven by water power or steam.[8]

In England, the main factors stimulating the change that brought about the transformation of the socio-economic system can be summarized in the following way.

The first factor is the development of science and technology. The 18th century, it is said, was the period of enlightenment, and of the rational analysis of problems. Scientific progress was considerable in England and in continental Europe. But the advance in technology was equally significant, particularly in England, especially in the application of scientific principles to production processes. The technological advances were in both agriculture and manufacturing, so that many authors, with reference to England, speak of both an Agricultural Revolution and an Industrial Revolution.[9]

In agriculture during the 1700s there was a transformation of the old system of field rotation and new crops were introduced. There were new forms of husbandry and livestock management that required the construction of stalls and agricultural warehouses. The improvement in carrying out agricultural work eventually involved increasingly common use of machines driven by steam or water power.

Now we come to manufacturing, to factories and the new forms of technological and economic organization of industrial production.

Already for some time in England, certain phenomena had developed that were paving the way for the arrival of the factory.

At the beginning of the First Industrial Revolution, the technical and economic organization of industrial production, which would continue in place until the end of the third decade of the 1800s, was structured as follows:[10]

a) craftsmen who usually worked under an entrepreneur master-craftsman or under a merchant who financed and organized production with the aim of selling the products;

b) cottage industry carried out in rural areas, distributed in villages and engaged in by families who also worked in agriculture. This type of manufacturing was also normally carried out under the supervision of a merchant who organized and financed production and sale;[11]

c) manufacturing facilities that were owned by a merchant entrepreneur who employed paid workers, who carried out mainly manual labour.

These three types of manufacturing all converged towards a new type of technical and economic organization of industrial production,[12] the factory, belonging to a capitalist entrepreneur, who undertook financial risk, and gathered a large number of paid workers in a workshop that increasingly made use of machines that were no longer made of wood but of iron and driven by water power or steam.[13]

In England before the end of the 1700s there were isolated cases of the introduction of machines, for example for the production of stockings, but these were used in homes and not in factories.

The sectors in which technological inventions and applications were of primary importance were those of cotton, wool, the mining industry and iron works.[14]

In the cotton sector, the most important inventions were the following:[15]

- the flying shuttle by John Kay (1733, adopted in 1760) was an improvement of the hand loom (for weaving) introduced into cottage industry. It did not lead to the construction of factories;
- the spinning jenny by James Hargreaves (1764), which improved the productivity of spinning; as in the previous case, the machines did not lead to the construction of factories as they were used by small rural cottage industries;
- the application of water power by Richard Arkwright to drive machines (spinning wheels) for spinning. This invention took place in 1767, and the application (1779) was of epoch-making importance as it was accompanied by the development of the large factory (300 employees for the mechanized spinning-mill). The date 1779 'can be considered as being decisive in the history of the English cotton industry because from this date the triumphant march of mechanized spinning began. This was the primary and indispensable condition to allow the new textile industry to start its wonderful expansion'.[16] This date (1779) therefore marks the appearance of the new technical and economic organization of industrial production: the factory. In the 20 years that followed, hand spinning (carried out for commercial purposes) almost completely disappeared and was replaced by mechanical spinning which was forty times more productive;[17]
- in weaving, the hand loom was replaced by the mechanical frame invented by Edmund Cartwright in 1785. However, its true industrial application took place only in 1806, in Manchester, when the first mechanized weaving activity began. In this sector, innovation came about more slowly, so that even by 1830 mechanical looms used in the cotton industry made up only 20 per cent of the total number in the whole of England.[18]

Innovation in the wool sector came about more slowly, with the exception of the flying shuttle for hand-loom weaving, which was introduced in the same period in which it was used for cotton. However, before 1800, machines for threshing, carding and the combing of wool had been introduced. On the other hand, the spinning and weaving of wool had to wait until after 1830 for the application of mechanized processes.

The efficiency and the capacity of industrial processes to expand depended not only on the use of machines, but also on two other fundamental changes: a) the use of steam rather than water to produce power; and b) the construction of iron and steel machines in place of those made of wood.

The water power available was certainly inadequate to meet the needs of production, due to a lack in England of really fast-flowing rivers. Innovation, therefore, depended on steam and on the creation of machines powered by this new type of energy. James Watt patented the first steam engine in 1764; he concentrated initially on its application to pumps for the extraction of water from mines, which then improved their production capacity and their profitability. In 1781, Watt patented a new invention that transformed the steam machine into an engine that could be used in every kind of application.[19]

In the second half of the 1700s, conditions were favourable for the improvement of mining techniques and for iron and steel works.[20]

The scientific and technological innovations described above were concentrated between the final phases of the 18th century and the first three decades of the 19th century, especially because of a series of factors that came together to create a system. Research and new technological innovations found prompt application because in that period conditions were ideal for the application of certain ideas. Leonardo da Vinci (1452–1519) conducted research that brought him to discoveries of genius: flying machines, primitive armoured cars, bicycles with chains and gear wheels and many other mechanical devices. But these ideas, with their staggering implications, were never applied because in that period the conditions were not right for their application.

3.3   The main catalysts of the process

The main catalysts for the application of science to productive activity in England were the following:[21]

- significant demographic increase during the 18th century and a strong increase in urbanization. In cities, a great quantity of labour was available, as people left the countryside also because of the so-called enclosures on the 'uncultivated land of common use' and on the 'open lands'. This made it easy and economical to obtain a concentration of labour for factories;[22]

- big improvements in the systems and means of transport to make them faster and more efficient;
- exploitation of colonies and the important development in the international trade in raw materials and manufactured goods;
- development of the London financial market, which attracted foreign capital and offered the possibility of raising capital to finance mines, industries and trade. In the second half of the 18th century, interest rates fell from 6 to 4 per cent and even 3 per cent.[23] This facilitated the growth of large enterprises, which in spite of some inconveniences and abuses, were the symbol of the new economic system that was developing: industrial capitalism;
- an important increase in domestic and international demand for cereals, and woollen and cotton products and the development of increasingly active trade that created the opportunity for domestic and foreign investments as well as lively competition between the various factories.[24] This stimulated research and technological innovation to improve the quality of products and reduce costs;
- the establishment of the capitalist spirit in factories and in the economic system as a whole. This spirit was characterized by the search for profit, by risk-taking and by the adoption of rational choices based on economic calculation, all in an operational environment in which economic liberalism held sway.[25] The typical representative of the middle class is truly particular. According to Werner Sombart,[26] he combined the characteristics of the merchant, the capitalist entrepreneur and the hero. This profile, described by the German author in 1913, in time was to be contrasted with 'a more sober and realistic image of the emerging middle-class capitalist and his animal spirits. This was also because it was not the only class to be occupied actively in commercial and financial speculation, in colonial enterprises and in industrial investments. Military duty and the administration of their own land, the comfort of an existence of opulent well-being and privilege, the monopoly of the highest offices of the court and the clergy, did not prevent certain members of the aristocracy from using part of their money in other initiatives. This happened in England, in the countries of the Baltic, in some German principalities and in France, where legal constraints were even stronger. However, Sombart was right in observing that the commercial and entrepreneurial

middle class distinguished itself from the nobility, though they were also engaged in business, not only because of a different system of values and mental habits but also because of a difference in motivation and social expectations that, with time, became increasingly incompatible with the codes of conduct of the aristocracy.[27]

With the first Industrial Revolution, capital became the strategic element of production of enterprises and of the economy. Therefore those who had capital acquired increasing power, not only in business organization but also at the level of the management of society as a whole. The capitalist entrepreneurs were undoubtedly opposed by the aristocratic class that owned the land and who felt almost predestined to govern society. The power of the capitalists seemed unnatural and was in any case regarded with caution and suspicion. Although the first Industrial Revolution marked the beginning of the eclipse of the power of the landowners, they would still continue to play a leading role for many years to come, before their influence progressively waned to the point of being confined to the margins of economic and social power. Well into the 1800s, industrial capitalism was not yet the dominant system. The old social system consisting of nobles, ecclesiastics, landowners, farmers and craftsmen was still presenting existence, though shaken. But capitalism had started its inexorable drive towards dominance.

It should be pointed out that during the 1800s, it was not only the industrial middle class that was affirming itself, but also the financial middle class:

If the strength of England was in the multitude of factories that populated the districts of the centre and north of the island, it was however the City [of London] that laid down the law, that regulated the pulse of its economy and not only that [. . .]. On the other hand, also in France, the world of high finance gave the same impression. In 1853 Proudhon declared that his era had 'taken the stock exchange and its operations as its ten commandments, for philosophy the stock exchange, for ethics the stock exchange, for politics the stock exchange, for country and church the stock exchange [. . .].

The most powerful castes of the English financial oligopoly (. . . Rothschild, Baring, Stern, Cohen, Hambro, Montagu) founded their prerogative essentially on their reputation for knowing how to earn for themselves [rather than inheriting land-based wealth]. It was their trustworthiness that enabled them to carry out such delicate and complex operations as the underwriting and quotation on the stock exchange of entire packets of foreign financial instruments on behalf of states or on behalf of commercial companies [. . .]. In Paris the Péreires had contended with the Rothschilds for first place in the great business undertaking of the Second Empire; and there were no sectors, from real estate to railways, from cotton to steel, on which the high Parisian bank had not cast their eye [. . .]. Together with the centralization of capital, there was therefore a closed circle of financiers, promoters and participants in a multiplicity of share combinations, pulling the strings and reaping the most abundant fruit of the industrialization process that began in the 1800s. Especially in Germany, they created some large merchant banks, that used part of the savings deposited by their current account holders to buy or control important blocks of shares in numerous enterprise.[28]

Notes

1. Luzzatto (1960); extract reproduced in Manca (1999), p. 269.
2. Le Prestre de Vauban (1707), pp. 71ff.
3. The passion for research in this period is revealed by the Egypt campaign of Napoleon Bonaparte. On this point, see Corzo (1994), p. 18.
4. The *Encyclopédie ou Dictionnaire raisonneé des Sciences, des Arts et des Métiers* was born as a result of the efforts of Diderot with the goal of defining, as far as possible, the order and the connections of human knowledge and to illustrate the principles of science and art. The *Encyclopédie* was the work of the most important thinkers of the times, such as d'Alambert, Voltaire, Rousseau, Quesnay and Turgot.
5. In 1791, the so-called Le Chapelier law was passed. It prevented masters and workmen from meeting, coordinating their activities and taking decisions aimed at protecting their common interests. On this point see Braudel and Labrousse (1980), p. 12.
6. Luzzatto (1960), p. 271.
7. Luzzatto (1960), p. 271.
8. In the opinion of Cipolla, 'up to the Industrial Revolution, people continued to satisfy their need for energy with plants and animals: plants to obtain food and fuel, animals to obtain food and mechanical energy [. . .] it is possible to risk affirming [. . .] that from eighty to eighty-five per cent of the total energy available to people prior to the Industrial Revolution was supplied by plants, animals and people themselves'. It was 'animated energy' obtained from 'animated converters'. With the Industrial Revolution, things changed completely: in fact, 'the Industrial Revolution can be considered as the process that allowed the exploitation on a vast scale of new sources of energy by means of inanimate converters': this was mainly hydraulic energy and based on steam. Cipolla (2005), pp. 50–2.
9. On the general influence of the scientific revolution in the two centuries preceding the Industrial Revolution, see Boas (1973); Hall (1976).
10. Luzzatto (1960), pp. 278–80; Ashton (1948).

11. In the case of a) and b) there was no workshop belonging to a capitalist entrepreneur.
12. Castronovo (2007, pp. 28–9) writes: 'The advent of this new form of enterprise, which tended to coordinate in a unitary and continuous way the different factors of production, marked a radical difference from the past. Up to that time the increase in productivity was so slow as to exclude the possibility of effective economic development and a general improvement in the standard of living. Though the expansion in trade had broken a chronic situation of immobility, it had however had a relatively limited impact. In fact between 1600 and 1700 the annual rate of growth in income never went higher than 0.5 per cent on average. In other words, it was necessary to go beyond this threshold, which had remained intact for centuries, in order to put in place the prerequisites for an absolutely different economic system from all the others that had preceded it.'
13. 'The Industrial Revolution, which came to England and southern Scotland in the last third of eighteenth century, brought into the factories and the factory towns the workers who previously had been producing goods in their cottages or food and wool on their farms. And it brought others who had been producing very little of anything at all. The capital that once had been invested by merchants in raw materials sent to the villages to be made into cloth or that had served to purchase the work of independent craftsmen was now in process of being invested in vastly greater amount in factories and machinery or in the far from munificent wages that kept alive, often only briefly, the workers. The dominant figure in this change, and thus increasingly in the community and the state, was not the merchant, whose orientation was to the purchase and sale of goods, but the industrialist, whose orientation was to their production' (Galbraith 1987, p. 57).
14. Concerning technical progress in the pre-industrial age and during the First Industrial Revolution see Lilley (1980), pp. 169–99.
15. Luzzatto (1960), pp. 281–8.
16. Luzzatto (1960), p. 282.
17. Luzzatto (1960), pp. 283–4.
18. Luzzatto (1960), p. 284.
19. Luzzatto (1960), p. 285.
20. Of fundamental importance was when Abraham Darby, in 1735, succeeded in manufacturing coke with fossil coal (abundant in English mines) instead of charcoal (rather scarce in consideration of the limited availability of wood). With the use of Watt's steam pumps and other innovative techniques, the mines produced an ever-increasing amount of fossil coal, which could then be used for the manufacture of iron. The iron industry consequently made giant steps in the production of machinery and tools that were essential for the efficient functioning of factories and for the creation of infrastructures and advanced products (bridges, cranes, ships, and so on). See Luzzatto (1960), pp. 286–7.
21. On this point, see Lilley (1980).
22. In the industrial firms the labour force was heterogeneous, unspecialized and there was a strong tendency to indiscipline that was tackled by tight organization. In the textile sector (cotton and wool) the workers were mainly women and children; very often they were helped by the parishes. On this point, see Ashton (1948).

23. Luzzatto (1960), p. 281.
24. On this point, see Ashton (1948); Heaton (1948).
25. The most important scholar of economic liberalism and of its effects on the economy and on the social system of the various nations was Adam Smith, in his *An Inquiry into the Nature and Causes of the Wealth of Nations* (1776). In the opinion of Roll (1966, p. 145), the success of Adam Smith 'would not have been so complete if the public he addressed had not been ready to accept his message. He spoke with the voice of the industrialists, who aimed at eliminating the restrictions that limited the market and the supply of labour and from all the constraints of the declining ancient regimes based on the merchant capitalism and great land owners' interests'.
26. Sombart (1978), quoted by Castronovo (2007), p. 17.
27. Castronovo (2007), pp. 17–18.
28. Castronovo (2007), pp. 50–3.

4
The Second Industrial Revolution (late 1800s and early 1900s)

Daniela Coluccia

4.1 Introduction

Historians usually talk about the Second Industrial Revolution (or second phase of industrial capitalism) to refer to a complex system of factors that came about between the final decades of the 1800s and the first decades of the 1900s.

These factors could be listed as follows:

- the use of electricity in the world of production and consumption;
- the development of new technologies, some of which are connected to the use of electricity; the more developed nations reach the development phase known as 'technological maturity';
- institutionalization of research and development within enterprises;
- growing use of capital in the production process, expansion of markets, the arrival of mass products and mass consumption and the advent of large corporations;
- the development of studies and practices in management – and, in particular, studies in the organization and motivation of personnel – with the aim of improving the efficiency of the factors of production of the enterprise and of satisfying the demands of the emerging class of paid workers.

These innovations strengthened and consolidated industrial capitalism and caused a considerable shift in power within companies and in society in favour of those that held the strategic factor of production, capital. This happened first in the USA and in Europe, but did not happen simultaneously in all countries.

In the last 30 years of the 19th century, industrial capitalism became almost dominant in England. However, it encountered difficulty in France, where it suffered because of its alliance with the lower middle class and small farmers. In Germany, industrial capitalism progressed at a slow pace as it had to make itself acceptable to the landowning nobility and obtain help from the State. In the USA, development continued and increased decisively after the American Civil War.[1]

With the so-called Great Depression (1873–1895) and later, up to the Great War, there was a marked slowing down of British capitalism and equally remarkable growth in Germany and America. French capitalism followed slowly. The ten-year growth rates of *pro-capita* production, from 1885–1894 to 1905–1914, were 11.4 per cent, 13.5 per cent, 17 per cent and 20.1 per cent respectively for Great Britain, France, Germany and the United States.[2] Global industrial production shares of the main industrialized countries between 1870 and 1913 changed as follows: Great Britain from 32 per cent to 14 per cent; France from 10 to 6 per cent; Germany from 13 to 16 per cent; the United States from 23 to 38 per cent; Russia from 4 to 6 per cent; Italy from 2 to 3 per cent.[3]

4.2 The use of electricity and increase in productivity

As was seen in Chapter 3, the efficiency and the capacity of expansion of industrial processes during the First Industrial Revolution were highly dependent on the use of iron or steel machines in place of wooden ones and by the use of energy derived from steam in place of water power. Productivity, therefore, increased significantly and the profits derived from these innovations increased investments, causing a positive cycle of wealth development. In the last decades of the 1800s an important innovation transformed the socio-economic environment: the use of electrical energy in workshops and homes.

This was a fact of extraordinary significance which gave industrial capitalism a driving force with far-reaching effects.[4]

From the dawn of humanity, man had tried to create technologies and tools capable of generating light in order to improve the productivity of economic activity (by freeing working hours from the cycle of night and day) and also security and the quality of life. For about ten thousand years the production of light had been connected to combustion that simultaneously produced light and heat. The artificial production of electrical energy therefore not only had made a long dream of humanity come true, but also had a profound impact on economics and society.

The wide and specialized use of electricity improved the productivity of machines, labour and production processes.

Electricity facilitated a radical change in the organization of production.[5] Each machine tool could now have an independent motor driven by electrical energy.[6] This made it possible to increase the specialization and efficiency of processes (high performance and low costs). Power stations were built, cables laid, and electricity started to be used in transport. In about 1880, there was a breakthrough in the transfer of electrical energy from where it was produced to where it was used. In 1877, Edison invented the incandescent light bulb using a carbon filament and thereafter a network of electric lighting was developed. The light bulb changed people's lives. Lighting became more efficient in about 1910, following the invention of the tungsten filament light bulb.[7]

4.3 Technological progress, economic discontinuity, oligopoly and high profitability

Between the end of the 1800s and the first decade of the 1900s, extraordinary scientific and technical progress was made in various sectors of the economy. There was systematic and generalized development of scientific and technological research, and an advance that brought the more developed countries to the stage of economic development that Rostow calls the 'phase of technological maturity'.[8] The characteristics of this stage are full and flexible domination of the most advanced technology, and the capacity to extend scientific knowledge and technological applications from traditional sectors (that in the past drove economic development) to new operative fields. In other words, an economy that has reached technological maturity 'has the human and material capacity to apply systematic knowledge to any type of production combination for the production of goods and services capable of satisfying human needs'.[9]

Between 1870 and the first decades of the 1900s, new inventions, ingenious applications, new industries and new products emerged at an incredible rate.[10] With the introduction of electricity, the telephone, the cinema, the radio, new systems of urban and intercity transport, elevators and the aluminium industry all made their appearance. But other production sectors were also coming into being: automobile, tyre, aeronautical, chemical, petroleum,[11] pharmaceutical, arms and explosives industries.

The new industrial capitalism went beyond local borders, crossed national frontiers, expanded on a vast scale and caused competition at a global level with the resulting conflicts and rivalries between the large companies of different nations. In addition a concentration of industrial capital took place with the creation of situations of oligopoly, the internationalization of capitalism, the development of large multinational enterprises and intense colonization. There continued to be enormous inequality, in economic terms, in the more technologically advanced nations (with the USA in the lead) and the tendency to develop a middle-class social system was very slow in establishing itself.[12]

The Second Industrial Revolution, as a result of its capacity to extend the available technologies to new industrial sectors, created strong discontinuity in economic life and in entrepreneurial objectives. 'What had been was obsolete. What was to follow would be very different. These discontinuities created opportunities to do things that had never been done before and to do old things in new ways. The smart and/or the lucky did not have to be in highly competitive business producing commodities at bond market equilibrium rates of return. In the jargon of economists, high disequilibrium returns replaced low equilibrium returns'.[13] In other words, entrepreneurs had the opportunity to prosper by creating positions of virtual monopoly for long periods of time and to make profits and achieve a rate of growth of their undertakings that was superior to the possibilities offered in markets in equilibrium. The use of increasingly advanced technologies permitted entrepreneurs to cut costs to a level that more than compensated for the fall in prices. Their current and prospective extra profits were fully perceived by the financial markets, which responded with a solid increase in the price-earnings ratio of shares. In a market economy the conditions of non-equilibrium always tend to disappear after a certain time, but in the period under consideration, the interval of time was very long and generated great wealth for the shrewder, more audacious and far-sighted entrepreneurs.[14]

4.4 The institutionalization of research and development within companies

One of the characteristics of the Second Industrial Revolution was the institutionalization of pure and applied research and development within companies. This revolution generated not only a progressive explosion of science and technology applied to various production processes and to many products, but it also put the activities of science and technology 'under control', in order that they were no longer 'left to chance', but were planned, developed and controlled within companies.

From the last years of the 1800s, the main sources of scientific research, applied research and development were companies and not so-called independent inventors.[15] The more prominent firms began to understand that scientific and technological progress was of strategic importance to achieving their goals of survival, expansion and profit. They understood that scientific and technological progress was a strategic variable to be strengthened and improved and therefore to be placed under control.[16] The largest companies, in particular, could no longer depend on the activity of occasional and independent inventors for research and development of new products and production processes. They consequently set themselves the task of institutionalizing centres of research and development within their organizations. In these centres, salaried groups of inventors and technicians put their creativity, genius and working abilities at the disposal of the company. They not only satisfied the interests of the organization but also succeeded in satisfying their personal motivation for success, recognition, prestige and personal fulfilment.[17]

Since the beginning, the process of 'internalization' of research and development has been typical of large corporations for a series of reasons that have operated as a system:

- important organizations can create integrated groups of researchers, who are able to face the various problems with an interdisciplinary approach;
- if research and development programs cover many different fields, then they are generally not within the capabilities of a small enterprise: even where a coordinating body is present, the costs would probably be much higher than they could afford;
- large companies, as a rule, have the human and financial resources to be able to carry out the more complex and more important research programs;
- large companies are also able to face the risks connected to the length of time necessary for research and development as well as the uncertainty of the results. This is because they are better able to utilize the unexpected results of research and the results of a number of research programs with different fortunes can compensate each other;[18]
- large corporations have a much higher possibility of defending themselves against imitation and of amortizing the costs of research and development before competition can cancel the benefits of innovation.

Finally, it should be pointed out that institutionalization of pure and applied research and development within enterprises has allowed science and technology to influence each other: technologies represent applications of scientific principles to production processes. Also, new operational needs stimulate new developments in scientific endeavours. Prior to this period, this did not happen. 'Previously, the economy had advanced on the brilliance of what we might call great entrepreneurial tinkerers (Watt, Bessemer, Arkwright). Technological advances were not closely coupled to scientific advances. Bessemer, for example, never knew the chemistry of what made his blast furnace work. He just fiddled around until it worked.'[19]

4.5   The growing use of capital. The beginning of mass production and mass consumption and the appearance of large corporations

The Second Industrial Revolution was marked by the growing use of machines and, more generally, of fixed capital in production processes. The determining factor in producing this was undoubtedly technological progress. Technology becomes more evolved, the more production processes can be broken down into elementary parts that can be 'treated' according to the results of available and specific scientific knowledge. In essence, the more possible it is to apply specialized scientific knowledge to specific operations the more effective technology is in terms of technical output, costs and profits.

The latest technologies – at the time of the Second Industrial Revolution – had an important influence on the cost structure of companies. Gradually, as they increasingly adopted mechanized automated production processes, costs that tended to be variable were replaced by fixed costs related to the services supplied by plant assets and by other services that were proportional to the production capacity installed (plant size), rather than to the volume of products made during the accounting period.[20] With the prevalence of fixed costs, production structures became less flexible in that they encountered a series of difficulties in promptly and economically adapting to external change in the demand of the market.

The adoption of increasingly advanced technologies also caused an increase in the 'minimum viable size' of a firm, the size below which the company could not meet or create the conditions for profitable activity. This phenomenon stimulated the concentration of supply, the creation of oligopoly in the more strategic sectors and the tendency of firms to find new outlets for their production in international markets.[21]

The use of new technologies caused a large increase in the demand for capital, not only for the purchase of machines, equipment and buildings, but also to finance research and development, which, apart from being very expensive, required a much longer development period compared to the past. A growing amount of money was also needed to undertake commercial activity and, more generally, to control the environment. The rigidity of investments, the uncertainty of research activity, the unpredictable and unreliable nature of market outlets and increasing competition encouraged larger firms to detach themselves, as much as possible, from the 'impersonal mechanisms' of the market. They made every effort to influence the market with a series of production and commercial strategies in order to make their investment choices less risky and make their expectations of economic equilibrium less precarious. It was necessary for products not only to be manufactured, but also sold in an acceptable time, in order to restore the value of the factors used in the process of production and to earn a fair profit to pay dividends to shareholders and to reinvest and so obtain sustainable and faster development. It was imperative not to obstruct the process of restoration and accumulation of capital in order to avert crises of shorter or longer duration.

The role of joint-stock companies was greatly enhanced by these growing financial needs as they were able to mobilize a large quantity of money on the markets. This contributed to increase the size of companies and caused important changes in the ownership structure of large organizations, which obtained money on huge markets from anonymous financiers, who had no desire to control the company they financed, but were driven to invest in shares motivated by the expectation of dividends and capital gains.

The effects of financial needs on the 'dispersion of share ownership' had already begun to be felt in large diversified corporations in the first years of the 1900s, a period in which they reached 'technological maturity' and began to develop strategies to remove themselves from the competitive mechanisms of the market with a view to facilitating the pursuit of their corporate goals of development and profit.

4.6   The development of studies and practices in the field of management

The Second Industrial Revolution saw the publication of numerous studies and operational applications in the field of management and, in particular, on the subject of business organization and the motivation of personnel.

During the long period of mercantile capitalism and the First Industrial Revolution, firms

> could be well-managed and controlled (by landowners, merchant capitalists and industrial capitalists) in a relatively simple manner: an adequate knowledge of mercantile techniques and accounting were sufficient to correctly manage exchanges, to collect accounting information, calculate business results, interpret facts and results [. . .]. In other words, the capacity to run and keep the economy of the enterprise under control was strictly connected to possessing the above-mentioned knowledge, which, undoubtedly, appeared to be the basic elements in running a firm.[22]

However, with the Second Industrial Revolution there was significant development in studies and applications in the fields of organization and motivation. And so began the study and concrete application of management techniques, and the start of a particular phase of thinking about the management process relating to the analysis and adoption of efficient organizational structures.

The main organizational innovations were connected to the need to achieve two objectives:

1) to introduce a system of scientific organization aimed at increasing the output of workers in charge of machines with the use of specialization of labour, coordination of tasks, and incentives, especially financial: task management or the theory of scientific organization of work arose from this; the founder of task management was F. W. Taylor (1859–1917);[23]

2) to rationalize the organizational structure of the firm, concentrating on specialization, on the formal coordination of roles, and on organizational departments and influences. This second group of theories and applications (known as the 'theory of the administrative organization of work') has its chief proponent in Henri Fayol.[24]

The work of Taylor could be defined as 'the physiological theory of organization' and described in terms of techniques aimed at moulding the physique of workers who performed operations on machines of varying complexity. His work 'takes the point of view of the engineer rather than the natural scientist, and prescribes procedures for the efficient organization and conduct of routine work'.[25] All this consideration of the physiological variable of the operator was in relation to the objective of increasing the productivity of his work.

The principles that inspired task management, in Taylor's opinion, were the following:

- the conflicts that exist between managers and workers in the factory derive, above all, from the constant pressure placed on subordinates without having established a production standard of reference;
- it is necessary, given the above, to decide the quantity of work to assign on a daily basis to the individual worker on empirical grounds. To this end, it is essential to study all the operations included in the tasks of workers scientifically to identify the best method and required time necessary to carry out each operation. It is naturally indispensable that management – and not the workers, as happened in the past – chooses the most suitable materials, the most appropriate capital goods, the best ways to use goods and people and the most adequate sequence for the different operations of production;[26]
- management has the task of recruiting, selecting and scientifically training the labour force. According to task management standards, because the tasks and the single operations in which these can be broken down are planned in method, time and sequence, it is essential that workers are chosen and trained to behave functionally, according to the requirements of the various roles of the organization;
- there must be a clear-cut separation of tasks between managers and workers; managers take care of planning and control of the activities, training and development of personnel; workers merely carry out the tasks assigned to them. This specialization is vital for an increase in productivity;[27]
- managers must motivate workers; more specifically, they must 'collaborate cordially' with workers, to stimulate them to work according to the prescriptions of organizational roles.

Conflicts with employees, in Taylor's opinion, would be eliminated or attenuated by the intrinsic quality of task management: the standards for performance are determined in a scientific and impersonal way, and pay and productivity bonuses are linked to them. This would therefore eliminate the root cause of controversies and prevent the innate tendency of workers to pretend to work, to drag their heels and make tasks take a long time.[28]

As can be seen, the fundamental aim of the scientific organization of work was to increase productivity by stimulating the 'human machine' to fully use all its physical energy and to operate with a specialized method, the required speed, suitable physical movements and adequate accuracy.[29] The theories of Taylor stimulated a total reorganization of industrial production. For example in 1913, Ford introduced the assembly line, which could be considered a rigorous application of Taylor's principles. These ideas turned out to be almost irresistible and were applied by the various industries as they are still applied today.

The 'theory of administrative organization of work', which started with the analyses and the writings of Henri Fayol (1841–1925), turned the spotlight on the whole system of the company and not on the combination man-machine. The attention shifted from the workshop (man-machine relationships) to the organizational structure of the company: to creation of departments and specialized roles, coordination of relationships and roles by means of lines of authoritarian (hierarchical and functional) and non-authoritarian influence systems of relationships between people (command). The problems posed by the creation of an information system were also studied, as were the facilitating of communications between different roles and different departments, the relationships between line and staff, the problems regarding the span of control (the number of subordinates to direct) and the creation of an organizational structure without a power vacuum and without the overlapping of tasks. Considerable emphasis was placed on the centralization of corporate planning, on the introduction of a hierarchy of authority and on analytical control of employees.

Also in this branch of studies, the working man within the enterprise seemed, in practice, to be a passive instrument to be inserted into the organizational structure. However, the great merit of Fayol was that of having analysed the management process. He can be considered the

> initiator of the functional analysis of administration and management. His contribution to the development of management theory is original and stimulating. His thought has influenced later speculation on the subject to a great extent. He studied the various management functions that up to then had been totally neglected and made it clear that these functions are the key elements to obtain rational and efficient administration. He affirmed that management skills gain increasing importance as gradual progress is made up the hierarchy ladder.[30]

To conclude, it can be said that both the studies and the applications of Taylor's theories as well as those of Fayol have made a contribution to the construction of organizational structures capable of stimulating the physical and technical performance of the human factor. They did not investigate the decision-making process, which affects the behaviour of employees and of the company, nor did they investigate the control that, in the course of time, would correct and keep the management process oriented towards business goals. It must be added that the notion of motivation analysed in these studies of personnel considered workers to be moved only by physiological needs and by the fear of hunger and loss of their jobs. However, although the interrelations among groups were not adequately investigated, these theories served the need for operational know-how in relation to the industrial capitalism of their period: knowledge of mercantile techniques, accounting, organization of labour and prevalently financial incentive systems. Essentially, this knowledge seemed sufficient at that time to run companies efficiently. But later, developments in science and technology, the growing dynamism of markets, the unpredictable behaviour of consumers and competitors, and the considerable risk connected to growth in size and to the rigidity of investments in fixed capital, all led to new developments in management doctrine producing important innovations in models of planning and control as well as more effective systems of motivation for employees.[31]

Notes

1. Concerning the United States, Krugman points out that during the Gilded Age (the golden age at the end of the 19th century), the economic system was characterized by great inequality in terms of income. With the passage to the Progressive Era, around 1900, things changed considerably from the political and cultural points of view. 'Theodore Roosevelt, who became president in 1901, was less reliably proplutocrat than his predecessors; the Food and Drug Administration was created in 1906; the income tax was reintroduced in 1913, together with a constitutional amendment that prevented the Supreme Court from declaring, as it had before, that it was unconstitutional. These changes, however, had little impact on either the inequality of income and wealth in America or the minimal role that the U.S. government played in mitigating the effects to that inequality. As best as we can tell, America in the 1920s, although richer than it had been in the late nineteenth century, was very nearly as unequal, and very nearly as much under the thumb of a wealthy elite' (Krugman 2007, p. 17).
2. Rostow (1978), p. 52. It should be noted that the information related to France concerns the decades 1861–1870 and 1890–1900; the data for Germany relate to the periods from 1880–1889 and 1905–1913.
3. Rostow (1978), p. 52. The capitalist way of producing, even if often accompanied by highly negative social and ethical phenomena, has definitely increased the production per capita of the various countries of the world. On the argument, see Beaud (1997), p. 100.
4. Thurow (2000), p. 3.

5. The first electricity generators were patented in about 1869. Zénobe Théophile Gramme (1826–1901) obtained a patent in 1867 for some devices related to electric dynamos, capable of driving electric machines with permanent magnets to produce light. In 1869 he improved his dynamos and patented the alternating current generator.

   Antonio Pacinotti (1841–1912) is the inventor of the machine that can be considered the prototype of the dynamic generators of electricity and electric motors (dynamos). Between 1860 and 1862 he tested his 'little machine' as motor and dynamo. On this point, see Lessico Universale Italiano, vol. IX, 1972 and vol. XV, 1975.

6. 'The second invention that changed the nature of economic advancement in the 1890s was electricity. Electrification allowed a whole new set of industries to emerge (telephones, movies) and radically altered the productive processes of every old industry. In the steam era, a giant engine powered a single central rotating shaft linked with machine tools through pulleys of long linear factories. In the new electric model of production, small motors could be attached to each machine tool, and very different and more productive configurations of machinery could be arranged on the factory floor. It was an earlier industrial version of what today is known as distributive processing in the computer industry' (Thurow 2000, p. 20).

7. Lessico Universale Italiano (1970), vol. VI.

8. Rostow (1962). In his opinion (p. 41), maturity is reached in about sixty years after the take-off phase. According to Rostow, the approximate dates that indicate the achievement of technological maturity are the following: Great Britain, 1850; USA, 1900; Germany, 1910; France, 1910; Sweden, 1930; Japan, 1940.

9. Zanda (1974), p. 1.

10. In Great Britain between 1880 and 1887 the number of patents granted each year was about 30,000 and about 16,000 in 1908. In the USA the number of patents was about 14,000 in 1880 and about 36,000 in 1907 (Bucharin 1966, p. 22).

11. The first oil pipeline was built in Pennsylvania in 1865 and connected an oil field to a railway station. In 1880, the network was only 200km long. The history of the oil industry started on 27 August 1859, the day on which E. L. Drake made oil gush out of a well in Titusville, Pennsylvania. Lessico Universale Italiano (1975), vol. XV and (1976) vol. XVI.

12. Krugman (2007), pp. 17ff. He reminds us that the tendency to equality and the creation of the middle class took place with the New Deal. In his opinion, the persistence of significant inequality up to the time of F. D. Roosevelt was linked, above all, to the policies adopted by the Republicans (Grand Old Party), which, in the period between the American Civil War and the Great Depression, won the presidential election 12 times out of 16 and 'controlled the Senate even more consistently, with Democrats holding a majority in only five of the thirty-two Congresses at the time' (Krugman 2007, p. 22).

13. Thurow (2000), p. 21.

14. Thurow (2000), p. 21.

15. Schmookler, in Mason (1970), p. 176.

16. 'Having invented systematic research and development, Germany maintained its scientific and technological lead for the first half of the twentieth

century. But no one was faster at shifting from elite classics-based education (Latin and Greek) to mass technological education than the Americans. Using this mass educational base, America replaced Britain as the world's wealthiest country early in the twentieth century, even though it was not the world's technological leader. [. . .]. The United States would not displace Germany as the world's technological leader until after the Second World War' (Thurow 2000, pp. 19–20).

17. Zanda (1974), p. 493; Laghi (2001), pp. 35–8.
18. Basic research especially, but also some applied research, generate benefits in the medium and long term and therefore are normally only within the reach of large enterprises with considerable financial power and the capacity to wait for the future benefits of research and development. See Zanda (1974), pp. 495ff.
19. Thurow (2000), p. 18.
20. On this point, see Saraceno (1967), p. 18.
21. In this period the average size of an industrial plant increased in all the nations with a capitalist system. For example, in Great Britain, between 1880 and 1910 the size of firms engaged in spinning and in blast furnace activity doubled. In the USA the average number of employees in an industrial enterprise rose between the end of the 19th century and the end of the second decade of the 20th century from 22 to 44 (Mathias and Postan 1954).
22. Zanda (2006), p. 39.
23. Taylor (1911a; 1911b; 1947). His main works are collected and translated into Italian in Taylor (1952). The principal followers of Taylor were: Gantt (1911); Gilbreth (1917), Gilbreth and Moller Gilbreth (1917; 1919); Emerson (1913).
24. Fayol (1956).
25. March and Simon (1963), p. 19.
26. Taylor (1952), p. 175.
27. Taylor (1952), p. 174.
28. Taylor (1952), pp. 243ff. and 157ff.
29. Taylor's theories are based on a purely economic conception of the world and only consider the physical variables of people: their feelings, needs, creativity, imagination and their ability to take rational decisions are ignored.
30. Zanda (1974), p. 192.
31. Critical discussions on classical organization theories are to be found in: Simon (1958), pp. 20ff.; March and Simon (1963), pp. 30ff.; Learned and Sproat (1966), pp. 3ff.; Pfiffner and Sherwood (1960), pp. 96ff.; O'Shaughnessy (1968).

5

The 'Managerial Revolution': The Origin and Growth of Managerial Capitalism (from the 1930s to the End of the 1970s)

Gianfranco Zanda

5.1 The first two decades of the 20th century and the Great War

In the opinion of Rostow,[1] countries that reach technological maturity (full and flexible command of science and technology and the capacity to expand the knowledge acquired from the traditional sectors that had previously borne the cost of economic advance to the new, more profitable sectors) can direct their socio-economic systems: a) either towards an aggressive policy aimed at consolidating the position of the nation at a world level; b) or towards a policy of social reforms designed to guarantee social security and to reduce working hours; or c) towards a policy that is favourable to the development of mass consumption (economic well-being). These policies are, in a certain way, competing for the use of the intellectual and material resources available. The various nations, on reaching technological maturity, can achieve an adequate balance of these policies. History has demonstrated that such a balance varies at different times and in different places because of a series of interacting factors.

It should be remembered that in Rostow's opinion, this stage of maturity was reached in Great Britain in the second half of the 1800s, in the United States in 1900 and in Germany and France in about 1910.

In the first two decades of the 1900s, in the most advanced capitalist nations, there was a perennial state of uncertainty. While preparing to adopt a political, economic and social model that favoured economic well-being (large-scale mass consumption), these nations were also coping with the tendency to embrace policies that were aimed at affirming themselves, also militarily, at an international level.[2] The final and tragic outcome of this was the Great War (World War I) of 1914–1918, which was caused by a complex system of events. These included: international commercial rivalry; the export of capital and the creation of operational units abroad; protectionism and diverging industrial and financial interests; the tendency towards international imperialism, as well as patriotic fervour. The desire to consolidate individual national capitalism (industrial and financial) at an international level had considerable effects. Above all, the capitalism of Great Britain, Germany, France and, to a lesser extent, of the United States extended the capitalistic relationships of production and trade on a world scale. These nations wanted to dominate economically at an international level. Civil conscience, in the end, did not oppose the war. Each nation being certain of its superiority, striving for the so-called vital spaces,[3] insane chauvinist tendencies and the conviction that the conflict would be brief, all contributed to the courage and drive necessary to enter armed conflict. In short, economic rivalry, nationalistic fervour, scarce and inadequate information and unfounded dreams of finding space and greater freedom drove each nation and produced an unprecedented catastrophe. These tendencies could not be stopped even by the rising organized working classes of different countries, which, as a whole, supported the so-called class struggle and the internationalization of workers. In the end, all the workers' groups and their organizations were neutralized and, at times, were even indirectly involved in the objective of safeguarding the 'common good' of the country. This common good was put on a par with the country's 'greatness' and with international expansion. It seemed, therefore, that particular interests were subordinated to the pursuit of a more elevated common interest that placed patriotism at the service of politics.[4]

In the richer nations, the USA, Great Britain, Germany and France, during the first two decades of the century, power in companies, and more generally in the whole of society, was held by those who had capital. Capital had, in fact, become the scarcest factor of production, the most difficult to obtain or replace and was therefore of strategic importance for the start-up or continuation of production activities. Industrial and commercial companies, in that period, carried out concentration operations. There were various acquisitions, many mergers and consequently companies grew in size. Large industrial and commercial corporations dominated the economy and attempted to create conditions of monopoly. Furthermore, they lived in symbiosis with the large banks.

In time, a close relationship developed between operational capital and financial capital which made the power of the great industrial and commercial corporations even stronger and permanently reinforced the role of the holder of capital within society and companies.[5] In the United States between 1898 and 1904 there was a wave of concentration that reduced the number of small and medium-sized enterprises, which merged to give rise to large corporations.[6] This was also because of a system of provisions that widened the operative horizon of enterprises as they facilitated acquisitions and mergers and allowed companies to hold shares in other companies.

5.2 From the Great War to the Great Economic Crisis

The Great War triggered the decline of Great Britain, France and Germany. At the same time, it strengthened the vitality and fervour of the United States, which rose to the ranks of a great world power.[7] The war generated serious socio-economic difficulties everywhere and when it finally ended it had not lessened the rivalry and rancour between the various nation-states that had been involved. During the 1920s, there was a fresh outbreak of nationalism.[8] There was also important technological and organizational progress in enterprises and an increase in the dynamism of market outlets. These events, working together as a system, created the pre-conditions for a crisis that developed slowly and was limited only to some nations. However it gathered pace and later culminated in the Great Crash of 1929 in the United States and in the Great Depression, which became generalized in all nations in the years 1929 to 1933.

In developed countries, companies had become increasingly capitalized and technically evolved. The organization of labour, along the lines recommended by Taylor, had reached its maximum level. Enterprises tended to become rather rigid due to the strong commitment of time and capital and the specialization of production at a moment when demand had become more erratic and therefore less predictable. Entrepreneurial risk grew and managers adopted various strategies to obtain acceptable levels of profit by increasing the size of firms and their range of operation in various internal and international markets. In addition, managers increasingly diversified production and controlled both the markets for raw materials and final markets.

However, Western economic systems did not find the necessary balance between total supply and demand. This was connected to monetary factors (such as war debt, inflation and interest rates) and to economic factors (such as production, sales and foreign trade). Taken as a whole, the world economic system was structurally oriented towards instability because there was no coordinating nation that carried out stabilizing operations, as Great Britain had done up to the First World War. Great Britain would have liked to do this, but was no longer able to do so, while the USA simply did not consider the possibility of playing such a role. So each nation dealt exclusively with its own internal interests and the general interest on a world scale was neglected.[9] The result of this was very strong competition between industrial and commercial companies on international markets, worsened by the crisis (starting from the First World War) in world agriculture due to overproduction, falling prices and reduction in profit rates on investments.

The rebalancing system of global supply and demand that had operated, in part, in the first years following the war became ineffective in later years and this was one of the causes of the great world crisis from 1929 to 1933.

At that time, economists, politicians and entrepreneurs believed that, left to itself, the economic system – without intervention from the public authorities – would automatically find a position of equilibrium and full employment. They thought that recession and inflationary tendencies could only be brief because the impersonal mechanisms of the market, without external interference, would automatically bring the economic system back to equilibrium with full employment of all the factors of production. In particular, the wonderful element that would automatically permit the savings produced at the time to be entirely invested (independently from the volume of savings themselves) was the interest rate on capital and its variations. Reductions in interest rates would permit the absorption of any quantity of savings produced by the system, in the form of demand for investments. But the stark economic reality at the end of the 1920s and the beginning of the 1930s showed in a clear and unequivocal manner that this mechanism was not working. As J. M. Keynes[10] had demonstrated in an exemplary manner, with an increase in income, the volume of savings tends to increase to a more than proportionate extent compared to income and the automatic reduction of the interest rate does not produce the desired effects. This is so, above all, because of two factors: 1) the level of interest rates cannot go below certain limits because of the 'propensity to liquidity' of savers, which does not allow interest rates to fall lower (given that not all savings are automatically invested); and 2) the demand for investment opportunities becomes gradually more rigid relative to interest rates as interest rates fall. In short, increasingly abundant saving cannot transform itself into investment either because of the rigidity of the amount of investments compared to interest rates, or because of the increase in the propensity to liquidity on the part of savers, who prefer to keep extra liquidity instead of investing at rates of return that are considered unacceptable. If an economic system is left to itself and there are no appropriate government measures to mediate state spending and revenue, supply and demand for capital will not reach the right equilibrium and there could be situations in which the supply of savings is greater than the demand for investment opportunities and vice-versa. In the first case, recession will be caused (deflationary vacuums) and, in the second, inflation will ensue.[11]

In the period of the Great Crisis, savings tended to exceed the possibility of investing and governments of the various nations did not take steps to introduce measures aimed at creating the necessary equilibrium. In all the industrialized countries, recession gradually crept in and then increased dramatically, generating reductions in production, high unemployment and severe social problems everywhere.[12] In particular, in the United States in 1929, the crisis, which by then had become structural, took a dramatic turn following the irrational speculation and panic that seized the Wall Street stock exchange. The collapse of the stock market was the sign of the American financial-economic crisis. With the help of the media, which was by then highly developed, the collapse spread to all financial markets and nearly all the industrialized economies, where it had been incubating for some time and where people were only waiting for the signs to become evident.[13] Thus between 1929 and 1933 the industrialized world experienced the Great Crisis: the price of shares on stock exchanges fell alarmingly, prices of goods fell by as much as 30 to 40 per cent and international trade shrank by two thirds in comparison to 1929. It should be pointed out that the leaders of national governments, in the years of the crisis, were not equipped to face the problems that arose because economic theory could not offer appropriate guidance. For example, in the United States in 1929, at the moment of the Great Depression, economics scholars had not yet developed a sound theory of economic depressions even with regard to the dominant ideological systems of the times[14] and were firmly tied to the theory of automatic rebalance to full employment and to Say's law of markets.[15] Clearly, therefore, at the moment of the crisis they were impotent:[16]

> Two of the leading figures of the time, Joseph Schumpeter, by now at Harvard, and Lionel Robbins of the London School of Economics, came forward to urge specifically that nothing be done. The depression must be allowed to run its course; this alone would effect its

cure. The cause was an accumulating poison in the system; the resulting hardship was what extruded the poison and put the economy back on the way to health. Recovery, Joseph Schumpeter avowed, was something that always came by itself. And, he added, 'this is not all: our analysis leads us to believe that recovery is sound only if it does come of itself'.[17]

After a period of adequate study, however, the collapse of the stock market and the great economic crisis of 1929–1933 taught many things. Above all, it taught that it was necessary – in the case of imbalance between supply and demand – not to leave market forces to themselves[18] and that it was essential that governments adopt systematic measures that would affect market trends and prevent both deflation and inflation. The provisions of economic and financial policy that the main industrial states would take in future would therefore be characterized by the adoption of the theoretical precepts of the Keynesian school:[19]

> The innovative importance of the Keynesian theory was in the fact that it contradicted the principle, that was generally accepted up to then, of balancing the budget on an annual basis as a guarantee of responsible management of public business and the financial solvency of the State. By this the Cambridge economist did not mean to deny the necessity to balance the accounts, but he maintained that balancing the public budget could be achieved by making use of positive balances, once the cycle has been stabilized; this could be achieved by means of the tax collected in the years when the economy expanded. The role which is thus attributed to the State, by means of the public budget, was a radical change from the past, fundamentally inspired by the principles of laissez faire. So much so that it gave the impression of perhaps being the prelude to a planned economy.[20]

The Keynesian theory gave rise to the illusion of being able to control markets in an adequate manner. Considering the growing complexity of modern society and the increasingly intricate interrelations of economic, political, social and religious affairs, the illusion was to disappear and reappear repeatedly during the remainder of the 20th century. This also occurred because of the mistakes made by those responsible for monitoring the economy, the unpredictable reactions of investors, financiers, producers and consumers, and the progress made in economic science.

5.3 The 'managerial revolution'

During the second and early third decades of the 20th century, there was a proliferation of studies and research on economic institutions and, in particular, enterprises. The analyses also began to examine the real world through the use of statistical and mathematical techniques in order to measure socio-economic variables. This gave birth to what came to be called the institutional school, which contributed greatly to making those principles of classical economics based on the 'invisible hand' obsolete, along with those automatic mechanisms of the market that were supposed to be capable of producing mysterious rebalances to the full deployment of the factors of production.

Furthermore, in this period, the focus of analysis was concentrated on the presence of large corporations and on the shift of power within these corporations from entrepreneur capitalists to employed managers who had no shareholding ties to the enterprise (the 'managerial revolution').[21]

On this subject, a book by A. A. Berle Jr and G. C. Means entitled *The Modern Corporation and Private Property*[22] was illuminating because it analysed the power of 'large mature corporations' and the level of concentration of the American economy: the top 200 organizations (excluding banks) held half of the entire patrimony of all American industrial and commercial firms and operated in a situation of oligopoly. More than half of these companies could be considered 'mature corporations', that is to say they were run by employed managers: the dominant figure in taking strategic decisions was no longer the capitalist entrepreneur but professional managers who did not own the company.[23]

In essence, the work of Berle and Means made three fundamental statements in a rather persuasive manner. These statements came into strong conflict with the principles of traditional classical economics: 1) the most important markets were characterized by oligopolies and not, as was supposed up to then, by competition; 2) power, in large corporations, and in particular those on which the prosperity of the industrial system depended, was exercised prevalently by employed managers and therefore, by then, power existed without property. In addition, this shift in power seemed irreversible; and 3) the managers had their own 'utility function' (system of corporate goals), which could differ from the simple maximization of profits and instead included social responsibility. These allowed them to gratify both their social motivations and their desire for success, status, prestige, power, economic gain and self-fulfilment.[24]

The statements of Berle and Means appeared, at that time, to be ideas of wide potential influence; they were also considered damaging, dangerous and deceptive by the economic establishment and therefore the prevalent tendency was not to refute them – possibly because that would have been difficult – but simply to ignore them.[25]

But what were the causes of the appearance of 'mature corporations' in the industrial economies of the most developed countries? Why did power pass into the hands of professional managers who were experts in running enterprises?

We will try to answer these questions systematically.

The event from which to start is the rapid development of *scientific and technological progress*. On attaining technological maturity, advanced companies could operate in any branch of production and in particular in the more profitable, new sectors. Product innovation and production process innovation were extraordinary. The new technological applications that, as was seen previously, had enlarged the minimum viable size of enterprises, had required capital investments that were no longer within the reach of single individuals or single families and resulted in the need for specialization of material goods and human resources. Scientific and technological progress required the introduction of specialized knowledge, information and abilities that are almost exclusively within companies. But the fundamental point is this: the constantly evolving technical and scientific knowledge necessary to maintain organizations at the forefront could no longer be the exclusive patrimony of a sole individual or a very few individuals placed in top positions. In companies of high scientific and technological capability this asset, by then, was represented by a group of specialists in various sectors of the corporation, who had to be organized and directed together as a unit towards the achievement of the strategies of profitability and development.

From another point of view, as was previously noted, *markets* (outlets, raw material, financial, labour and so on) had become very dynamic, very difficult to predict, and volatile. In particular, demand for consumer goods had become very discretional and rather elastic and it was necessary to study, analyse and influence it. Business adaptation to the dynamism of the environment also required the use of strategies that were capable of affecting its evolution, in order not to be at variance with the organization forecasts on which company planning and investments had been based, but rather to conform to them to as much as possible. The relationship with markets and the development of adaptive and/or coercive strategies required the introduction of personnel with specialized information and skills.

It was also necessary to organize the *specialized skills of individuals*, to coordinate and direct them harmoniously, develop synergies and prevent particular interests of individuals (personalizing dimension of the organization) from prevailing over the general interests of the enterprise (socializing dimension). All of this required a) the establishment of efficient organizational structures (systems of roles and lines of authoritative and non-authoritative influence); b) the adoption of an effective process of planning and control; c) the creation of adequate systems of information to support decision-making, operational activities and control; d) the introduction of effective systems of motivation and incentives for personnel aimed at developing imagination, fantasy and the creativity of specialists and lead them to making a high contribution in terms of time and dedication to the well-being of the organization. However, the creation of an effective organization required specialists, and that meant the inclusion of people with additional professional skills within firms.

In the largest and most developed capitalist companies at the beginning of the 1930s (and the same holds true even for later years), specialized knowledge was indispensable. However, it could not be condensed and be the exclusive preserve of the individuals in the top management of the organization, but was widespread among many people located in various points of the enterprise system. The behaviour of large manufacturing firms was therefore determined by many specialized and coordinated individuals, who were included in the organizational structure in various ways. That is to say, rational behaviour was strictly dependent on a pluralistic decisional structure, organically integrated and articulated around a plurality of centres of decision-making and control.[26] Such a solution assigned important powers to the so-called techno-structure,[27] gave enterprises high sensitivity to environmental evolution and allowed them to operate in conditions of readiness, flexibility and profitability.[28] Naturally, the results of the enterprise were largely dependent on the way in which corporate specialists used their discretional powers in decision-making and on the quality of the organizational instruments adopted by management to reconcile the conduct and needs of single individuals with the interests of the enterprise as a whole. The techno-structure was the heart of the decision-making process and of control in large corporations. But this, in turn – though it influenced strategic, tactical and operational decisions – was coordinated by a closed group of persons placed at the top of the organization called the 'economic subject'.[29] More precisely, while the decision-making process of a certain level of importance was the result of the participation of a number of specialists, the need to harmonize, coordinate and guide decisions with a view to achieving the general corporate objectives imposed the introduction of a hierarchy of objectives, decisions and authority.[30] The more important decisions (strategic decisions) were, in fact, taken by the 'economic subject' (a close coalition of managers constituting the head of the organization). Below this level, decisions were taken regarding tactics and, further down were operational decisions concerning the definition of the operational objectives and policies of corporate sub-systems. Decisions at lower levels could be regarded as the concrete application of the decisions taken by managers of higher levels. Both the relationships between the various organs that take decisions at different hierarchical levels as well as the relationships that exist between the various specialized individuals that had taken part in a single decision-making process were 'organic' in nature: the influences were reciprocal; but those of the higher levels in the hierarchy had a greater conditioning force. In essence, the organs at the head of the organization, with their decisions aimed at limiting and conditioning the freedom of action and the discretionary powers of the organs at a lower hierarchical level, so that the decisions taken by them were coordinated and functional in line with the general goals of the corporate system.

In view of the above, it follows that the conduct of the large organization, in which a techno-structure prevails, was the result of a system of decisions taken by numerous specialists included in the organizational framework of the corporation; but the *head of the corporation (top management)* represented the primary source of direction and coordination. It was the head that:

- made strategic decisions (the mission of the corporation, general objectives, corporate strategies regarding markets and customers to serve, products to manufacture, services to provide and sell, choice of technology, choice of factors of competitiveness, choices concerning the use of the human and material resources available to the corporation);[31]
- controlled the real functioning of the corporate system by imposing a hierarchy of objectives, decisions, departments and command on the basis of authority and of other non-authoritarian influences.[32]

The group of top managers appeared as the central unit of management and control and directed and monitored the evolution of the corporate system. This delicate and complex task, naturally, required very high managerial competence in the fields of planning, organization, control and leadership as well as an extraordinary ability to recognize changes in the environment and within the enterprise in relatively brief periods of time. Furthermore, it required the ability to pinpoint the strengths and weaknesses of the firm as well as the tendency to avoid 'managerial inertia' – self-satisfaction, self-praise – that leads managers who could otherwise have been winners to becoming prisoners of the formulae that had brought them success in the past.[33]

It is clear that – in the period in which the 'mature corporation' appeared and established itself – the professionalization of the function of management related to all levels, but above all to top management. Therefore, companies at the forefront in the various fields of technology, marketing, information and organization were forced to place high-level management professionals in the highest organizational positions. In other words, the management of large corporations implied that the managerial function was increasingly informed by scientific methods, specialized knowledge and the progressive relinquishing of decisions based on experience, good sense and the capacity to predict – almost clairvoyance – of the traditional entrepreneur, who was guided by intuition and a flair for business. The professionalization of the managerial function was the consuming fire that devastated the old world of the owner-entrepreneur; instinct, tenacity and courage, which though still necessary, were no longer sufficient to guide complex organizations operating in a dynamic environment.[34] The owner-entrepreneurs of enterprises without this professional capability marked time; progressively delegated the real power to specialist managers who were not owners; and, slowly and quietly, vanished. The 'mature corporations' became dominant in this way. Obviously this process did not affect all sectors or all companies. The owner-entrepreneur continued (and still continues to our day) to survive in agriculture, in the professions, in the construction sector, in small and medium-sized industrial manufacturing firms, in a very large part of the retail trade, in domestic services, and so on. The large mature corporation made its appearance and developed in the sectors that were and still are the driving force of the economy and of society and that were characterized by the use of sophisticated technology, huge investments of capital, research and innovation, and the presence of professional managers.[35]

The economy of the more developed nations, with the appearance of the large corporations, then simultaneously comprised all the following participants: a) mature companies; b) proprietor-managed companies;

and c) companies managed by capitalist entrepreneurs together with non-owner professional managers.

The appearance of the large mature corporation was also facilitated by two important factors: 1) the consolidation of the public limited company; and 2) the atomization of share ownership. Such phenomena are closely linked to the spectacular increase in the requirements by these corporations for capital as a result of scientific and technological progress.

Regarding the first of the two phenomena, Berle[36] has pointed out that the Industrial Revolution had made the collective organization of human and material resources indispensable. To carry out sophisticated production, and to be able to distribute products effectively and better satisfy growing demand, it had become necessary to set up an organization that had an economic and financial capacity that was normally much greater than that of the single entrepreneur. The public limited company made it possible to gather considerable amounts of financial resources relatively easily and quickly while, at the same time, limit the risk of investors to the value of the capital invested. The public limited company, at the beginning of the 20th century (and later even more so), was not so much an instrument that allowed the association of a number of capitalists with the aim of managing a company together, but rather an expedient to gather large quantities of capital and, at the same time, to limit investment risks. This is especially true in the sectors of high technology which are also characterized by significant investments. It was therefore not an association aimed at joint management, but rather an instrument to allow the common organization of economic resources.

The fragmentation of ownership took place especially in companies that needed to muster huge amounts of capital, much greater than the financial capacity of individual owner-entrepreneurs or their families. Gradually, as the company made recourse to the capital market and as the contributions of the new shareholders became more important, the fragmentation of capital increased and therefore there was a progressive reduction in the percentage of shares held by each old partner compared to the value of the capital of the company. The majority of the new shareholders were geographically separate and did not make the investment with the intention of taking part in the running of the company. Their aim was to receive an adequate economic return on their investments. One incentive for those investments was the fact that those who ran the company were high-profile professional managers, capable of guiding the company towards objectives of excellence.

In time, the fragmentation of shareholding was accompanied by the shareholders' growing absenteeism and their lack of organization in controlling shareholders' meetings. The result was that the quota of share capital necessary to control the company was much lower than 50 per cent. At times it was sufficient to have 20 or even 10 per cent to gain control. All this made it even easier to shift power from the shareholders to the professional managers. These managers, armed with their capacity and prestige and through the help of the banking system, especially in the United States, obtained voting proxies from shareholders, who continued to trust managers as long as dividends paid were sufficient and the share prices satisfactory.

In conclusion, the managerial revolution, with the separation of ownership from the control of the company, was brought about by a complex system of interdependent events that interacted and could be listed as follows: extraordinary scientific and technological progress; dynamism and volatility of markets; growing complexity of corporate decision-making; the need to employ professional managers with specialist knowledge in the running of companies; a high requirement for capital that had to be raised on the financial markets; fragmentation of share capital; absenteeism of shareholders (which is also connected to the religious, philanthropic and cultural tendencies of the old proprietor-entrepreneurs and their heirs, who continued to keep their investments of capital in companies precisely because they were run by professionals who were capable of managing them effectively); and the ability of executive managers to obtain voting proxies, nominate themselves and keep their office (perpetuate themselves).

5.4 The power of non-owner managers in the large corporations

'Depersonalization of ownership' or a split between the powers that, by tradition, were expressions of ownership occurred in large mature corporations. As Berle and Means[37] observed:

> Power over industrial property has been cut off from the beneficial ownership of this property – or, in less technical language, from the legal right to enjoy its fruits. Control of physical assets has passed from the individual owner to those who direct the quasi-public institutions, while the owner retains an interest in their product and increase. We see, in fact, the surrender and regrouping of the incidence of ownership, which formerly bracketed full power of manual

disposition with a complete right to enjoy the use, the fruits, and the proceeds of physical assets. There has resulted the dissolution of the old atom of ownership into its component parts, control and beneficial ownership.

In this way, the large corporation ceased to reflect the personality and the capacity of owners and their patrimonial history. The prosperity and the development of corporations, by then, depended on the quality of managers and, above all, on the quality of the mechanism of self-generation (and self-perpetuation) of high-ranking corporate executives. Large corporations ended up no longer depending on the capacity of any particular manager for their development and prosperity, but, by virtue of the mechanism of self-generation of managers, they consolidated their position as a permanent organism in the environment in which they operated.[38] The mature corporation, finally, became an entity with its own autonomous life and its successes existed beyond the people who temporarily managed it. If the mechanism of executive self-generation worked efficiently, it was highly unlikely that a corporation would disappear. It was more likely that less able executives lost their position and were replaced by more capable managers.[39]

As was said previously, the managerial revolution began during the first years of the 20th century, but it most clearly manifested itself at the end of the 1920s, above all in the case of Standard Oil of Indiana. The episode involved the Rockefeller family and the president of the company, Colonel Steward. The Rockefellers held 14.9 per cent of the shares with voting rights; Steward had become leader of the corporate techno-structure. He threatened not to make available to the Rockefellers the proxy mechanism on the basis of which the control of the shareholders' meeting was assured. Only after a no-holds-barred battle, at enormous financial cost, did the Rockefellers succeed in prevailing against Steward. This event represented a prelude to the split between ownership and power within Standard Oil of Indiana.[40]

Thereafter, the phenomenon of the public company became increasingly common,[41] especially in highly dynamic sectors that required the application of advanced technologies, high investments of capital and, above all, high-profile managerial capabilities. Furthermore, it became very important because of the fragmentation of shareholdings.[42] Something amazing had happened: the capitalists had had their power of control within the capitalist system expropriated. Power had shifted into the hands of employed managers in the context of a managerial system that exhibited the tendency of self-perpetuation (because it was able to control the self-generation mechanisms of managers), as well as making itself increasingly independent from the capitalists, in that its specialized and professional functions were not easily controllable by the holders of capital.[43] It should also be pointed out that the independence of the non-proprietor management increased as corporations grew in size. In the capitalist economy, starting from the 1920s, the tendency towards saving was to be abundant, that is, savings tended to be higher than the possibilities for investment. That fact changed the relationship between capitalists on the one hand, and landowners and the world of labour (employees and managers) on the other. Capital became weaker. Besides, the large corporation did all it could to procure capital for itself, by internal means, through self-financing, which became increasingly important. The truth is that consistent savings had also been made by the large companies that controlled the dynamics of these savings directly in relation to the need for investments. Large companies, in other words, not being able to rely on the savings capacity of the market, tried to produce savings financing themselves and were consequently able to control the sources of these savings to a great extent, detaching themselves more and more from shareholders.[44]

In the dominant sectors of mature corporations, the shift of power from the owners of capital to appointed managers was, at least at the beginning of the process, rather neglected by scholars.

On the one hand, there was the classical theory of economics that held that the basic condition for the control of an enterprise was the right of ownership: therefore, the capitalist-proprietor had the right to coordinate the factors of production, which, essentially, were subject to his choice. This economic theory, nevertheless, guaranteed that the capitalist-proprietor, in essence, had the right of control within the enterprise, but did not hold any effective power to influence sales prices, wages, interest or profits (that is, the reward for the factors of production, land, labour, capital and entrepreneurial skills): it would be the impersonal market forces and competition that decided the value of such variables.[45]

On the other hand, there was the theory of Marx that stated explicitly that power in companies and in society was solidly in the hands of the capitalist classes, who could manipulate or suspend the mechanisms of competition and strongly influence prices, wages and profits.

Essentially there was unanimous agreement concerning who held power in the enterprise and in society – the capitalist-proprietors. However, there was strong dissent concerning the capacity of capitalist-proprietors to influence the rewards of the factors involved in the production combination in their own favour.

In spite of the fact that there was clear proof (supported by studies) of the shift in power from capital to the managers in large manufacturing corporations, there was

> great reluctance to admit of a significant and enduring shift of power from the owners of capital. Some observers have sought to maintain the myth of stockholder power. [. . .] Others, including all Marxians, argue that the change is superficial, that capital retains a deeper and more functional control. [. . .] Some have conceded a change but have deferred judgment as to its significance. Yet others have seen a possibly dangerous usurpation of the legitimate power of capital that should, if possible, be reversed. Comparatively few have questioned the credentials of capital, where direction of the enterprise is concerned, or suggested that it might be durably in eclipse.[46]

It was difficult to admit this at first, either because it seemed unnatural and therefore had to be opposed or because personal interests demanded that a reality that there was no willingness to accept was either denied or neglected. The typical reaction of the psyche faced with an unpleasant novelty is denial, but this reaction did not succeed in changing or stopping the reality.[47]

Industrial managerial capitalism and the mature corporation increasingly became the most important features of the world economy, at least until the end of the 1960s.[48] The capitalist system, led by non-proprietor managers, gave an enormous boost to the development of production and of consumption and, also by means of Keynesian intervention by various governments, generated continuous socio-economic progress from the end of the Second World War. Capitalism, as Shonfield observed,[49] had acquired, in that period, greater self-control. It had also maintained a constant impetus that allowed it to survive as well as to achieve considerable consensus. Its capacity to strongly and continuously increase the total amount of wealth allowed it to solve, in part, the problems of the distribution of wealth and the related social friction. Consequently, it obtained more approval than protests. Managerial capitalism, which had characterized the large corporation from the mid-1930s to the end of the 1960s, produced an observable reduction in income inequality (economic democracy) in the more developed nations. In particular, in the period mentioned, in the USA the so-called 'great compression'[50] began; that is, the narrowing of the gap in income and consequently the creation of a middle-class society that once had seemed an impossible dream.[51] Not only did this not produce any negative backlash on the economy as a whole, as many had thought, but on the contrary, it prepared the way for an enormous economic boom that lasted an entire generation.[52] In fact, during the period of managerial capitalism, in capitalist countries there was considerable economic development and the realization of high rates of employment. Some have spoken about 'economic miracles' in that the more brilliant economies had very high growth rates (for example, Japan grew at a rate of 11–12 per cent, Italy, on average at a rate of 4 per cent) in an environment marked by social peace, which is the fundamental drive behind economic development. 'Managerial capitalism' was synonymous with 'professionalized management'. It was also associated with the concept that the large 'mature corporation' was an almost public institution, one therefore, to be managed with a commitment to social responsibility.

5.5   The growing interest of scholars and managers in the decision-making process and human resources management

From the 1930s there was increasingly rapid development in science and technology. Production cycles received the investment of enormous amounts of capital, a prolonging of the time necessary for research and the development and use of very specialized factors of production. The markets for raw materials, sales, finance and labour were pervaded by continuous change and were difficult to predict and therefore it was necessary to 'protect' company results from changes in the environment to the greatest possible extent. In order to do this, the growing risk was tackled by systematically evaluating the internal and external environment and creating a system of planned management based on the adoption of strategies (adaptive and coactive) to keep markets and operational structure under control, so that what had been planned in the end was achieved.[53]

The problems of corporate management in this period had become very complex and risky and the solutions to these problems involved the use of information, knowledge and specialized professional experience that could not exist totally within the capabilities of top management,[54] but were possessed by a series of groups of specialists within the organizational structure.[55]

As is well known, in the case of routine problems, the efficient firm has a pre-existing plan of the means and the human resources ready to face them. Often standard operating procedures are used that establish who must decide, who must operate, where, how and according to what sequence. At times, if the problems are very complicated and the decision-making process cannot completely follow a procedure, however, corporate policies can be used to guide the decisions of specialists.[56]

In the presence of 'non-structured', unusual problems, the well-organized corporation searches its 'memory' for the most adequate solutions and otherwise provides a procedure involving the contribution of all the parts of the company with competences related to the problems to be faced. The solution may come from people in finance, production, marketing, research, accounting, and so on, or from a group of people with different specializations. In any case,

> faced with a non-structured problem for which there are no pre-arranged routine solutions, many organs of the corporation's system are mobilized so each can offer its own contribution of information and intelligence in order to overcome the difficulties presented by the problem. In this way, decisions are more rational, and the decision-making structure of the firm becomes more elastic, more independent in study and research, more sensitive to environmental evolution and more available to respond to the needs of the organization.[57]

With the appearance and establishment of the large corporation, the decision-making system of the enterprise has been increasingly analysed, studied and improved in theory and practice. It has been recognized that the effectiveness and efficiency of firms in complex and dynamic situations is closely linked to the way in which specialists use their decision-making faculties and, therefore, to the way in which the decision-making system is structured. It was discovered that the quality of the decision-making system is closely related to the leadership model adopted by managers and to the management style of top managers. Finally, the main factors that made it difficult for the behaviour of single individuals to adapt to the needs and objectives of the enterprise were clearly identified and adequate provisions to adapt the 'personalizing dimension' (interest of the individual) to the 'socializing dimension' (interest of the enterprise) were introduced.

Scholars and managers discovered that the following are the main internal factors that make the operation of the corporate system difficult.

In the first place, the average person in the organization does not behave like a machine. He has particular motivation and objectives that do not necessarily coincide with those of the corporation and given that he is vested with greater or lesser decision-making powers, he may exhibit unpredictable behaviour that may not be in line with the general interests of the corporation.

Secondly, a person in the organization has the tendency to distort not only the information that he sends to his superiors in the hierarchy, but also the information he receives from his superiors that he has to forward to lower levels in the organization structure. Then he also tends to distort the information that he gathers, works on and sends to people and organs connected horizontally or transversely within the organization structure. All of this causes serious lack of coordination and efficiency in the decision-making process.[58]

In third place, the person in the organization tends to interpret his role in a personal manner and this can be the cause of a power vacuum, overlapping of tasks, lack of coordination, friction and tension.

Also people who take decisions that have consequences for a part or the whole of the organization system tend to evaluate the state and the tendencies of the environment in a personal way (and therefore differently from the other managers, executives and supervisors). As a result, different decision-making premises emerge, which are sometimes incompatible and, therefore, generate incoherent decisions.

A further complication is that many decision-making organs (located in various points of the organization hierarchy) possess specialized 'exclusive' competences. As a result, their discretionary powers are wide and their conduct becomes unpredictable and difficult to control by superiors.

All of these discrepancies – especially in the large corporation directed by managers – have been met with effective managerial provisions that can be listed as follows:

- systematic definition of organization roles and lines of authoritarian and non-authoritarian influence that connect the various institutional organs; this provision creates the organizational structure;
- determination of the objectives to be reached in the course of time and specification of the so-called working rules (policies, procedures and rules); in this way a rational process of planning and control at a strategic, tactical and operational level is developed;
- creation of an adequate information system (accounting and extra-accounting) capable of producing the necessary material to support the processes of decision-making, execution and control;[59]
- research, selection and employment of personnel with capabilities in line with the needs of the organization and their training in a manner that conforms to the requirements of organization roles;[60]

- introduction of management models that induce employees to inter-nalize the organization values and make the maximum contribution in terms of energy, imagination and creativity in carrying out the tasks assigned to them.

With the success of the large corporation and of professional managers, there was an enormous drive to rationalize management and to introduce more up-to-date management theories and techniques. Emphasis was placed on planning, control, organization, information and motivation of human resources. The problem of the management of the enterprise became increasingly influenced by 'systems theory'.[61] As well, the impor-tant problem of external information in favour of stakeholders and the preparation of balance sheets (that present the economic and financial situation of the enterprise in a clear, truthful and credible manner) was considered. There is therefore no doubt that industrial managerial capi-talism, with its need for rationalization of management, has produced a series of efforts to make the managerial function 'scientific'. This has contributed considerably to the progress of economic activity.

Increasingly from the 1930s scholars and managers drew atten-tion to management models to guide employees in the processes of decision-making, execution and control. It should be underlined that large corporations directed by managers were the object of studies and experiments in the field of leadership but also the driving force of innovation in this field, especially through the action of managers who, at that time, had to run organizations that progressively became more complex and in which the traditional models of management no longer worked adequately. The time had come to review the human side of companies in a systematic way.

At this point the human factor must be considered.

At the end of the 1920s, perhaps also as a reaction to the classic theories of organization and as a reply to the newly emerging problems in the large corporations, interesting studies and experiments were developed concerning the human factor of enterprises. The human-istic school, which analysed humans not from the physical but from a psycho-sociological point of view, came into being.[62] Attention was focused on the motivational and social aspects of business behaviour. It became evident that an enterprise is not only a structure of tasks, responsibilities and power but, above all, a social system, a compli-cated intertwining of human relations, a convergence of motivations and of particular objectives, that do not automatically coordinate and integrate. Rather, they need to be harmonized and made coherent by means of the action of managers. Therefore, it was recognized that the management of an enterprise of a certain size was a complicated process that aimed at balancing and merging the general objectives of the institution with the objectives and the motivations of the single individuals and the groups that make up the organization of the firm.

Great attention was paid to the motivation of people, as it was considered the crucial aspect of productivity. The existing organizational systems, based on Taylorian prescriptions, neglected social and psychological motives and tended to exalt the productivity of people on the supposition that the average person was moved only by economic motivations, by the spectre of unemployment and by the fear of poverty. In factories there were visible and important signs of frustration that arose from the existence of obstacles and the rigid organization prescriptions that prevented workers from reasonably satisfying their motivations: social motivation, self-esteem, respect of others and self-realization.

Psycho-social investigations and applications became more numerous and systematic after the experiments carried out between 1927 and 1932 by the team of Elton Mayo[63] at the Hawthorne factory of the Western Electric Company, near Chicago.[64]

The fundamental propositions to come out Mayo's experiments can be stated as follows:

- productivity is not closely linked only to the physical conditions of the worker and to the physical characteristics of the working environment, but it is definitely linked to the satisfaction of the worker's social and psychological motivation;
- an employee inside an organization assumes 'corporate conduct', in the sense that the worker tends to share the feelings, values, vision and evaluation of the group to which he belongs. The worker becomes tied to and faithful to these elements;
- formal and informal leadership are essential factors in stimulating the behaviour of components of a group and creating and controlling the values and attitudes to be shared;
- the information and participation of people in the decision-making processes are indispensible instruments of motivation and development of efficient behaviour.

The Hawthorne experiments gave rise to the hope of an improvement in the quality of management and, as a consequence, an improvement in human relationships in companies. Very often, however, the training programs in human relations have not produced the desired results.[65]

In the 1940s, 1950s and 1960s some basic research was carried out on human motivation and, in particular, the motivation of employees. These studies have formed the basis for management models aiming to improve both the efficiency of the organization and the morale of employees. In this regard, we should note the works of Maslow (1943 and 1954), Lewin (1935; 1936; 1951), Herzberg (1966 and 1959 with Mausner and Snyderman), Hull (1943), Etzioni (1961) and Monsen (1964 with Saxberg and Sutermeister).

With regard to the development of management models, a growing impulse came from theory and practice starting from the 1940s. These models were constructed gradually as more knowledge was acquired from studies on motivation, decision-making and control in the company, which was considered as an open, probabilistic, socio-economic system, capable of self-regulation.

The need to prepare adequate management models came strongly to the fore because the traditional Taylorian-type models had entered a state of crisis, particularly in new production sectors and in the more dynamic companies.

The management process, as is well known, consists of functions of planning, control, organization and leadership of employees. The function of leadership appears to be strategic for the success of the firm: it inspires the type of planning, control and organization that will be adopted for the running of the firm. It also determines how the employees are motivated, how to develop and apply their intelligence, creativity and energy to the work and how to supplement corporate objectives with those of the individual. In fact,

> the quality and effectiveness of decisions, control, the organization system and of the operational activities depend to a great extent on the style of leadership adopted. Leadership is, therefore, regarded as a 'causal variable', and it affects the health of the organization and its results. Leadership is the spark that triggers the achievement of satisfaction and productivity. Consequently, if there is inadequate leadership, the whole organizational system will be affected negatively. In this case, leadership represents the plant of evil from which stems the poison of disagreement, which breaks down the organization system and reduces the productivity and satisfaction of the employees.[66]

In the opinion of Bakke and Argyris,[67] models of efficient management should create conditions of organizational structure (nature of roles and quality of lines of influence) and of operation (planning and control) that are capable of gratifying the needs of workers and of simultaneously realizing the objectives of the firm. In other words, a good managerial model must create a 'fusion process' between the personal needs of employees and those of the firm; it must merge and supplement the 'socializing dimension' (interest of the enterprise) with the 'personalizing dimension' (the interests of those who hold organizing roles). If the physiological and safety needs are reasonably satisfied, the behaviour of the people who operate in the company will be oriented towards needs of a higher order: social motivation, success in work, self-confidence, independence, prestige, status and self-fulfillment. It would therefore seem to be indispensable to create organization structures and processes of decision-making and control which satisfy both competing motivations and the interests of the organization.[68]

The indicators of the efficiency of a management model are connected to the levels of morale and productivity shown by employees in their work.

As McGregor observed, while according to Taylor and Fayol management consists 'in doing things in order that subordinates do certain things', and in concrete terms this manifests itself in the centralization of decisions, in issuing orders and in the use of rewards and sanctions, according to the philosophy behind the new approach to management, the task of the manager is that of creating the conditions in terms of structure and functioning that allow workers to have 'rewards that are intrinsic to the work'. In both the traditional and modern concepts, the aim is identical, that is to say, how to merge/integrate the interests of individuals and those of the company. However, what distinguishes the two management approaches is the way in which this integration is to be achieved: traditional management involves the centralization of decisions, authority and external control of the behaviour of employees; modern management is decidedly based on confidence in the capacity of employees, decentralization and self-control and therefore the activity of an effective manager is seen to be the 'process of creating opportunities, releasing potential, removing obstacles, encouraging growth and guidance'.[69] The manager, in the view of the modern approach, still maintains a role that is no less important than in the past: the modern manager

assumes the role of the master, the educator, advisor, coordinator and, only in exceptional cases, that of authoritarian boss who imposes certain behavior on employees and continuously controls and corrects what has been done. The new role of the manager is certainly more evolved, but it is also more complex, more difficult and more demanding.[70]

A model that works, in essence, produces satisfying business results and a high 'degree of acceptance' of managers by employees.

A great number of variables influence the relationship between superiors and subordinates and, consequently, the satisfaction and productivity of employees. But, according to what has been demonstrated by research carried out by the Institute for Social Research at the University of Michigan, the quality of the relationship under discussion depends strongly on the realization of the following conditions: leadership must be based on a real interest in the well-being of subordinates; managers must be competent and behave impartially without indulging in favouritism and discrimination; the effective leader must have influence in higher levels of management in order to be able to help employees satisfy their aspirations; the effective manager must continuously do everything possible to develop the qualities of employees and, in particular, promote growth from a human point of view; the effective leader uses constructive control aimed at improving the professionalism of employees; the good leader must continuously encourage the participation of subordinates in the solving of problems regarding their activity, their professional development and career advancement.

Among the various proposals from the management models developed during the period of the large managerial corporation, we should note those made by Argyris (1953; 1964), Barnard (1938; 1949), Bendix (1956), Blake and Mouton (1964), Drucker (1954; 1964), Green (1972), Leavitt (1958), Likert (1961; 1967), McGregor (1960), McGuire (1964), Tannenbaum, Weschler and Massarik (1961) and Vroom (1964).

These proposals have been the doctrine that inspired several generations of scholars all over the world and have guided the behaviour of many managers.

The application of advanced management models has been important in large managerial corporations, even if difficulties and resistance to change have been encountered. We will return to this point in Chapter 10.

The blending of the needs of employees with those of the company has had mixed fortunes depending on the level of the employees concerned. While for workers above operative levels, organization methods and decision-making and control mechanisms have allowed for an important degree of integration between the needs of individuals and those of the company, for workers at an operative level – those who carry out repetitive and routine activities – the desired integration was not easy and the problem has only been partially solved by means of job rotation, job enrichment and by the introduction of group specialization.[71]

5.6 Managerial motivation and the goals of the corporation: theoretical outlines

As we have seen, industrial managerial capitalism created a strong boost to the development of science and technology and to the rationalization of the management of the large company. This boost has contributed to tangible economic and social progress. The advent of the large managerial corporation – as Berle and Means wrote – was characterized by the split between property and power, and the eclipse of owner-shareholders[72] and the assumption of control (strategic and operational) by managers without capital and with motivations and strategies that were not always in line with the interests of shareholders.[73]

The majority of scholars of business behaviour maintain that the objectives of the production organization change according to whether the management is in the hands of owner-managers or professional managers who have no links with the company through an investment of capital. In the latter case, naturally, the enterprise in question is a 'mature enterprise'. The scholars mentioned state that if the enterprise is run by the owners, the goals of that enterprise would be represented by the achievement of maximum profit or by the maximum value of its shares. On the contrary, according to the hypothesis in which power is exercised by professional managers, the goals of the enterprise would change: there would be the pursuit of the maximum rate of growth in terms of size and such a strategy would be conditioned by the achievement of profits adequate to satisfy the expectations of capital markets.

For a deeper understanding of the issues involved it is necessary to examine the relationship that exists between the motivational make-up of those who manage large companies and the goals assigned to them.

It is well known that the identification of the motivational profile of managers is the starting point for the specification of their so-called 'utility function'.

It is also well-known that the holder of power in a company is also able to establish the mission and the general goals of the organization. From these general goals are derived the strategic objectives that constitute the point of reference for the tactical objectives that, in turn, inspire operational objectives. This sequence of objectives produces a chain of ends and means: the lower objectives are the means by which to realize the objectives on the next level, until the final goals of the enterprise are reached. Also, there is a close connection between the motivational system of managers who are in charge of running the firm, on the one hand, and the goals assigned to the enterprise, on the other. The chosen objectives can be viewed as the instruments necessary to satisfy the motivation of managers. Given that the top executives are those who specify the mission, the general goals and the general objectives of the enterprise and the strategies to achieve them, it would seem entirely plausible to argue that they assign to the company, aims and objectives capable of gratifying their own motivation. In essence, the 'utility function' of top managers is strictly dependent on the system of motivation of the managers themselves.[74]

It would seem correct to say that the motivational system of those who manage large corporations, whether they are owners or professional managers, consists of five fundamental needs: physiological, safety, self-esteem, respect of others and self-realization. These needs are arranged in a hierarchy.[75] Physiological needs do not normally influence the behaviour of managers, who, therefore, have an attitude of indifference towards them. A physiological need that is reasonably satisfied is no longer a need and does not affect human conduct. Instead, it is the need for safety that arises and, until this has been reasonably satisfied, the other needs at a higher level on the motivational scale are not relevant.

For managers at a high level, the need for safety can be understood in two ways: a) that the enterprise that they manage continues to survive; b) that they, the managers, continue to have power in the company.[76] A need for safety puts a brake on aggressive management policies and acts as a reminder, therefore, to act with prudence.[77]

What is the goal that managers assign to the enterprise to satisfy the need for safety? It would seem entirely plausible to maintain that such an objective consists in the realization of a particular (adequate) level of profitability to achieve the following:

- the payment to shareholders of normal[78] and usual[79] dividends, so that the level of the valuation ratio[80] does not fall below a safe level;
- the financing of the investments that are indispensable to adapt business to environmental changes, while also maintaining the leverage ratio at a safe level, that is, at a level that excludes both financial embarrassment as well as stimuli for the reduction of the value of shares.

As can be seen, the objective that managers give as a priority for the company is the realization of a profit (or better, of profitability), that is minimum/adequate and not maximum. The level of return must, in fact, be such as to satisfy the need for safety. This adequate/minimum level to be achieved can be determined – it is said – with reference to the above-mentioned valuation ratio and leverage ratio.

If dividends paid by the enterprise are normal and usual and if the capital market approves the management of the company, the valuation ratio increases or at least remains at a safe level: the shareholders trust in the management, keep their investments in the enterprise, and are actually willing to supply new capital to finance the investments necessary to help the business adapt to the dynamism of the environment (competition included). Furthermore, in this case, the leverage ratio is not affected by negative signals of risk. If capital markets evaluate its management positively, the company continues to survive and those who manage it do not run the risk of losing control, as would happen in the case of eventual takeover bids by dissatisfied shareholders, or by new investors who believe they can 'extract' more value from the enterprise.

On the other hand, if dividends are not normal and usual and if there are negative factors that, operating as a system, give rise to doubts concerning the validity of the management, capitalists do not remain inert: they begin to ask for information, organize, carry out studies and sometimes they see signs of crisis and are immediately assailed by fears of a fall in the value of shares. Firstly, they predict a temporary crisis, then they hear that the crisis will not be short-term. Fear then triggers irrational behavior. Shareholders then come to sell their shares; share prices fall; the valuation ratio falls; struggles develop for the control of the company; internal and external groups of capitalists organize themselves and set in motion the 'takeover' process. There may follow a change of management. But in addition a fall in the valuation ratio also affects the leverage ratio. This happens because the enterprise is forced to use credit to a greater extent to finance indispensable investments and also because the use of credit tends to generate an increase in the cost of credit itself. This creates financial embarrassment and risk for the company, increases the perception of risk among financiers and produces further negative effects on the value of shares on the stock exchange and on the valuation ratio that is linked to it.[81]

Undoubtedly, the satisfaction of the need for safety is obtained by means of achieving a minimum level of profit, which allows for the maintenance of the valuation ratio and the leverage ratio at levels adequate for satisfying the expectations of shareholders and also for minimizing the risk of financial embarrassment and takeover bids by internal and external groups that aspire to control the enterprise.

But, having reasonably satisfied the need for safety (survival of the enterprise and conservation of its controlling power), top managers, whether owners or professionals, increasingly feel a higher order of need: social (the desire to maintain internal and external relations with people and more generally with stakeholders, the need for acceptance, to feel part of the community); for self-esteem (need for knowledge, competence, self-confidence, independence, success in work); respect of others (prestige, status and power); for self-actualization (the need to realize all the potential of one's personality; to complete a development plan for the enterprise, to be of service to others, to be creative and to influence the internal and external environment according to personal values).[82]

To satisfy these needs, managers assign objectives to the company that are capable of reasonably satisfying these desires. These objectives are pursued simultaneously:

a) growing rates of return;
b) increasing rate of size development;
c) a policy of responsibility towards employees, clients, suppliers, the environment and the local communities in which the company operates.[83]

Achievement of profit (and, more generally, dividends and capital gains) is an important means of satisfying social and psychological motivations (need for social gratification, self-esteem, respect of others and self-actualization). It represents

> a powerful means to be accepted by the social environment, to develop interaction with others within and outside the enterprise [. . .]. It allows for improvement in status, which is the position occupied in the hierarchy of the social system [. . .]. Even prestige is closely linked to the economic factor: the aptitude of an individual to stimulate admiration and respect is also in relation to his wealth. Money also allows the satisfaction of the desire for power; in other words, it confers the possibility to control people and environmental factors, to initiate events and not to respond passively to them [. . .]. Profit also allows managers (owners and non-owners) to satisfy the need for self-actualization [. . .].[84] Just as a musician has to compose music in order to 'realize' himself, so the entrepreneur must succeed

in achieving the objectives of the company. Because, usually and traditionally the company is an organization oriented to making profit, the group that controls it fulfills itself by achieving the expected return rates. If this task is not accomplished, professional pride and self-esteem are frustrated to a greater or lesser extent.[85]

The size increase of the company – kept within certain limits and over specific periods of time – appears, on the one hand, to be an instrument used to obtain an increase in the rate of profit and, on the other hand, an autonomous objective that is capable of directly gratifying the social, self-esteem and self-actualization motivations. Expansion, pursued within certain limits linked to the rational functioning of the company, generates positive effects on profits and profitability. In this way, considerable savings can be made related to economies of scale. With vertical development, market risk (regarding prices and quantity) can be partially eliminated by keeping supplies and/or sales under control. Size increase normally involves the differentiation of products and above all operational diversification[86] which permits entry into new markets (new in an absolute sense for all companies or for the single company). This allows the company to deal with risks adequately and to make higher profits as new sectors are generally more attractive and more promising. In addition, size increase stimulates scientific and technological progress, the creation of centres for research and development, and the exchange of information, experience and innovations among the various divisions of the company. In other words, diversified development allows the firm to use all the technological, financial, commercial and human resources available in a more efficient way and to manage and renew them more rapidly; in this way, the firm gains differential advantages over the competition and a considerable capacity to influence the environment in a manner that conforms to company objectives. Size increase, if not too rapid and kept within limits that allow the organization to function efficiently and, above all, if kept within the limits of the coordination capacity of top management, tends to increase total earnings and the profitability of the company or, in any case, to increase total earnings and keep profitability essentially constant. Both size and profitability increase are complementary objectives which, if pursued in a sensible and systematic manner, strengthen each other.[87]

In the case of the objectives of social responsibility, it must be pointed out that these are goals that the managers assign directly to the company and are not financed by the personal incomes of managers. These objectives, in other words, are realized by attributing the costs directly to the profit and loss statement of the company, which assumes directly the tasks of social responsibility.[88]

More precisely, these objectives concern:

- protection of the natural environment and, in particular, the requirement not to release polluting and/or toxic substances into the air, on the land or in water;
- the development of safe working conditions that conform to the higher principles of the ethical treatment of employees; payment of wages that are in line with human needs and productivity;
- the introduction of management models aimed at integrating the interests of the individual with those of the firm, to create structural and operating conditions that stimulate creativity, imagination, the energy of workers and the development of management processes that are inspired by the principles of equity;[89]
- formulation of a personnel policy that offers job security and therefore minimizes the dangers of unemployment and precarious employment;
- development of fair relationships of collaboration with main stakeholders and, in particular, with consumers (fair prices, safe products, and so on), with small financiers that buy shares and bonds, with suppliers and with banks;
- the development of company behaviour that is respectful of the interests of the local community in which production units are located. This is about putting in place a strategy of social legitimacy (of coherence), which is indispensable to operating successfully.

In other words, it is a question of formulating socially responsible behaviour (that is not only in line with the minimum conditions imposed by law, but goes beyond these obligations) and also of investing in the human capital of the firm, in the environment and in relations with the various stakeholders.[90]

From our analysis it emerges that – apart from the question of whether those running the company are proprietors or financiers – the 'utility function' of managers (considered as the set of objectives to be pursued) is not mono-dimensional and is different from that which generally characterizes economic theories on company behaviour; that is, it does not follow a mathematical model. These theories are based on the maximization of some function/objective subject to certain conditions that need to be met as a prerequisite.[91]

At this point it must be understood whether the three fundamental objectives indicated in a), b) and c) above are mutually compatible or in conflict and therefore incompatible.

In the following sections we will examine the relationship between rate of size increase, profitability of capital invested and the objectives of social responsibility, in the light of the theory of motivation. We will first examine the relationship between profitability and size increase (section 5.7); then, we will analyse the relationship between objectives of social responsibility on the one hand, and profitability and size increase on the other (section 5.8).

5.7 The relationship between profitability and increase in company size

This topic must make reference to a particular time frame, which, for simplicity, could be identified as the period in which the long-term planning process of the company is based. In this period of time, a very high rate of size growth comes into conflict with the objectives of profitability (or with the increase in the value of shares). Conventional theory attributes the cause of this phenomenon to the decreasing returns on the 'costs of expansion' connected to costs of commercial activity, organizational restructuring and research and development.

It is certainly true that an inappropriate rate of growth, in a particular period,

> would force the company to practice commercial policies (of product, price, advertising, etc.) that are increasingly expensive in order to attract and promote demand from the market; the 'rate of success' would tend to diminish with the increase in the 'rate of diversification'. All this would be to the disadvantage of the profitability of the firm. There is no doubt that a very high rate of development would impose hurried and inefficient organizational restructuring and would not allow the constitution of a united, coordinated, competent management group, capable of facing the business problems of the company rationally.[92]

However, in large enterprises, according to the observations of Penrose,[93] the rate of development is in practice defined in relation to the capacity of the managerial group to find new management forces and to absorb and integrate them in order to achieve and maintain, over time, a compact, coordinated and competent management structure. Penrose points out that, in a particular period of time, the capacity of the existing managerial group to integrate new resources is a limit to development.

In our opinion, the rate of growth that can be achieved seems to be limited by two factors:

1) the physical, technical and managerial capacity of the existing management group;
2) the capacity of this group to integrate new managerial forces.

If the first condition is not met, serious consequences could be produced for the physical health of managers. Also the group

> will no longer be able to control events: the situation tends to get out of hand, the initiatives of the group will become ineffective and its decisions contradictory [. . .] and very soon conditions will arise that can threaten managers' job security and their full control of the company.[94]

With regard to the second limit, if the rate of growth is not consistent with the speed with which the integration of new managers takes place, the organization system will display a strong tendency towards disorder and lack of coordination. Therefore dangerous tensions could develop that reduce the power of the managerial group, which could even result in the loss of control of the organization.

Whenever these two factors are not respected, the need for safety, which is a priority motivation, reappears.

It is evident that all managers (proprietors and non-proprietors) have no interest in going beyond such limits. These criteria, therefore, define the highest rate of development achievable in a certain period of time.[95]

Accepting this, it is plausible to conclude that if managers derive no benefit from going beyond these limits, because that would conflict with their motivational system, then the objective of increase in company size would tend not to be in conflict with the objective of profitability (or increase in share value).[96]

This can be analysed by comparing the rate of growth and the rate of profitability in a certain period of time. It can be seen in the following graph (Figure 5.1) that if the rate of growth remains within the limits of the capacity of the management group, there is no fall in profitability. In our opinion, the need for safety is important in two ways: the first regards the risks that come from the financial world and the second concerns the personal capacity of managers and their ability to integrate new, competent

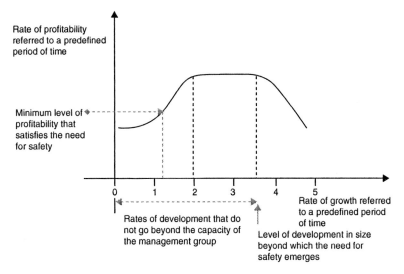

Figure 5.1   Rate of growth and rate of profitability

and well-controlled managers in the existing managerial group. In other words, the need for safety is satisfied if two conditions occur:

1) realization of an appropriate level of earnings to allow both the payment of normal and usual dividends as well as the financing of indispensable investments while maintaining the valuation ratio and the leverage at safety level;
2) maintaining the increase in company size, in the reference period, within the limits of the physical, technical and managerial capacities of the managers who are in control, and the capacity of managers to integrate new managerial resources while maintaining efficient control of the company.

5.8   The relationship between objectives of social responsibility and rate of profitability and company size development

Let us consider, at this point, the objectives of social responsibility and let us see how they affect profitability and development in company size.

There is no doubt that the pursuit of these objectives signifies costs for the enterprise, costs that have to be displayed in the profit and loss account with an inevitable negative influence on earnings.

But if the problem is observed over a long period of time, and especially if the enterprise is considered as an 'open' socio-economic system whose results are closely connected to attention paid to the environment and to the quality of its human capital, the outlook changes, and in a radical way. The costs mentioned above represent investment in human capital, in the development of relations with the environment, the local community and with stakeholders who formulate expectations with regard to the behaviour of the company. The result is that these costs, that in a short-term view seem to be costs without corresponding benefits, represent a source of future material and intangible advantages. These costs, on the one hand, develop internal resources that boost the productivity of the organization and, on the other, they allow the creation of external conditions and relations of synergy with stakeholders. The company is therefore enabled towards achieving satisfying objectives of profitability and stable development in size. In practice, if this is considered in a wider context and with a far-sighted perspective, economic priorities are not in conflict with social concerns and corporate behaviour inspired by strong reference to ethics.[97]

5.9 The 'utility function' of professional managers of dominant large corporations from the 1930s to the appearance of 'financial shareholding managerial capitalism'

It follows that:

- the motivations of managers inspire the definition of the objectives of the company, and can be considered as the means to satisfy them;
- for professional managers, the prime motivation is safety. This is satisfied by assigning to the enterprise the objective of realizing a minimum/adequate level of profit, to allow payment of normal and usual dividends to shareholders, financing indispensable investments and maintaining the valuation ratio and the leverage ratio at a safe level. Safety is guaranteed by maintaining increase in size, in the period of reference, within the limits of the personal capacity of managers and their ability to integrate new managerial resources while keeping control of the company;
- motivations of a higher order (social needs, self-esteem, respect from others and self-realization) are gratified by assigning to the company, and realizing *de facto*, a system of objectives that can be summarized

as follows: development of profitability, size increase and social responsibility. The relationship between motivation and objectives is very complex and cannot be described in a rigid and analytic manner, unless the intention is to carry out a purely academic exercise. This would lead to different results arising from the introduction of certain assumptions that vary according to the particular environmental situation, the specific personality of individual managers, their individual and family history, the level of their aspirations, and so on. Predicting the behaviour of managers is extremely complicated;

- much economic and managerial doctrine[98] maintains that, in the 'mature corporations' (that dominated the world economic scene from the 1930s until the end of the 1960s), management power shifted into the hands of a small group of non-proprietor top managers, who, presumably, did not administer the means of production in the exclusive interest of shareholders. In particular, a professional manager does not necessarily maximize profits; rather, 'such an action would frequently be exposing him to risks that could put his position in the enterprise at risk'.[99] Much of the above doctrine also maintains that the management group of the 'mature corporation' tends to attain the objective of the maximization of the rate of size increase subject to some constraints imposed by the motivation of safety. The theory explicitly affirms that the group that holds control – as long as it observes the limits imposed by the need for safety – is motivated towards realizing increasing rates of growth, even at the expense of profitability. Such behaviour should then be reinforced by the fact that larger size should allow managers to increase their influence on the environment and have greater autonomy and flexibility of behaviour. Although it is not at all explicit in the prevailing theory on company behaviour,[100] it can be deduced that if professional managers tend to 'maximize' the rate of size increase, even to the detriment of the rate of profitability (both because they obtain greater economic benefits and because they acquire greater power over the environment), then they would also be motivated – again at the expense of profitability – to pursue important objectives of social responsibility, in order to create favourable relationships with stakeholders and facilitate their strategies of development and control of the environment.[101]

Modifying the graph that was presented previously, the 'utility function' of professional managers, can be represented as follows.

As can be seen, the chosen level of general growth, as defined in advance by professional managers, would be realized at the expense of

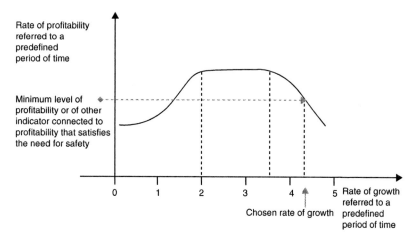

Figure 5.2   Rate of growth and rate of profitability (modified)

the 'maximization of profitability'. The decrease in profitability, as has been said, could also have been affected by a policy of social responsibility aimed at facilitating the relationship with stakeholders and at realizing the objectives of corporate growth more easily.

Some brief observations follow concerning the theory illustrated above (Figure 5.2).

Apart from the criticisms that could be raised regarding the concept of 'maximization' – concerning which, reference can be made to the brilliant works of H. A. Simon[102] – the statements made in the last point of this section should be analysed and evaluated in the light of the following remarks, which in turn, should be examined in depth to verify their soundness:

- professional managers could show a propensity for development in size to the detriment of income if their rewards structure was closely connected only to the size of the company (turnover, value of net capital and so on). But what happens if their rewards structure is indexed to revenues or to the value of shares? In mature managerial capitalism, what were the prevalent conditions? The reality of enterprises has demonstrated the presence of cases with different solutions regarding the parameters which are taken into consideration in determining the reward structure;
- if the size increase relative to a pre-fixed timeframe is kept within the physical and professional capabilities of managers and of their ability

to integrate new managerial resources, it is highly probable that size development and profitability will not enter into conflict. It is more than likely that they will operate in a manner that is mutually advantageous. Furthermore, conflict tends not to be present in that the manager, whether proprietor or professional, is considered a profit maker;

- the assumption of social responsibility, if practised with a long-term point of view and inspired by the higher principles of ethics, does not enter into conflict with the objective of profitability; rather it can 'support' the achievement of a very satisfying profitability and also facilitate the policies of general growth of the company;

- the behaviour of managerial companies can be realistically explained if consideration is given to the relationship between the motivational system of managers and the objectives that they themselves set for the company, in order to gratify their own competing motivations. As was seen previously, after having satisfied the need for safety, managers turn their attention to gratifying a superior order of motivations (of belonging, acceptance, interaction, knowledge, competence, success in work, independence, self-confidence, social status, prestige, power and self-realization).[103] To this end, they pursue objectives of profitability, general growth and the assumption of social responsibility. It is important to underline that the relationships between individual objectives and the motivational system are very complex. We do not believe they can be described in an unambiguous manner by means of analytical instruments, especially because the behaviour strategy of managers (all managers) is strongly connected to the environmental situation, their personality, culture, individual and family history, level of ambition, and so on. Undoubtedly, the choice of the objectives to be assigned to the company and their connection to competing motivations, is to a great extent a subjective matter.

The Ford case is emblematic in this respect. Henry Ford (1863–1947) in 1903 founded the Ford Motor Company, which by 1926 was the largest automobile manufacturer in the world. Gifted with great inventiveness, Ford introduced efficient methods of production along the lines of Taylor's theories. From 1914 he granted profit-sharing to employees. His objective was to make automobiles that all could buy at very affordable prices. This was the policy behind the Model T Ford up to 1926, followed by the Model A.[104]

Henry Ford paid his employees much better salaries than his competitors and guaranteed a minimum wage. In 1914, for example, he increased wages considerably, taking them from $2.89 a day for nine hours of work to five dollars a day for eight hours of work. Ford also gave advantages to customers by continually lowering the price of cars: the price of the Model T fell from an initial $900 to $440 in 1916. He aspired to making reasonable profits and was very sensitive to the interests of stakeholders.

Ford founded the company with the participation of the brothers John and Horace Dodge, who were the majority shareholders. The administration was prevalently in the hands of Henry Ford and John Dodge. In 1916, the Dodge brothers, who were about to launch their own automobile company, and therefore needed high dividends, entered into a head-on confrontation with Henry Ford, who had decided to cut dividends and favour consumers by lowering the prices of the Model T. The controversy ended up in court. The Dodge brothers were of the opinion – according to what the law seemed to state – that profits ought to be directed to shareholders and that they could not be lowered by the administrators to favour customers, employees or other social groups. Ford held that the corporation was an institution with autonomous legal personality, and in his opinion such an entity was different from the proprietors and should be managed with equity and far-sightedness in relation to its objectives of survival and development. In other words, because the corporation had by then assumed importance and power in society as a whole, it should be managed with consideration given to the interests of the various stakeholders and not only those of the shareholders. The Supreme Court of Michigan, in 1919, agreed with the Dodge brothers: the management of the company must serve the interests of shareholders; the enterprise must be administered, above all, for the benefit of the shareholders; those who manage the company have no authority to operate in the interests of groups that are not shareholders. In essence, it was affirmed that those who manage the corporation must act in the 'best interests' of the firm, that is, in the best interests of its proprietors. However, contrary to what the judge originally decided, the Court did not prohibit Ford from increasing the company size as, obviously, it did not deem this to be in conflict with the interests of the owners.

The case of Ford vs Dodge is very interesting in relation to what has been said above. Both Henry Ford and the Dodge brothers were manager-owners and, at least until 1916, had managed the enterprise with a 'utility function' that left ample room of manoeuvre for the objectives of social responsibility and growth, even at the expense of profitability. Only the contingent need of the Dodge brothers, who in 1916 found themselves faced with the necessity to make a large investment to create an automobile factory of their own, changed their 'utility function' and, therefore, their preference as to what was in the best interests of the Ford Motor Company.

The events illustrated above demonstrate clearly that the 'utility function' of managers reflects to a large extent the contingent environmental situation, and the values, personality, aspirations and history of managers themselves.

In conclusion, it would seem that the analytical models available on the behaviour of managers in the period in which the large mature corporation was at its zenith have a limited capacity to predict managerial behaviour. To better understand how the large mature corporation operated in the period in question, it seemed appropriate to develop a hypothesis of a theory of managerial behaviour on the basis of the relationship between motivation of managers and objectives to be assigned to the enterprise. We are aware that our conclusions need further development. To achieve this, we believe it is important to make use of already available or future empirical research in order to construct an ample case study that supplements analytical models that have been developed and that allows the formulation of a managerial behaviour theory that is explicative, predictive and reliable.

Notes

1. Rostow (1960).
2. Cipolla (2003), p. 164.
3. On this point, see Leroy Beaulieu (1891).
4. In other words, the anti-capitalism, anti-imperialism and internationalism of the workers' movements represented fragile clay vases among the iron vases of nationalism.
5. Hilferding (1961), pp. 309ff.
6. Marchand (1998), p. 7.
7. Great Britain and France recovered quickly, because of their efficient industrial apparatus, their banking systems and their colonial empires. Germany re-emerged from the 1922–23 crisis thanks to foreign loans, its scientific research and its capacity to develop technology in various fields. Immediately following the First World War, Japan emerged as a new industrial power.
8. There was also a reduction in international solidarity, and the dream of internationalism of the workers' movements was put to a hard test. Often during the wars between nations and in the operations of colonial conquest, national working classes found themselves opposing each other, a situation which was difficult to reconcile with the myth of international unity. Many general strikes against the war, though adequately prepared and publicized, in fact turned out to be failures and thus created divisions within workers' movements.

9. Kindleberger (1982), pp. 257ff.
10. Keynes (1936) criticized the classical theory of automatic equilibrium achieved by the variation of interest rates.
11. Experience and theory have taught that it is not right to leave market forces to themselves and rely on the variations of interest rates, but that it is necessary to introduce some provisions capable of influencing market mechanisms in order to manage both the tendency to recession and to inflation. State intervention was essential in this respect, through the manoeuvre of government revenues and spending aimed, precisely, at keeping in balance the amount of savings produced in each period and the volume of investments. But all this did not happen between 1920 and 1933. The classical theory of economic equilibrium was considered a dogma. Therefore any government action aimed at interfering with market competition mechanisms was frowned upon. Indeed, every possible evil was attributed to attempts to erode the processes of competition and the freedom of the market.
12. Cipolla (2003), pp. 177–8.
13. 'The crash of the stock exchange in 1929 and the resulting recession in the United States were the last straw. With the loss of the greatest consumer nation on the planet, exports fell in the whole world. Balance of payments deficits rose in Europe, Japan and Latin America. As international loans were reduced to the minimum, countries under the gold standard had to make the corrections required: wages and prices had to go down so that the country could export more and generate the necessary surplus to re-establish an appropriate equilibrium in the trade balance. But with the labor force no longer willing to accept a significant cut in wages, the best alternative available to government was a block on imports and support for exports. The United States set the example with the Smoot-Hawley protectionist law. Obviously, if all countries behaved in this way, world trade would collapse, and this is precisely what happened. The world entered into a negative economic spiral and the recession transformed into depression' (Rajan and Zingales 2004, p. 243).
14. Krugman points out that in the United States during the period called the Long Gilded Age (the final decades of 19th century to the beginning of the New Deal), anti-State ideology was widespread and well-established. 'It was an era in which respectable opinion simply assumed, as a matter of course, that taxation had devastating economic effects, that any effort to mitigate poverty and inequality was highly irresponsible, and that anyone who suggested that unmitigated capitalism was unjust and could be improved was a dangerous radical, contaminated by Europeans' ideas. [. . .] the Red Scare after World War I had the incidental effect of discrediting or intimidating ordinary liberals, people who believed that capitalism could be made more just without being abolished. [. . .] But in the United States the gospel of free enterprise remained dominant' (Krugman 2007, pp. 32–3).
15. Say (1854).
16. The Great Depression was also linked to the confusion of the time regarding inflation. See Shiller (2008), p. 97.
17. Galbraith (1987), p. 195.
18. 'It took the searing experiences of the Great Depression to teach Americans that unfettered financial markets can implode and bring whole economies down with them' (Thurow 2000, p. 4).

19. Keynes' ideas began to be gradually accepted from 1936. In that year Harvard University celebrated its 300th anniversary and decided to assign some honorary degrees. The young economists proposed Keynes; but his candidacy was not accepted. 'But the response of the younger Harvard economists was specific; it was through their agency that the Keynesian system was to come to the United States. As Wisconsin would be the source of Social Security and Yale of monetarist innovation, Harvard, previously a citadel of the high orthodoxy, would be the germinal point for Keynesian economics in the United States. There were, of course, older converts. But most of the economists of established reputation stood firm, and quite a few saved themselves from temptation by not reading *The General Theory*' (Galbraith 1987, p. 238).

20. Castronovo (2007), pp. 84–5.

21. One of first authors who used the term 'managerial revolution' was Burnham (1941). A fundamental work on the 'managerial revolution' is Chandler (1977). Although the term 'revolution' is used, in reality it was a progressive and not a sudden process. In 1964 Robin Marris asserted: 'Naturally, there was never a managerial revolution. Like the Industrial Revolution, the development from traditional capitalism to the contemporary form has involved the slow replacement of one kind of economic organization by another, a process that is still continuing' (Marris 1972, p. 4).

22. Berle and Means (1932).

23. In their research relating to 1929, regarding the nature of existing control in the 200 largest American corporations, Berle and Means (revised edn 1968, p. 106) pointed out the following situation:

Type of Control	Number of Corporations
I Private Ownership	12
II Majority Ownership	10
III Minority Ownership	46
IV Legal Device	41
V Management Control	88
In Receivership	2
Total	200

24. There are many interesting examinations of this subject, including: Baumol (1959), pp. 45ff.; Campbell et al. (1970), pp. 340ff.; Caselli (1966); Drucker (1964); Galbraith (1967), chs. V, VI, VII, VIII, XIII and XIV; Marris (1963; 1965; 1972); Maslow (1943); Monsen et al. (1964); Papandreou (1952), pp. 183–219; Rothschild (1947); Williamson (1964); Zanda (1974), pp. 363–424.

25. Galbraith (1987), p. 197–98.

26. On this point, see Beer (1967); Bertini (1975); Saraceno (1967).

27. The term was used by Galbraith (1967), pp. 60ff.

28. Caselli (1966), p. 47; Fortuna (1975).

29. In our opinion, the maximum power in the mature corporation was not (and is not) held by the techno-structure, as Galbraith (1967) maintains (chapter VI and, in particular, chapter V, pp. 58–59), but is in the hands of the small group of managers who constitute the so-called 'economic subject'.

30. Simon (1958), pp. 5ff.
31. On the concept of strategic decisions we have referred to: Ansoff (1965); Canziani (1984); Coda (1988); Hofer and Schendel (1978); Lacchini (1988).
32. Zanda (1974), pp. 295–334; Paoloni (1990), pp. 123ff.
33. Adapting to change is not always easy; it depends mainly on the quantity and quality of the resources available and also on 'managerial inertia', or the tendency of top managers to remain attached to their own 'success formula', which, in the past, allowed them to achieve excellent economic and financial results. As Confucius maintained, the symptoms of failure already exist when success is achieved. This is due to 'self-satisfaction', which dims the strategic vision of managers and their ability to foresee environmental trends. Self-satisfaction is the result of the mysterious effect of success (realization), which stimulates feelings of invulnerability, superiority, arrogance and myopia.
34. On this subject, see S. Zanda (2009) chapters I and II, in particular, section 2.4.
35. These sectors are defined by Galbraith (1967, p. 10) as the 'Industrial System' which is the dominant element of the 'New Industrial State'. In particular, on pages 9–10 he writes: 'This is the part of the economy which, automatically, we identify with the modern industrial society. To understand it is to understand that part which is most subject to change and which, accordingly, is most changing our lives. No exercise of intelligence is to be deplored. But to understand the rest of the economy is to understand only that part which is diminishing in relative extent and which is most nearly static. [. . .]. The two parts of the economy – the world of the few hundred technically dynamic, massively capitalized and highly organized corporations on the one hand and of the thousands of small and traditional proprietors on the other – are very different. It is not a difference of degree but a difference which invades every aspect of economic organization and behavior, including the motivation to effort itself'.
36. Berle, preface to Mason (1970), p. 13.
37. Berle and Means (rev. edn 1968), p. 8.
38. On this point, see Zanda (1974), p. 274.
39. This is even more valid for mature corporations operating in the most industrialized nations after the first two decades of the 20th century.
40. Berle and Means (rev. edn 1968), pp. 75–8.
41. In 1963, an analysis of 200 large corporations showed that public companies were expanding. The study reported that 169 corporations were controlled by managers without ownership and that only five were controlled by shareholders with a majority stake. See Caves (1970), p. 14.
42. See Larner (1966). Robin Marris reports that at the end of the 1930s, in two thirds of large and medium English companies and in four fifths of large companies in the United States, not even the 20 major shareholders had a sufficient number of shares to acquire an absolute majority. Since then, the dispersion of shares has continued to increase and, at least in Britain, the tendency seems to have accelerated (Marris 1972, p. 23). See the following studies on the division of share ownership: Berle and Means (1932), book I; Gordon (1945), ch. V; Gordon (1940); Sargant Florence (1961), pp. 68ff.
43. They could only judge the quality of the management by considering the value of distributed dividends (their normality in comparison with competitors and the past) and the market share price.

44. Galbraith (1967, pp. 37–9) writes: 'The individual serves the industrial system not by supplying it with savings and the resulting capital; he serves it by consuming its products. On no other matter, religious, political or moral, is he so elaborately and skillfully and expensively instructed. [. . .] Control of the supply of savings is strategic for industrial planning. [. . .] Money carries with it the special right to know, and even to suggest, how it is used. [. . .] All of these dangers and difficulties are avoided if the firm has a secure source of capital from its own earnings. It no longer faces the risks of the market. It concedes no authority to outsiders. It has full control over its own rate of expansion, over the nature of that expansion and over decisions between products, plants and processes.'

45. Authors in the classical tradition assumed that enterprises were very small and that they could not therefore affect the course of the market, which, however, determined in an anonymous and automatic way the returns of the productive factors. In short, according to classical economic theory owners did not have substantial market power and company control was never analysed because it was not an issue.

46. Galbraith (1967), p. 50.

47. In Galbraith's opinion, the shift of power 'has been disguised because power has not gone to another of the established factors as they are celebrated in conventional economic pedagogy. It has not passed to labor. Labor has won limited authority over its pay and working conditions but none over the enterprise. And it still tends to abundance. If overly abundant savings are not used, the first effect is unemployment; if savings are used, one consequence is a substitution of machine processes for unskilled labor and standard skills. [. . .] Nor has power passed to the classical entrepreneur – the individual who once used his access to capital to bring it into combination with the other factors of production. He is a diminishing figure in the industrial system. [. . .] Power has, in fact, passed to what anyone in search of novelty might be justified in calling a new factor of production. This is the association of men of diverse technical knowledge, experience or other talent which modern industrial technology and planning require' (Galbraith 1967, pp. 58–9).

48. Interesting observations on the separation between ownership and control in Italian companies are found in Coda (1967), pp. 7ff.

49. Shonfield (1967).

50. The term was introduced by two economic historians, Goldin and Margo (1992), pp. 1–34, quoted by Krugman (2007), pp. 7–8 and 38–9.

51. Krugman, (2007) p. 39. Furthermore, Krugman, on pages 38–9, points out that 'America in the 1950s was a middle-class society, to a far greater extent than it had been in the 1920s – or than it is today. [. . .] ordinary workers and their families had good reason to feel that they were sharing in the nation's prosperity as never before. And, on the other side, the rich were a lot less rich than they had been a generation earlier. [. . .]; the narrowing of income gaps was a defining event in American history, something that transformed the nature of our society and politics'. The indicators regarding changes in the income of various social classes and the reduced inequality existing in the 1950s in comparison with the 1920s are reported by Krugman (2007), pp. 40–51.

52. Krugman (2007), p. 39. On pp. 54–55, we can read that 'during the postwar boom the real income of the typical family roughly doubled, from about $22,000 in today's prices to $44,000. That's a growth rate of 2.7 percent per year. And incomes all through the income distribution grew at about the same rate, preserving the relatively equal distribution created by the Great Compression'.
53. Capaldo (1965), pp. 34ff.
54. Caramiello (1965), p. 61.
55. These organizational centres, even if guided and oriented by top management (usually the economic subject), could, within their competence, find and define business problems, develop alternatives in order to solve problems, make choices and take risks.
56. A policy is a principle (or a system of principles) that guides and delimits discretion in taking decisions. A policy establishes the overall guidelines or boundaries which provide general direction to the decisions carried out in the company. It keeps business decisions moving along the goals determined by managers. In other words policies are general statements which guide the thinking of subordinates in decision-making. Procedures are quite different. They guide action, while policies relate to the process of decision-making. In particular, a procedure is a system of prescriptions that establishes the phases needed for a certain activity to be accomplished, the actors to be involved and the related time sequence of phases and tasks. On the nature and role of policies and procedures see Davis (1958), pp. 158ff. and 697ff.; Goetz (1949), pp. 84ff.; Koontz and O'Donnell (1959), pp. 458ff.; Terry (1955), pp. 89ff.; Zanda (1968), pp. 126–35.
57. Zanda (1984).
58. Pfiffner and Sherwood (1960), pp. 298ff.
59. The creation of an effective information system requires access to data and information in order to produce rational decisions and to coordinate decisions of subordinates.
60. On the relationship between the effective recruitment of personnel and the amount of authority to be used to control workers, see Etzioni (1967), pp. 129ff.; D'Alessio (1980), pp. 67ff.
61. On this topic we suggest the following works: Ackoff and Eckman (1961); Beer (1967); von Bertalanffy (1971); von Bertalanffy and Rapoport (1959); Barile (2006); Boulding (1956); Boulding (1953); Churchman (1971); Golinelli (2000), book I; Huant (1960); Rapoport (1966); Simon (1965); Wiener (1948; 1950); Zanda (1974), chapters VI, VII and VIII.
62. Sexton (1970); Barnabé (2007), pp. 49ff.
63. See Mayo (1933; 1944 [with G. F. Lombard]; 1945; 1947).
64. An overview of the Hawthorne experiments is found in Roethlisberger and Dickson (1939).
65. Landsberger (1958).
66. Zanda (2006), pp. 77–8.
67. Bakke and Argyris (1954).
68. Drucker (1972), p. 44.
69. McGregor (1966), p. 15.
70. Zanda (1984), pp. 88–9.

71. Regarding the lower level of the organization (worker's tasks), we are still very far from a reasonable integration between individual and company needs. Companies are engaged in developing new technologies aimed at diminishing repetitive, meaningless activities and at the motivational appeal of success, sense of competence, independence, and so on. The new technologies and the new forms of organization will probably give rise to various social and managerial problems concerning the need to hire and train employees able to operate with new technologies and new models of organization.

72. Berle and Means (rev. edn 1968), pp. 112–18 and 299–313.

73. Capital owners have been confined to the fringe of company management; in some large corporations they have maintained the power to nominate the top managers who take the strategic decisions; in other corporations, these top managers have acquired the power of self-nomination and self-perpetuation.

74. Caselli (1966), chapter I; Salvati (1967), pp. 138ff.; Zanda (1974), chapter VIII.

75. Maslow (1943), pp. 146ff.; McGregor (1960), pp. 36ff.

76. Zanda (1974), pp. 373–7.

77. We can ask ourselves whether the reminder to act with prudence, which can also be regarded as a reluctance to take risks, is more important for the owner-manager or the non-owner manager. Only a few authors have studied the problem, with contrasting conclusions. In our opinion, at present we lack reliable experimental verification of the various hypotheses.

78. A dividend is 'normal' when it is congruent with dividends paid by similar companies or when it is in line with the current conditions practised in the financial markets.

79. A dividend can be considered 'usual' when it is in line with the dividends paid in the recent past to the shareholders of the company.

80. The *valuation ratio* is the ratio between the market value of shares and the book value of equity. It is an indicator of the appreciation showed by the capital markets relative to the quality of the management and the results achieved by the company.

81. It should be noted that exorbitant *leverage* tends to increase risk; but increased risk stimulates, in turn, an increase in the rate at which profits or future cash flows are discounted. The increase of this rate generates, naturally, a decrease in the economic value of the company.

82. The need for self-realization manifests itself in many ways and is closely related to the personality of managers. It is not necessarily associated with the presence of or links with other people; moreover, it is not inevitably a creative motivation.

83. For an interesting analysis of the process that generates value for the various categories of stakeholder, see Stampacchia (2007), pp. 109ff.

84. Manager-owners undoubtedly enjoy the benefits deriving from increasing rates of profit; other conditions being equal, the higher the profit, the higher the dividends and share price. Normally in mature corporations, the rewards of professional managers are closely linked to achieved profits; Also compensation related to stock options and exit-bonuses is strongly

dependent on the level of the profit. Therefore there is no doubt that the pursuit of increasing profit rates is a fundamental instrument for the gratification of the motivations of both owners and professional managers.

85. Zanda (1974), p. 397; see also Paoloni (1990), p. 140.
86. On the role of diversification, see Marris (1972), pp. 149ff.
87. The level of profitability determines the value of shares, in the long term. Therefore the objective of increasing the share price can take the place of the objective of increasing profitability.
88. For an interesting analysis of the connection between economic objectives and the values of company players, see Catturi and Di Toro (1999); Riccaboni (1995).
89. Zanda (1984).
90. For a detailed analysis of integration between the principles of the Christian Social Doctrine and modern management theory, see Alford and Naughton (2006).
91. An interesting analysis of theories regarding the company is found in Galassi (1968), pp. 209–42.
92. Zanda (1974), p. 402.
93. Penrose (1959). According to the author, absolute limits to the development of the company do not exist. However there is a temporal limit to growth: this is defined by the capacity of the managerial group to integrate new managerial forces.
94. Zanda (1974), p. 403.
95. Zanda (1974), p. 403.
96. 'To affirm the contrary would mean to admit that new sectors and new possibilities of expansion do not exist, in reference to which the investments show, at least, equal profitability in comparison with the current situation. It would mean, moreover, to affirm that the abilities of programming, organizing, controlling and leading of the management team in charge are badly used [. . .]. But the first hypothesis seems unrealistic; the second would denote that the managerial group in charge has gone beyond the limits of its physical and managerial capacity' (Zanda 1974, p. 404).
97. On this point, see Onida, (1971), chapter II.
98. Baumol (1959), pp. 45ff.; Baumol (1962) pp. 1078–87; Berle and Means (rev. edn. 1968), pp. 3ff.; Monsen et al. (1964), pp. 546ff.
99. Monsen et al. (1964), p. 546.
100. This still refers to the above-mentioned doctrine.
101. This means the acquisition of a solid 'social legitimacy' that permits the company to have broad room for manoeuvre relative to stakeholders.
102. Simon (1958), pp. 75ff; Simon (1952), pp. 1130–9; March and Simon (1963), pp. 137ff.
103. These are the motivations defined in the so-called 'hierarchy of needs' of Maslow (1943; 1954).
104. In 1945, his grandson Henry Ford Junior was appointed president of the company. He followed the style of his grandfather: improvement of work organization and relations with stakeholders and employees.

6
The Appearance and Establishment of 'Financial Shareholding Managerial Capitalism'

Gianfranco Zanda

6.1 Preliminary remarks

As previously stated, 'managerial capitalism', based on the large public company, dominated the economic scene from the 1930s to the end of the 1960s. This model of capitalism has been studied analytically and regularly revised. The discussion is still open and no definitive conclusions have been reached; however it would seem reasonable to maintain that managerial capitalism

> has marked a period of considerable economic expansion, of satisfactory profitability for enterprises, of growth in employment and real wages and of improvement in working conditions. It also seemed to many that the 'utility function' of managers was to a certain extent oriented also to social relations and to respect for the higher needs of the workers. The view of managers was directed to the long term; the level of profits was appropriate, even though in keeping with certain assumptions about social responsibility.[1]

In essence, the 'managerial revolution', on the one hand, has modified the relationships between shareholders and professional managers and, on the other, has contributed to 'convert the strategies of large corporations towards objectives of growth and profitability planned over a longer period and with such horizons as to embrace a vast network of circuits and international relations'.[2] In addition: large 'mature companies' have generally operated with the objective of guaranteeing the 'going concern' (the continuity of the firm) and with industrial and commercial entrepreneurial strategies which, normally, ruled out opportunist and speculative behaviour. In Western countries they have assured, especially from the end of the Second World War, full use of resources, satisfactory salaries and innovative technology. Furthermore, they have given renewed driving force to the economic system.

Again, in economic reality

> the 'invisible hand' of the market – the hidden and providential balancer of the different and conflicting interests of the various economic subjects in their free unfolding – is being replaced (as Alfred Chandler said) by a 'visible hand', represented by the large companies, by their growing power to plan and construct the mechanisms of demand and supply.[3]

Even though it has given rise to concern regarding the freedom of consumers and savers, this phenomenon has contributed to creating greater stability of the economic system, considerable social peace and a progressive tendency to reduce inequality in economic terms.

These processes were stimulated in the West, in the period 1945–1970, by political systems that facilitated the declaration of civil rights and of economic democracy. In our opinion, these political orientations have been as important as the role played by large corporations in achieving technological, economic and social progress.

The 'large mature corporation' has become synonymous with a quasi-public institution as well as with professional management. This is Dore's view of managerial capitalism:

> In the 1960s [. . .] share capital was dispersed, expectations concerning an adequate level of return for shareholders were reasonably stable, and satisfying these expectations was seen as merely one of the responsibilities of managers, together with supplying employment at decent wages, producing goods that were safe and reliable at reasonable prices, contributing to the progress of local communities and effecting economic growth by promoting innovation and being in constant dialogue with government officials. The expression 'management as a profession' reflected the notion according to which companies were, in a certain sense, public institutions; the people who managed them had responsibilities towards society, therefore ethical integrity was necessary on the same level as was expected of doctors and lawyers, as well as moderation in fixing their own compensation.[4]

It is possible to say that mature corporations, in the period from the end of the 1930s to the beginning of the 1970s, played an important role in social life; supplying a mass of goods and services to satisfy human needs and influencing people's behaviour by encouraging new lifestyles.[5] Consequently, the issues of the responsibility of managers of large corporations and their control arose. The companies of the 19th century operated in a system of small units that competed with each other, and the conduct of managers was under the vigilant control of the owners and, above all, was subject to the regulation of the mechanisms of a competitive market. In public companies the managers progressively freed themselves from the owners' control and, given the enormous dimensions of the production organizations, they had considerable influence on markets, communities, the State and on the values and aspirations of people. Thus the conviction grew that because the market and owners were not capable of controlling managers, it was necessary to think of some intervention that would tackle this problem.[6] This question was to become even more important with the advent of shareholding managerial capitalism characterized by the 'financialization' of business.

6.2   Internal and external crises of economic systems and the fall in profits

In the mid-1960s, Western economies began to slow down and to lose stability. The response to this was so-called 'post-industrial modernization', when countries worked to increase productivity through the introduction of modern technologies that would save labour: robotics applied to assembly lines and information technology and computers used in factories and offices. From a political and social point of view, Anglo-American capitalism shifted towards 'deregulation' and the weakening of public intervention, while the capitalism of the rest of western Europe continued to maintain the 'social state' by rationalizing and obtaining efficiency through the reduction of costs, especially in the area of public administration.

Between the mid-1960s and the end of the 1980s, there was an evident and important fall in profits. This became generalized and struck the industrialized Western world, even if it appeared with different intensity in different nations and sectors.

Gross profits before tax, in the more industrialized countries, showed a reduction of about 40 per cent. In particular, in the USA between 1965 and 1982 the rate of profitability of non-financial enterprises fell from

24 to 12 per cent.[7] If we consider as a profitability indicator the ratio of gross domestic product to investment in fixed capital, in Great Britain we see a fall of about 40 per cent in the period 1963–1988 and one of 50 per cent in Japan between 1960 and the end of the 1980s.

The causes of this very important phenomenon are very complex. They must be placed in the context of a crisis that was not foreseen by the capitalist system, which, over time, had probably partially lost the driving force that had characterized it for so many years. In fact, the capitalist system, starting from the first years of the 20th century, had acquired an incredible 'growth capacity', especially in relation to the establishment in the economic landscape of large corporations quoted on stock exchanges.[8] From the mid-1930s, it had also added an adequate 'regulation capacity'. As we have said, in the period from immediately after the war (1945) to the mid-1960s, the Western capitalist world experienced a real economic boom and very high rates of employment. There was talk in various countries (for example, Japan and Italy) of true 'economic miracles'. More generally, the period has been seen as the 'golden age of capitalism'. Economic growth was accompanied by peace; the two circumstances reinforced each other, thus creating a virtuous circle that produced remarkable results. Some of the economists of the time interpreted this as the result of the systematic application of Keynesian theories to economic systems.

Gradually, however, from the mid-1960s, the Western capitalist system saw its operating mechanisms produce results that were below expectation, to the point of reaching a real slow-down in its economic, financial and political components. In particular, over time, a reduction in profits took place.

The fundamental causes of the destabilization of the capitalist system and the corresponding fall in the level of profits can be listed as follows:

- at first in the United States and then in the countries of the West, the efficient combination of high technology and low costs came to an end, together with the growth of mass consumption.[9] More precisely, there was a slowing down of the demand for consumer goods: the rates of growth progressively stopped and stabilization of consumption was reached. Additional investments in the Taylorian model of production could only give decreasing returns, with a resulting negative impact on profits.[10] The development of new models of consumption caused further crisis in the existing system of mass production and consumption. The production apparatus was highly specialized and rigid and could not adapt quickly and appropriately to market changes, while the risk facing companies was increasing and employment tended to lose stability. This last fact, naturally, also produced negative effects on demand. It is true that the large corporations did all in their power to make the single individual serve the industrial system by inducing him to consume the products manufactured. It is true that, as 'on no other matter, religious, political or moral, was he so elaborately and skillfully and expensively instructed';[11] however, when the demand for goods of mass consumption was completely saturated, it was inevitable that a phase of stagnation and lower profits would be ushered in. It should be pointed out that the mass production of conventional goods (or rather, traditional mass-market goods such as radios, televisions, tape recorders, refrigerators, washing machines, and so on) has fallen remarkably in the more industrialized countries. This is because various technologies have been adopted in other countries of the world, which have started production – often at very competitive costs – and have competed with the products of the more economically advanced nations;

- from the mid-1960s and during the 1970s, in Western capitalist countries, there was an unexpected workers' protest movement. This shattered the social peace that had existed in almost all western countries from the post-war period onwards. The problem of the redistribution of income between profits and wages was posed in an urgent manner. Ultimatums were issued calling for the narrowing of the salary gap, the improvement of working conditions and the extension of social and insurance rights. Companies became almost unmanageable and the control of units of production therefore became problematic. The demands of workers and trade unions were insistent and effective. This contributed to the weakening of companies and even further reduction in the level of profits and investments. Trade unions supported demands for rights and found fertile terrain in the world of labour. The average worker, in Western industrialized society, was freed from primary needs and therefore enjoyed economic well-being. The relative ease in finding alternative employment as well as legislative guarantees made employees less 'attached' to companies, and more willing to undermine the authority-subordination mechanism and to question decisions regarding their work. In spite of the fact that the industrial relations policies of the large corporations were highly developed, the action of trade unions produced remarkable results, with significant consequences for the conditions of labour and the level of remuneration and profit;

- at the beginning of the 1970s, the problem of the coordination of the prices of international trade arose, especially with regard to the price of oil and of other raw materials. It therefore became necessary to fix the 'terms of trade' between the developed nations and developing nations in a stable and satisfactory manner. This worldwide problem had been solved up to the First World War, especially by Great Britain, which succeeded in coordinating the terms of international trade using political mediation, but also through pressure connected to its military power. Later, particularly at the end of the Second World War, the USA progressively took on the role of coordinator of the terms of trade on a world scale. However, from the mid-1960s, the countries producing oil and other commodities began to question the role of the USA. Price increases, sometimes sharp, were called for in response to the growing demand from rich countries. What appeared most worrying for the developed countries was that the commercial counterparties by then were acting on their own initiative and had become organized consortiums; for instance, oil-producing countries formed the OPEC cartel.[12] The price of basic raw materials, especially oil, rose disproportionately and, very often, quite suddenly. This provoked serious problems for company costs and profits, causing a noticeable reduction in currency reserves and disequilibrium in the balance of payments of developed countries. In the same period the price of food increased, due either to shortage of production in developing countries or to prolonged periods of unfavourable weather conditions. It can be seen that these inflationary forces had been generated by external shocks. Their deep effects spread to the economic systems of developed countries, which was made worse by policies adopted in these countries indexing wages and salaries to inflation.[13] These conditions continuously stirred up inflation at the beginning of the 1980s, when rates reached double-digit levels.[14] For companies during the 1970s, the increase in the cost of imports caused a sharp reduction in the 'residue', that is, the part of value that should be divided between profits and wages. This worsened the problem of internal distribution between workers and the capitalists who received the profits, creating a very heated social climate and reinforcing the protests of workers and trade unions. This situation, undoubtedly, had negative repercussions on investments;
- at the beginning of the 1970s, the system for international payments progressively entered a crisis. The system of the gold exchange standard or rather the dollar exchange standard – based on conversion

of the dollar into gold at fixed prices and on the conversion, at fixed exchange rates, of the main Western currencies into dollars – was abandoned. The preconditions developed for the destruction of the payment system at a fixed rate of exchange, which had been introduced on 1 July 1944 with the Bretton Woods agreement, in which 44 countries, all members of the United Nations, participated at the request of President Roosevelt. The conditions for this change are to be found at the beginning of the 1970s when the balance of payments of the USA began to be negative[15] and central banks in Europe gradually accumulated enormous dollar reserves. As well there was the development of the Eurodollar market which was fed by loans in dollars granted mainly by European credit institutions[16] to economic operators and speculators. Therefore, when the mass of dollars became excessive compared to US gold reserves, confidence in the capacity of the USA to convert the dollar vanished. On the appearance of the first signs of a crisis, in 1971, the American President, Richard Nixon, declared the dollar non-convertible. This was because the level of US reserves was, by then, insufficient to respond to every possible request for conversion, and steps had to be taken to counter speculation on the dollar. Therefore, the value of the reserves in dollars held in various central banks became highly unstable. Consequently various states began to use the mark and the yen as reserve currencies and also to strengthen their gold reserves. All of this undermined the foundations of the fixed exchange system, worsened the international trade price system and triggered an increase in speculation on the floating exchange rates.[17] Strong political orientations and authoritative neoliberal economic theories justified the system of floating exchange rates:[18] they trusted in free-market forces to solve the problems of the system of international payments in the best way; they believed that the market, with its 'invisible hand', would determine the equilibrium of exchange rates. But the market, left to itself, does not always solve the problems of equilibrium. In the presence of floating exchange rates, an environment was created in which financial speculation, some of it quite savage, became the order of the day. It generated disproportionate profits, stimulated the 'financialization' of business activity and contributed to making the economic system of various countries increasingly unstable. All of this affected risk and the confidence of investors negatively, especially those operating in the context of the real economy;

• the massive demands of workers regarding the redistribution of income and improvement in working conditions, the crisis in the system of international prices, the disturbance of the system of exchange rates and of international payments, the growing lack of confidence of investors and a clear fall in the level of profits were accompanied by two more worrying factors: inflation and stagnation from the beginning of the 1970s until the end of the 1980s. These two events occurred simultaneously and, for the first time in the world of economics, there was talk of 'stagflation'. This concept is absurd in the terms of conventional economic theory in that, in the course of history, periods of depression have been unfailingly characterized by a fall in prices and vice-versa. During this period, inflation was considerable;[19] in some of the most developed industrialized countries rates of above 20 per cent were recorded, and in various developing nations inflation rates reached three digits. Politicians and economists, at that time, were of the opinion that they could deal with stagnation, mainly because of what they had learned from the experience of the crisis in the 1930s. However, they felt very uncertain about understanding and responding to inflation. Therefore, inflation gradually became the main enemy of economics, and consequently much attention has been dedicated to it. In the period under consideration (1970–1990), rather than there being a real depression, there was stagnation. The growth in gross domestic product in the most industrialized countries fell considerably and stabilized at around 2 per cent. At the time, the prevalent monetarist economic theory identified the causes of inflation, above all, in the increase in the money supply and in the connected Keynesian government policy. As a result, the general remedy proposed essentially took the form of restrictive monetary and fiscal policies, aimed at reducing aggregate demand and public expenditure. This is clearly in striking contrast to Keynesian economic theory, which sees the fundamental causes of inflation as the uncontrolled increase in the cost of labour and the price of commodities. Inflation was constrained[20] only at the beginning of the 1990s, when wages and international prices of raw materials were brought under control. This created the conditions to increase profits. Profits also rose, as will be seen later on in this work, because of the 'reawakening of shareholders' of large corporations, which influenced a change in the distribution of income (the relationship between wages and profits) in line with a political and economic environment inspired by the following principles: to leave the market free and carry out incisive deregulation to enable this; to reduce public spending; to control monetary growth, even at the expense of full employment; to leave exchange rates to float; to not disturb the 'natural' and efficient functioning of the mechanisms of the free market by means of State intervention;

- the world student protest movement of the 1960s to the 1980s probably affected the profitability of the large corporations. It contributed to the creation of an atmosphere that was not favourable to the accumulation of capital and the maximization of profits. It also underlined the need to give more consideration to people within companies and society. It also re-proposed the extremely complex problem of reconciling the company hierarchy of power with the need for equal human dignity;

- in addition, the activity of consumer organizations, opinion mobilizations and activist groups (for the defence of workers, and for the protection of the environment and, more generally, of human rights) considerably influenced the limitations placed on profits;

- finally, the level of profits was also affected, to some extent, by certain examples of managers who sincerely pursued objectives of social responsibility.[21] There is no doubt that much of the hidden behaviour of companies was the result of a cold calculation of economic convenience: in these cases the strategies of social responsibility were insincere; they were designed only to support and improve profitability and were pushed only when the costs involved were equal to or less than the economic benefits. We are of the opinion, however, that many responses were sincere, because they were fundamentally inspired by the higher principles of ethics. In these cases, managers were conscious of leading an important economic institution in terms of its relation to society as a whole and therefore felt the duty to manage their organizations to serve the interests not only of shareholders, but also of the other 'human groups' linked to the company. In essence, the principle of managing according to the 'best interests of the corporation' was interpreted in a broad sense, as not only encompassing the interests of owners and especially of the controlling shareholders, but also considering all the expectations of stakeholders.[22]

6.3 The reaffirmation of the principle of the maximization of profit and of the value of the company. The return to 'investor capitalism'

Already from the mid-1960s there was a return to the so-called 'investor capitalism' with individuals, families, nation-states and, above all, institutional investors holding shares. This was a response to the significant contraction of profits and pressure from an increasingly dominant political environment dedicated to the deregulation of the economy and the defence of the interests of risk capital. The holders of capital tried to increase the level of profits and, in order to do so, became interested in influencing the management of companies indirectly and, in some cases, also directly. They did not trust the professional top managers who, in their eyes, seemed guilty of not unrelentingly pursuing profit, and of not 'maximizing the value of shares' and therefore the value of the company on the stock exchange.

In this way, an old problem, which seemed by then to have been solved and which had been analysed by Adam Smith[23] and taken up again by others in the 1920s and 1930s, was again raised. In *An Inquiry into the Nature and Causes of the Wealth of Nations* (1776), Smith expressed strong concern about the fact that the owners of large corporations had delegated power more and more frequently to professional managers with specialist competences. The reason for this, in his opinion, was that those professionals would not manage other people's money in a parsimonious manner, their vigilance would be inadequate and this would lead to waste and inefficiency. In 1919, as we have seen (Chapter 5), in the controversy between Henry Ford and the Dodge brothers, the Supreme Court of the State of Michigan ruled that an enterprise must be run, above all, for the benefit of shareholders and not with the primary goal of benefiting the other stakeholders. The 'non-owner managers' – the Court maintained – therefore had no right to act in the service of interests that were not those of the owners. Profit was the first goal of the company and, therefore, the discretionary power of managers should be used above all to achieve this primary objective.

These ideas were taken up as early as the mid-1960s, exactly when profits began to fall, and they stimulated the reawakening of the shareholder interest in the running of firms. For example, Theodore Levitt[24] considered it serious and dangerous to attempt to assign functions of social responsibility to companies. This attempt – in his opinion – could create, under the pressure of ideological considerations, significant damage to companies and to society as a whole. For Levitt, goals of a social nature are irrelevant to companies.

Milton Friedman,[25] a scholar of international renown and influence, and Nobel prize-winner for economics in 1976, maintained that managers have no obligation connected to social responsibility, if we exclude obligations deriving from the law. He believed that the growing moralism developing in companies was in fact immoral. He stated unequivocally that the only goal of managers is that of increasing the wealth of shareholders and asserted, equally clearly, that contrary ideas on this subject constitute 'a subversive doctrine'. Finally, the only case of a strategy of social responsibility that could be acceptable is an insincere one, that is, when it is devoted to the maximization of the wealth of shareholders.[26]

The desire of owners to 'return' to managing large companies in order to increase the rate of profitability and the value of shares led to the following:

1. Putting in practice a system of corporate policies to increase operational efficiency: measures for the organization of the work that tend to increase productivity and reduce costs; programs of industrial relations with the aim of dealing with trade union action and improving the mobility and flexibility of labour; marketing policies to increase prices and support demand; relocation of production, even abroad, with the objective of reducing the cost of labour, services and raw materials;[27]
2. Indirect and, at times, direct participation of shareholders (especially coordinated institutional investors) in the strategic management of large companies. Only administrators and managers with a commitment to pursue the interests of shareholders and to consider the expectations of other stakeholders (consumers, employees, local communities, etc.) only within the limits of the economic convenience of the company were to be appointed. Fundamentally, the 'managerial techno-structure' remains and continues to ensure that companies have the scientific, technological, financial, marketing and organizational knowledge required to manage enterprises as effectively as possible. But two things diverge, compared to managerial capitalism:

   a) controlling shareholders influence strategic decisions either because they take these decisions directly or because they have tight control over those who take these decisions and have the power to appoint, dismiss and reward the managers at the higher levels of the organization.[28] The 're-conquest' of corporate control by shareholders takes place by means of a continuous penetrating process, supported by 'propaganda' that underlines the need to 'fight' the inefficiency of non-owner managers, all in the interests of the company and of society as a whole. Gradually, this propaganda, from being a simple collection of opinions, transformed itself into a new theory of company goals and behaviour. Increasingly, legal decisions, studies by important economists, the curricula of business schools and, in particular, the programs of some political parties, combined in the development of this theory and its transmission;

b)   the choice of members of the techno-structure is made so that management positions are offered to those who have 'internalized' a model of behaviour that reconciles 'the best interests of the firm' with those of the owners and, in particular, with the interests of the shareholders that control the company;

3. A new model of corporate behaviour is developed and adopted, based on the two following fundamental principles (the first of which was outlined previously and will be briefly referred to here):

a)   the company is an organization that has as its fundamental objective the 'maximization of the value of shares on the stock exchange'.[29] Any pursuit of interests other than those of shareholders (including social responsibility, especially when it is sincere) is irrelevant to the enterprise, and may in fact be dangerous for the corporate institution;

b)   the business model, aimed at maximizing the value of the company, is different from that adopted in the past by the large industrial corporation; the investment of capital is not made only in the production and in the sale of goods and services, but also in creating a system of financial operations.[30] The so-called 'financialization' of business[31] and, therefore, the growth in the value of shares is increasingly pursued through financial operations (acquisitions, mergers, separations, break-ups, purchase and sale of packets of shares, and so on) and less and less through production and sale of goods and services.[32] The large industrial corporations proved that the profitability of the financial sector was higher than that of industrial companies. Therefore they dedicated themselves to producing profit by using money. In order to do this, they created autonomous subsidiaries or sections of the company specializing in financial operations for this purpose, which achieved high rates of profitability and, in the end, absorbed a considerable part of the company's investments. This, among other things, led to less attention being given to industrial processes and technological innovation. The attraction of easy financial gain in the short term has often distracted attention from the consolidated industrial operations. Currently, the strategies of financialization adopted by top managers are increasingly speculative rather than entrepreneurial. Managers have lost sight of the principle of continuity of the firm (going concern). They aim instead, with a short-term point of view, to make the value of the income of the company and the quotation on the stock exchange as high as possible, in order to make sales of packets of shares (also controlling share packets) and earn high capital gains.[33] The strategies often include the acquisition of companies and their restructuring and organization into branches that are sold on the market to realize huge gains. This essentially speculative behaviour is reinforced on the financial markets: the various players compete in a process of company overvaluation. This activity is not always characterized by correctness, transparency and respect for norms, and causes financial bubbles, which are very often not controlled by the market, which then gradually tends to lose its capacity for self-regulation. In the new model of behaviour, unlike what normally took place in the past, managers are essentially limited to short-term decisions. Six-monthly or even quarterly controls are imposed by the group that holds power in the firm (composed mainly of representatives of shareholders and especially investment funds) to measure the performance and efficiency of managers. Because reaching the pre-established goals is the necessary condition for a manager keeping his job, he is forced to improve the value of shares within the very short term. Such behaviour is also reinforced by the fact that the compensation of managers is often connected to the value of stock options[34] and to other monetary rewards indexed to the growth in the market value of the company. In essence, managers tend to identify themselves with the values and objectives of investors with controlling rights. Under the persuasive pressure of financial incentives, they no longer conceive of the large corporation as a quasi-public institution and no longer consider the aim of social responsibility towards stakeholders as relevant. The managers in question have disproportionate self-esteem and, with the permission and/or collusion of controlling shareholders, tend to give themselves unreasonably high compensation.

> Politicians, scandalized, exhort investors to reduce the excesses of managers; but if top managers applied the brakes, that would also mean putting in doubt further growth in the compensation of capital owners. According to a recent estimate, the remuneration of the average American CEO is equal to 475 times the average salary; thirty years ago, it was only 25 times as much.[35]

6.4 Shareholding managerial capitalism based on the 'financialization' of business: some remarks

From the 1970s, the management of large enterprises evolved to produce a clear modification of the 'managerial capitalist system': it became a system that could be defined 'financial shareholding managerial capitalism'.

This system can be briefly summarized as follows:

- indirect return and, in some cases, direct return of shareholders to the management of companies and the use of the 'techno-structure' functionally with the objective of the 'maximization of the value of shares on the stock exchange' (or to create the maximum value for shareholders);
- growth in the value of shares, which is increasingly achieved by means of financial operations (very often speculative in nature) and less by entrepreneurial activity based on the production of goods and services; administration and control of managers based prevalently on a short-term view.[36]

At the end of this account of the evolution and decline of managerial capitalism and the advent of financial shareholding managerial capitalism, the following conclusions may be drawn.

With the establishment of shareholding managerial capitalism, capital returned to govern and control large corporations. The separation between ownership and control was constantly eroded, even if the 'techno-structure' – though highly limited – continues to be the element on which the efficiency of corporate decisions is based. More precisely, the group that holds power in the large industrial corporation tends to consist of external capitalists who do not participate directly in the management of the corporation (mainly institutional investors, banks and insurance companies); they have the capacity to control the management of the company and appoint the majority of the board of directors and the top managers. These capitalists are therefore able to guide the strategic decisions of the company in which they have a controlling interest. As said, the members of this group are external and carry out negligible management activity in the company controlled. They have a single overriding motivation: to earn as much as possible from their share investments. They therefore assign to the controlled companies the objective of maximizing profit and the value of shares.[37] As they are not working inside the company, they do not have an institutional view of the companies controlled, but consider them instruments or 'legal packaging' from which to obtain the money for the management of the financial companies in which they are mainly engaged. Their 'utility function' is consequently the objective of maximizing profit and the value of shares. The goals of increase in company size, technological and product innovation and social responsibility are ignored. This 'utility function' is very different from that which is characteristic of both 'managerial capitalism' and large industrial enterprises managed and run directly by a capitalist entrepreneur.

With the new model of capitalism, the interests of managers at the higher levels and also middle management increasingly tend to coincide with those of the shareholders that hold power. This happens especially because the controlling capital owners can appoint and remove directors as well as managers and can stimulate management to maximize the value of shares with stock grants and stock options.[38]

During the 1990s, this convergence of interests contributed to the increase in the price of shares in the USA and in EU countries by four to six times.[39] Even the fall in profits experienced in the 1970s and 1980s was recovered from, both in the United States and in the other industrialized countries.

This new form of capitalism also had the effect of provoking, in the opinion of Gallino,[40]

> the breakdown of the Keynesian-Ford compromise, which had served as the guiding principle for managerial capitalism [. . .]. The essence of that compromise was a pause in the capital-labour conflict, which had allowed the working classes to achieve a consistent and growing quota of the growth in national wealth in the form of real and increasing wages, better working conditions and the expansion of social protection.

Managerial shareholding capitalism progressively spread in the United States and because the formula of the maximization of share value also pleased countries in the EU, the new model of corporate management also developed there.

But with time, in this new context of reorganization of the most developed capitalist economic systems, on the horizon appeared the 'irresponsible' corporation. In obstinately pursuing its goal of profit by means of financialized management and with a short-term perspective, it has brought about behaviour that does not take adequately into account the values, expectations and interests of employees, consumers, local communities and the natural environment. It is an enterprise without a soul, without human language and whose behaviour is often inspired by the calculation of the difference between the cost of sanctions in the case of violation of the environment or social laws and the benefits that could be obtained from the violation itself.

6.5   The problem of irresponsible corporations

This is a phenomenon that remained latent for a long time and which attracted general attention at the beginning of the 1990s, particularly in the context of 'financial shareholding managerial capitalism' dedicated to 'maximizing' the market value of shares through increasingly aggressive strategies.[41]

This new development concerns large corporations, generally quoted on the stock exchange, that operate at a multinational level and have considerable capacity to influence the external environment.[42] These companies are generally enormous industrial organizations that appear to be insensitive to the needs of people and without respect for the natural environment, and which stubbornly pursue the objective of maximization of share value, ruthlessly opposing the interests of other stakeholders.[43]

The large irresponsible corporation is inspired by a system of values deriving from a particular conception of corporate management and of careful ideological and managerial training in which the political system, university institutions and also business schools are all involved. More precisely, an irresponsible corporation starts from the following principles, which shape its behaviour:

- a corporation must pursue the maximization of income and share value;
- the law excludes any objective connected to the satisfaction of other interests; corporate law speaks clearly: favouring the interests of employees, the community, consumers etc, is only allowed on condition that it is to the advantage of shareholders. Managers, when they venture into this field, must therefore carefully correlate costs with benefits and demonstrate their 'correct' behaviour on the basis of rational calculations of economic convenience;
- stakeholders, who are not control-shareholders, are protected by the law, which imposes conditions and minimum limits that must be observed by the corporation; the law also specifies adequate sanctions corresponding to the gravity of the violation;

- managers – although this has never been explicitly stated – must make every effort to transfer to stakeholders who are not shareholders (consumers, employees, suppliers, local community, environment, etc) the largest possible amount of costs that affect the income statement;[44]
- the corporation must behave opportunistically in the field of politics; it must interact with political parties not on the basis of values and ideologies, but in a manner that is coherent with its economic interests.[45]

From the above, it can clearly be deduced that the model of the irresponsible corporation is founded on a culture that does not draw inspiration from the higher principles of ethics and which actually prevents sympathy with the needs, values and aspirations of those interest groups that are not shareholders.[46] The language and logic of business are cold, arid and aseptic and are guided by pure economic rationality. In essence, according to this model, the behaviour of a manager inspired by human principles, and therefore open to social values, would be non-rational, would not correspond to the law or be correct – except when it is a case of behaviour that is not sincere and is based on the calculation of the difference between the costs and the benefits of respecting or violating the law and the ethical principles of managerial conduct.[47]

Irresponsible corporations tend to prefer markets and work locations where the laws and rules aimed at imposing respect for fundamental human needs and at safeguarding the natural environment are unclear or obscure. They obviously also prefer markets and places of work in which the laws and rules can be circumvented by dubious marketing and public relations operations. In markets and places where the laws and rules are clear and sanctions are severe, they develop lobbying[48] activities and corporate policies aimed at attenuating and, if possible, eliminating any form of regulation. Even if norms and rules cannot be eliminated, companies actively engage in doing everything possible, through their great powers of influence, to dismantle the controls aimed at verifying observance of norms. In every case, the decisions that affect the interests of stakeholders that are not shareholders, as well as environmental variables, are subject to a rigid examination of economic convenience.

In the world of business from the 1990s, especially in the United States, violations of laws for reasons of economic convenience have been numerous. Corporate policies that are insensitive to human needs or not respectful of the natural environment are widespread, as are policies involving the uncontrolled waste of non-renewable resources and the pollution of those so-called 'free use' resources like water and air.[49]

As an example, there is the case of one of the greatest and most famous corporations of the world: General Electric.[50] Its catalogue of violations of the law between 1990 and 2001 is impressive. These violations range from the pollution of water, to fraud against the US government in defence contracts, from the supply of defective aeronautical equipment, to defects in the planning of nuclear plants, and from fraud to money laundering in the context of the illegal sale of aircraft to Israel, to illegal credit-recovery practices and pollution of the soil. Bakan lists 41 cases of illegal behaviour and the respective court sentences requiring the corporation to pay damages.[51]

Steve Proulx, in his 'black book' on the principal American multinationals, comments on the not exactly edifyingly behavior of 23 corporations. One of the cases reported is that of Disney.[52] The President of Disney, Michael Eisner, wrote the following in 2002: 'from the moment that the integrity of our products have always merited the loyalty and the trust of consumers, the integrity of our commercial practices should merit the loyalty and trust of investors.' Since 1923, Disney has been a respected symbol of entertainment for children and also for adults. It has now become, in the minds of ordinary people, the machine for manufacturing dreams. In 2002, Disney had more than 110,000 employees; spent $2.3 billion on advertising and its brand-value was estimated at about $30 billion.

But in spite of this, love for the factory of dreams is not unanimous and protest groups of various political tendencies have organized boycott campaigns. The most important accusations concern the conditions faced by Disney workers. An issue that has tarnished the image of the company is the questionable management of employees, over a period of eight years, in the Shah Makdum factory in Dhaka, Bangladesh. The National Labour Committee (NLC), a New York organization concerned with respect for human rights,[53] revealed that women worked there in pitiful conditions. Adolescents were used to sew Disney clothes and forced to work 14–15 hours a day, seven days a week. They were often beaten and threatened if they worked slowly. They were paid 5 US cents for each item; these were then sold to western children at $17.99.[54] The women protested and asked the owners of the manufacturing plant to better respect their human rights. In particular, they asked for the elimination of physical punishment and a day of rest each week. The NLC reported that Disney cancelled the contract with the manufacturers. The manufacturers then dismissed the employees. Later, the owner of the manufacturing plant apologized to the employees and introduced improvements in the conditions of work: cleaning of washrooms, supply of soap to workers, installation of fans, filters for the purification of water, introduction of a day of rest each week, access to a cafeteria where workers could eat a meal seated at tables. After these provisions, the working conditions were better than the average for Bangladesh.[55] The National Labour Committee recognized the improvement in working conditions, but, in spite of this – writes Proulx: 'Disney did not raise even a finger: if the giant of dreams does not give the contract back to the manufacturer, he will be forced to close shop and leave more than three hundred workers on the streets.'[56]

Disney, in fact, controlled the manufacture and had every chance to make the local factory owners guarantee certain minimum conditions that respected the fundamental needs of the workers. It had the possibility of making the manufacturer introduce organizational solutions that could reorganize factories that destroy health, spirit and hope. It was therefore a deviation towards irresponsibility; perhaps the managers of Disney were not aware of this because they were blindly programmed to maximize the value of shares.

6.6   The main provisions to adopt

It is highly probable that the irresponsible corporation is an extreme creature produced by the philosophy that is at the basis of 'financial shareholding managerial capitalism', which blindly pursues objectives that maximize share value in the short term. Perhaps, as different scholars have been stating for some time, it is the pathological result of the evolution of an economic institution (the large joint-stock company), which is potentially dangerous if left to itself and which, therefore, must be subject to clear and precise rules. In this context, Bakan writes:

> the corporation is an *institution* – a unique structure and set of imperatives that directs the actions of people within it. It is also a *legal* institution, one whose existence and capacity to operate depend upon the law. The corporation's legally defined mandate is to pursue, relentlessly and without exception, its own self-interest, regardless of the often harmful consequences it might cause to others. As a result, [. . .] the corporation is a pathological institution, a dangerous possessor of the great power it wields over people and societies.[57]

In other words, according to Bakan, the corporation symbolizes a productive organization characterized by two aspects that are in striking contrast:

1) on the one hand, it has the capacity to be very useful to society because of its ability to produce goods and services efficiently and so keep people out of a state of need;
2) on the other hand – with its fundamental mission to pursue the interests of controlling shareholders – its activity, if not adequately controlled, has disturbing implications for society. Naturally, every democratic society should do everything to contain potentially dangerous phenomena and increase, as much as possible, those factors that are of service to the people and so keep the corporate institution in the service of satisfying human needs.

In any case, an irresponsible corporation, such as those unfortunately found today in the world of business, is a company that paradoxically considers immoral all behaviour by managers that does not ensure the maximization of the interests of controlling shareholders.[58] It tends to stimulate behaviour among managers that favours 'domination' over the environment and which does not consider the often negative consequences of its activity on those stakeholders that are not controlling shareholders. Managers of this kind interpret and apply the 'contractual theory' of companies in a rigid manner: according to this theory a company is regarded as a collection of contracts, among which the fundamental one is that between owners (shareholders) and managers. Managers must work exclusively in the interest of the owners/ shareholders. Contracts with other stakeholders must be managed in order to maximize the wealth of shareholders; from this it follows that the interests of stakeholders are opposed by a clear corporate policy.[59]

To conclude, the irresponsible corporation is an organization that develops strong conflicts with the less-protected or weaker groups of stakeholders. It is an entity that considers respect for the environment as extraneous to its tasks. It is an organization that has no sensitivity for any eventual human cost that it is involved in causing and that, in the long run, does not serve either the corporate good or the good of controlling shareholders.[60] In the opinion of Gallino,[61] such an enterprise 'risks compromising its own future and that of the world economy, on account of the aggressive competition that it has created, the excessive financialization of its activity and the corresponding slow-down of accumulation'. This point will be returned to later.

The irresponsible corporation has stimulated the development of important movements of ideas and the adoption of measures by nongovernmental organizations and public authorities that have hampered and will continue to hamper its strategic design and process of expansion.

The future responses and factors that could modify the behavior of irresponsible corporations effectively can be summarized as follows:

a) corporate self-regulation aimed at developing social responsibility towards employees, the community, consumers and the environment. Codes of ethics could be created that involve companies and there could be agreements between companies to promote greater attention being given to the more defenceless stakeholders. In the opinion of the supporters of this strategy, the acceptance of social responsibility on a voluntary basis is more effective than compulsion; such an approach would be faster, more realistic and have greater impact. On the other hand, the adoption of compulsory provisions by public authorities – according to various opinions – would be slow and ineffective and would be accompanied by corruption and the influence of the lobbying apparatus.[62] The voluntary adoption of responsibility enjoys considerable approval in the Western world. This is clearly seen from the formal documents drafted by public authorities and associations of entrepreneurs.[63] In our opinion, however, irresponsible enterprises, left to themselves, are not capable of developing adequately virtuous behavior. It is necessary to intervene and provide other contextual conditions to make the voluntary provisions produce useful effects. We must not forget that, by definition, and from the evidence available, the large irresponsible corporation is an organization without a human language, that relentlessly pursues its particular goals;

b) the development of 'counter-powers' in the economic, political and social fields that are capable of dealing with the dubious actions of corporations and eliminating problems at their source. Among these must be included trade unions, which, if reorganized and adequately regulated, are of important potential. There are also organizations and movements of consumers and savers, advocacy and action groups for the defence of the environment and for the protection of human rights, schools and student movements, foundations and non-profit associations, and others. All these organizations can contribute to a better awareness of the problem of social responsibility and help to develop a climate of change and fresh ideas, capable of waking up the average citizen from the torpor that makes him insensitive even to the most obvious and worrying interrelations between politics and the 'club' of businesses. A new and genuine voice – able to effectively oppose the dominant language of the large multinational, excessively preoccupied as it is with the maximization of profit in the market – could be so-called 'social enterprises'. In the opinion of Yunus, 'an alternative voice is absolutely necessary to restore to the market at least an appearance of par condicio'.[64] Such a voice – in Yunus's opinion – could be represented by companies with social aims, which would supplement in an effective way the action of the various advocacy groups and organizations previously mentioned.[65] For example, an organization that produces for the market, with social aims relating to the environment, could make clients more informed about ecological risk and offer products that are compatible with environmental protection. Also, a company with social aims that operates in the sector of micro-credit could illustrate the needs that it is attempting to satisfy with its programs and how urgent it is to effect a reform of the traditional banking sector. A company with social goals that offers medical assistance at low cost could inform the public about how to maintain good health without spending money on doctors and medicines, through prevention, correct diet and physical exercise;[66]

c) enlarging the field of intervention of various national governments and of international institutions by passing laws, regulations and directives aimed at protecting the interests of various stakeholders in a more decisive way. Such intervention should clearly establish the rules for the operation of the market economy, the limits to its reach and the system of control to be used. However, because the legislative framework, as useful as it is, does not on its own guarantee that market operators spontaneously pursue objectives that they do not desire (for example, the goals of stakeholders), it is necessary that adequate stimuli to encourage them to do so are introduced. The norms should not have a minimalistic character – as happened in the past – but the level of protection for stakeholders should be raised, over time, to become more complete and effective. Sanctions should be more severe and in line with violations. Deregulation and the attenuation of the force of norms should become increasingly difficult to achieve.[67] It should not be easy – as unfortunately it still is – to weaken the norms that aim at protecting the common good and the interests of weaker groups. Lobbying should become very complicated and very risky. In short, the violation and weakening of rules should also become a great problem for the more powerful and unscrupulous corporations. What has been said above clearly requires a clean political environment, uncontaminated by the influence of lobbies and attentive to the real needs of citizens;

d) more effective, fast and incisive controls regarding the application of norms. Irresponsible enterprises should find it very difficult to get around controls, especially because the problem has now been brought to general attention. The growing quality of norms in defence of stakeholders who are not controlling shareholders and the efficiency of controls should progressively transform the unpredictable competitive arena by making it progressively less an untrustworthy jungle and by creating the conditions for more equitable and transparent competition;

e) creation of a cultural environment that stimulates 'the awakening of the conscience' of managers, to help promote the adoption of strategies of social responsibility that are really sincere and take into account the objectives, values and motivations of the various stakeholders.[68] Thus the 'utility function' of managers should differ from that of 'economic man', who maximizes profits in a blind and extreme manner in the interests of the owners/shareholders that control the company. Such a utility function should therefore be multidimensional and informed by ethical principles,[69] to social empathy and to the protection and improvement of environmental resources. This reawakening of the conscience of managers, this re-appropriation of their freedom and of their intrinsic values, should form the basis for the reform of corporate management and, more generally, for the development of a modern theory of 'business behaviour' inspired by an enlightened interpretation of the institutional conception of the company. Such a theory should consider the company as a complex socio-economic system,[70] which aspires to survival and to satisfying dynamically the needs of the various socio-economic categories that interact with it. The company should be guided by responsible top managers who pursue, with a long-term strategy, the goals of corporate survival, of appropriate (not maximum) profit and of social legitimization through the satisfaction of the expectations of the various groups of stakeholders that have links with it.[71] In particular, the new theory should stimulate the 'revisiting' of the legal model of the joint-stock company, with a view to improving the protection for the weaker stakeholders.[72] The role of top managers of large corporations should, therefore, be redesigned as follows: because they have acquired great power internally and in society, it would be suitable to consider them as supporters of the survival and the development of the company-institution, as administrators that do everything possible to ensure an appropriate (and not maximum) remuneration of risk capital that harmonizes the interests of the various social groups involved with the company, with a long-term view.[73] It can be seen that this role is probably more easily played when the management of the large corporation is firmly in the hands of professional managers, and within a so-called 'mature corporation'. But what happens if a large enterprise is dominated – as often happens nowadays – by manager-owners? In our opinion, on this hypothesis, things will not change very much, if there is also trust in the awakening of the conscience of management, and also if the factors that have been illustrated in points a), b), c) and d) of this section operate.

***

Robert Reich states that corporate social responsibility seems to have become, for many observers, the effective response to the problems of capitalism, to the extent that it can be considered 'a new form of democratic capitalism'.[74] In his opinion, this is completely erroneous and he feels that this interpretation highlights a limited knowledge of the logic of super-capitalism. In fact, this way of thinking 'distracts attention from the more arduous but more important challenge to formulate new rules that protect and make the common good flourish and prevent super-capitalism from invading the political arena'.[75] According to Reich, the progressive establishment of corporate social responsibility, carried out by self-regulation and by agreements between companies, is strongly connected to the loss of trust in democracy. In his opinion, even progressive thinkers are convinced that it is easier to induce managers to practise self-regulation and implement social responsibility than to stimulate the government to dictate rules that direct large corporations to adopt behaviour favourable to the needs of workers, the environment and the community. In reality, Reich believes that the main reason why governments are not able to make the necessary laws is the systematic strategy used by large corporations to prevent public authorities from adopting rules that restrict the room for manoeuvre of managers. Therefore, Reich asks himself, why should large companies become sensitive to the social, environmental and labour issues on which they had systematically worked to prevent government intervention. The answer is that acceptance of social responsibility by companies usually takes place when it is instrumental, when it is connected to the maximization of the profits and the wealth of shareholders. Also – according to Reich – the citizens of large, powerful countries are completely wrong if they believe they can achieve a better result with a policy that encourages corporations to improve their behaviour by means of self-regulation rather than by intervention via the democratic process, leading to the passing of regulatory measures inspired by respect for ethical and social principles.[76]

Reich's opinions appear mostly correct. In our opinion, however, in order to promote effective social responsibility, it seems more productive to use all the strategies illustrated in the present section simultaneously, also giving more importance to those indicated in points c), d) and e) above.

6.7 The predominance of the financial economy over the real economy. Irresponsible behaviour of global finance and its impact on the recent economic and financial crisis

It is common opinion that the present crisis that has struck the world economy started in the context of the Anglo-Saxon capitalist system. In particular in the USA, Great Britain and Canada, the financial sector has gained predominance over the real economy. In these countries, the earnings of companies are produced to a considerable extent from finance and its derivatives. The main players in finance, in the 20 years that preceded the present crisis, achieved very high profits; for example, investment banks in the USA and Great Britain, from the mid-1990s, reached rates of profitability of between 15 and 20 per cent, while the profitability of the real economy had rates of about a third lower. The dominance of the whole financial sector compared to the non-financial sector can be deduced by considering the trends of profits in financial and non-financial companies in the USA from 1946.

> In the first five years – that is to say up to the end of 1950 – the proportion of profit of financial companies out of the total profit oscillated, with small fluctuations, at around an average of 9.5%. Later there was an acceleration, to reach the maximum value of 45% in 2002; and then a fall (33% in 2006) due only to a rapid increase in profits in the non-financial sector. In reality, the inexorable growth of profits in the financial sector has continued unhindered. They increased at a rate of 16.7% annually between 2000 and 2006 (from

200 to 505 billion dollars), in comparison to an annual growth of 9.4 per cent in the period 1990–1996.[77]

It is difficult to describe and identify the heart of the world financial system in a rigorous way. It can be said that it is composed of a group of institutional investors and of a system of insurance companies, commercial banks, merchant banks and mixed banks, all of considerable size, operating at an international level.

Among the main institutional investors must be included:

a) autonomous pension funds, whose subscribers belong to both the private and public sectors;
b) mutual funds, which are open to all savers and that, generally, require modest subscription quotas;
c) speculative funds (hedge funds), which have various configurations and normally require high subscription quotas;
d) private equity funds, which specialize in the purchase and sale of companies and/or partnership shares and in the takeover of companies that are then restructured, re-launched and then – also through break-ups – sold, with a view to achieving high capital gains;
e) foundations that manage gifts, legacies and trust funds;
f) sovereign funds of various foreign states.

It has been estimated that the total amount of capital managed by institutional investors alone is very close to the value of the world gross domestic product for 2007: $53 trillion.[78] It has also been estimated that these investors are owners of half the capital of companies listed on international stock exchanges.[79] This allows managers of funds to exercise a dominant influence on the companies in which they have a controlling interest. In particular, it allows them to impose the logic of the maximization of profits and share value at the expense of the aspirations and interests of stakeholders.[80]

To better interpret the operation of the financial system, it must be emphasized that banks are closely linked to institutional investors and as we will see later, in many socio-economic contexts the principle of the separation between merchant and savings banks is outdated. In fact, it is normal for banks to participate in the capital markets or even constitute pension funds, mutual funds, hedge funds and other types of funds structured in various ways. Thus they become true 'economic subjects' (actual power holders) that direct the activities of companies in which they have a controlling interest by defining the criteria for the investment of savings and, in particular, the quantitative parameters of profitability.

It should also be pointed out that banks have offered various funds a great quantity of derivative contracts, some simple, others very complex. These have fed an immense and turbulent market, whose collapse is one of the factors of the crisis of 2008, which is still continuing.[81]

The process of financialization of the economy has been developing progressively since the 1980s, particularly in the USA, Great Britain and Canada and, to a lesser extent, in Germany, France, Japan and Italy. Historically, the Anglo-Saxon model of financial capitalism has always been praised and imitated by other states, creating real convergence.

The increasing predominance of the financial sector over the real economy was stimulated by a system of closely interlinked causes, including:

a) growing profitability of financial intermediation and financial services;[82]
b) high technical complexity of financial operations that require highly specialized competence and involve high risks. This has driven up the rewards and commissions available to operators;
c) development of economies and international trade, which have required more sophisticated financial and insurance instruments;
d) the progressive establishment, since the 1980s, of the concentration of share capital in the hands of various pension funds, investment funds, speculative funds, private equity funds, banks of various types, insurance companies, and so on; this is the opposite of what happened in the more industrialized economies between the 1930s and the end of the 1960s when there was dispersion of share capital, the separation between ownership and control and the arrival of the mature corporation;
e) reawakening of shareholders of the large industrial corporations (especially Anglo-Saxon), which have come together[83] and put considerable pressure on managers to obtain increasing rates of profitability in the short term,[84] especially with financial engineering operations that are very often speculative;[85]
f) close connection between the remuneration of top managers and short-term profitability in large industrial companies, increasingly oriented not towards the production of goods and services, but to effecting new and ingenious operations of financial engineering developed by top managers or imposed by the funds or the banks with controlling interests;

g) the growing and unbridled greed of financial operators (especially banks and institutional investors), who, in order to pursue their own immediate gain, looked for business opportunities in an indiscriminate and exaggerated manner, in line with the 'impersonal discipline of the market'; to this end they requested and obtained deregulation of the financial markets. This allowed operators to accept increasing risks, which were often badly calculated, and behave frequently without ethics or responsibility;

h) change both the theoretical orientation of economists and entrepreneurs as well as the political orientation of governments of the more important states, especially from the 1980s, in relation to the role and control of large corporations. In academic circles the appeal of the 'institutional theory' is losing ground. According to this theory, the large company is an almost public institution, whose managers – although the need to achieve a normal profit remains – must satisfy the system of expectations of the various stakeholders and therefore must behave according to norms of social responsibility. On the contrary, especially in the United States, the theory (originating from Milton Friedman) that maintains that managers have the sole duty to satisfy their shareholders and every other behaviour is considered immoral and even against the law,[86] is prevalent.

The crisis that exploded in 2008 was triggered by the American property bubble, although the system of conditions that could produce a financial and economic shock already existed. This bubble acted as a detonator and the results rapidly crossed the borders of the United States to establish themselves at a global level.

In the United States, in 1999, the principle of the separation between merchant banks and saving banks was set aside.[87] Large banks, hedge funds, insurance companies and other institutions took more and more risks and used 'financial leverage' rashly, with the aim of satisfying their ambition to become global financial leaders and to make increasingly high profits. There were corporate crises; the US Federal Reserve intervened – directly and indirectly through the contributions of other banks – to save some large financial institutions that were in difficulty. This reinforced the aggressiveness of financial institutions and, unfortunately, contributed to the development of 'imprudent and irresponsible confidence to trust in the knowledge that, if an enterprise became "too big to fail", the government would intervene'.[88] Motivated by the desire for success and with the confidence that protection would be received, the institutions in question financed consumer credit for the purchase of real estate, cars, etc. Especially in the real estate sector, loans were of enormous amounts and involved both families and companies. In this sector, competition was unrelenting and banks 'chased' clients and only analysed superficially the capacity of clients to repay loans, relying on the fact that the mortgages on the real estate (to which the loans granted were connected) would guarantee the payment of the loans themselves as well as large earnings. In brief, credit was consciously granted even where there was doubt concerning the capacity to repay and about the rate of interest, which seemed inadequate to compensate for the risks. Consequently, sub-prime loans were made, based only on the guarantee of the (allegedly increasing) value of the underlying real estate. These loans were taken out by people who were unaware of the risks; in world financial jargon, these clients are called Ninja (no income, no job, no assets).[89] In the USA the value of real estate increased until 2007. Unfortunately, from that date, the enchantment wore off and the value of real estate began to fall noticeably, provoking ballooning risks and remarkable losses for the credit institutions.

To understand the real nature of the financial crisis for American banks (and also for those of other countries that had imitated them), it is also necessary to consider another phenomenon of decisive importance. This is the distribution/transfer of risk connected to the collection of consumer credit. More precisely, banks developed a new business model that was encouraged by the American authorities. In fact, the Federal Reserve did not feel it was necessary to regulate the financial market connected to the operation of such a model. It also believed that the model was a valid instrument to split up credit risk among many subjects and thereby strengthen the total security of the system. The new business model included the creation, also by means of external corporate vehicles (special investment vehicles), of a series of 'structured financial packages' to be sold and distributed to third party buyers. The packages (also called 'structured investments') systematically assembled the different credit held by the bank (especially and above all the sub-prime loans), and created a 'complex financial product' which was later subdivided into many 'quotas' to be sold to third parties. The risk, in this case, tended to be distributed. A particular financial product much used were bonds based on guaranteed debt from real estate (collateralized debt obligations). This product appeared on the financial markets at the end of the 1980s. In this case, the bank, which granted the loans and had the underlying credits, issued, either directly or through one or more special investment vehicles, these bonds, which were then sold to third parties. These bonds were connected to the underlying credit and gave the purchaser the right to receive part of the interest produced by that credit and, on the expiry date, their subscription value. In this way, the risk on the underlying credit was divided and transferred. The complexity of the operations for issuing the 'bonds based on debt guaranteed by real estate' is strictly dependent on the structure of the package of the underlying credits on which the bonds are based. Often, such bonds are put on the market in different tranches with different ratings and prices in relation to the priorities that bondholders have to collect the income and, more generally, the cash flow deriving from the complex whole of underlying credit of the package.

The sale of the 'quotas' of products, by now having become 'toxic', ended up 'polluting' the financial market, particularly because there were numerous financial institutions involved in creating these 'structured products'; furthermore, some institutions were simultaneously creators of 'financial packages' and purchasers of 'quotas' of financial packages created by third parties.[90]

This business model worked for many years and permitted numerous banks, up to 2006–07, to make enormous profits. It was facilitated because the Federal Reserve did not regulate the market and approved of the method used to distribute the risks, and also because the rating agencies probably acted without sufficient attention and, often, driven by the objective of maximizing earnings from the institutions who paid their fees, had fully guaranteed the 'structured packages', often assigning them a maximum rating.

It must be pointed out that the American financial sector was characterized not only by the presence of the above-mentioned 'structured instruments' (securitization and collateralized debt obligations) connected to loans guaranteed by real estate, but also by the progressive development of derivative credit products such as the credit default swap. These products were used to hedge against risks on the value of goods, securities and cash flow, but unfortunately they were also massively used for exclusively speculative reasons. In other words, they were increasingly used by financial institutions to bet on the probability of default by companies, and on the probability that certain rates or particular exchange rates would occur. If a bank stipulates a credit default swap to protect the current value of a share packet of X dollars held in ownership by paying a premium, the bank uses a hedging instrument. But if it stipulates the same contract with a financial institution and bets on the maintenance of the value X of the same type of shares, which however it does not hold in ownership, in this case it is a merely speculative contract. On this hypothesis, the operation is carried out with the purpose of later selling the contract to third parties and earning the difference.

From 2007, debtors began to not honour their commitments in relation to sub-prime loans. The value of real estate fell drastically. The value of financial instruments, particularly the speculative instruments, showed growing volatility and then a very sharp fall. In 2008 there were bank failures and nationalization of banks and insurance companies in the USA and in the UK. There was the awareness that risk assessment had been carried out by financial institutions and rating agencies in an inappropriate manner, by trusting in the capacity of sophisticated mathematical and statistical models to predict market trends, based mainly on historical data and on hypotheses concerning the behaviour of the subjects involved in operations on the financial market that were not always realistic. It is true that the occurrence of negative events had, on the basis of the quantitative models used, a probability of less than one in a million. But, unfortunately, the size of the markets, the greed of traders, the uncontrollable behaviour of various operators, and the lack of serious rules and effective control made the prediction of the value of financial instruments decidedly inadequate.

The financial sector, as it came to be formed in the more developed countries, seemed to be an enormous, dangerous and predominantly speculative superstructure that operated above the real economy and managed the relationship between the producers of savings and those who utilize them, above all, to satisfy self-interest.[91] In the opinion of Dore, it is a

> vast superstructure of speculative transactions hinging on producers and consumers of goods and non-financial services, who need: a) credit; b) insurance against uncertainty; c) profitable investment for their capital. And, after all, it is the producers and consumers who largely pay the cost of the activity generated by this immense superstructure, to the benefit of those who make it work.[92]

The financial crisis of the Anglo-Saxon countries has also had an impact on the rest of the world because the American financial model has been imitated in many other states, to varying degrees. In addition, the so-called toxic products, eventually devoid of any value, were widely available at an international level.

The financial crisis has had a devastating effect on the real economy and, above all, on credit to enterprises and consumers. The banks that offer ordinary credit have done everything possible to put their balance sheets in order, they have analysed the value of financial products and have jealously guarded their available liquidity. Many have restricted or eliminated interbank credit and have become extremely rigorous and parsimonious in providing loans to clients. The credit crunch has now become a problem for the real economy worldwide. Central banks are putting liquidity into the credit system in order to re-launch the driving wheel of credit.

Currently, the real economy is continuing to suffer the serious consequences of the expansion and disorder that have characterized the financialization of the world economy.

The correction of the disaster triggered by irresponsible global finance is a very complex problem and requires time. But, in all probability, the crisis will not be either as long or as deep as that which took place in the years of the Great Depression. This is because the various states are technically better 'equipped', compared to the 1930s, to understand and to face economic depressions. Furthermore, the majority of states – even if to different extents – have a public sector that is more significant compared to the period of the Great Depression. Their governments provide welfare and they seem to be capable of facing the great task of re-launching demand, rebuilding consumer confidence and, above all, investor confidence within a brief period of time. During the recent crisis, governments have intelligently interpreted the nature of the problems and adopted coherent policies: they have cut interest rates (contrary to what happened between 1931 and 1932, when governments, limited to the 'gold standard', increased interest rates); they promptly intervened to prevent the collapse of some financial companies that were going to cause a systemic risk; they have supported employment and revitalized demand. We hope that these same governments will commit themselves to continuing to stimulate the economy for as long as necessary to end the crisis.

***

There is no doubt that the global financial system, made up of large banks (of various types) and by a multitude of institutional investors, has developed very negative behaviour, which has put at risk the future of the real economy.[93]

However, the governments of various countries have intervened promptly with encouraging results.

At this point, we take the opportunity to indicate the strategies that could be followed to mitigate the negative behaviour of the financial system. These strategies, with the necessary adjustments, are, in our opinion, very similar to those that could be adopted (and in many cases have already been adopted) to counteract the irresponsible behaviour of large industrial corporations:

1) first and foremost, it is useful to promote self-regulation with the aim of encouraging virtuous behaviour. This should be on a voluntary basis, by the creation of ethical codes and agreements between enterprises favourable to putting financial organizations on the right path of responsibility and moderation;
2) in the second place, it is to be hoped that the conditions are produced that allow the creation and strengthening of adequate 'counter-powers', represented by movements of savers and consumers, trade unions, schools, associations and foundations that offer micro-credit;
3) thirdly, it is necessary to rely on government intervention and of the national supervision agencies as well as international institutions to define rules for the operation of the financial markets (national and global): rules that are transparent and establish the parameters of respect, specify the system of control to be set up and the incentives to be eventually introduced to stimulate the various subjects operating in the market to behave in a virtuous way. More specifically, some remedies to be introduced could include the following:

- impose adequate capitalization on financial institutions as well as the reduction of leverage; in other words, the parameters in force should be reconsidered with the aim of containing the general corporate risk;
- reduce the system of operations that banks are now allowed to carry out and permit only speculative funds to take part in certain forms of highly speculative activities with great risks; in particular, the problem of the amount of direct or indirect participation of banks in industrial, non-financial and service enterprises should be considered;
- regulate speculative activity in a clear way, especially hedge funds, because today no clear regulations exist; it is necessary to establish the principle that speculative activity is carried out by managers, largely with the money of outsiders; the managers should remember that they are 'agents' and must therefore bear in mind the underlying interests of their 'principals';[94]
- improve the system of evaluation of the reliability of clients that take out loans, by choosing statistical and mathematical models

that are appropriate for measuring risk and determining rates of interest. Also, create the conditions that allow the authority in charge to control the financial system more incisively and effectively than in the past;

- regulate the business model now adopted by the large banks to distribute or transfer credit risk. As we have seen, at present, many large financial institutions use 'special investment vehicles' to prepare 'structured financial packages' composed of a system of credits of variable quality held by the same banks. These 'complex financial products' are later divided into quotas and sold to third parties in different tranches with different ratings and prices. This business model should be revised in order not to allow banks to free themselves of credits (that they have imprudently or negligently granted) by means of inserting such credits into a complex financial product made up of a specially arranged mix of good, average and bad credits;
- consider seriously the possibility of introducing some form of tax on international speculative transactions, the revenue from which could be utilized to finance the development of the world's poorer nations;[95]

4) fourthly, it is necessary to do everything to develop a political and cultural environment that considers the role of the State as an important instrument for regulating the economy. In fact, many of the provisions already mentioned could not be adopted if public intervention were excluded. The financial markets urgently need regulation. On the contrary, further deregulation would have very negative consequences both on the scale and the duration of the current economic-financial crisis. Therefore there should not be an *a priori* rejection of State intervention, but rather informed acceptance, since it now appears to be indispensable to conserving and restoring vigour to capitalism based on a market economy: the State creates the rules for the operation of the market, controls their application and develops incentives to induce the various organizations operating on the market towards virtuous behaviour. To this end, it is necessary to devote a great deal of attention to the improvement of the technical capacity and the moral integrity of the people who constitute the political apparatus. Without incisive intervention in this field, there is the risk that the currently widespread neo-liberalism will take further hold, with its belief that the intervention of public authorities is unreliable and inconvenient and that public administration is, generally, inefficient, corrupt and easy prey to groups of lobbyists that pursue particular interests;

5) finally, but equally importantly, there is the need to create the conditions to stimulate the 'reawakening of the consciences' of managers, with the aim of developing corporate strategies to favour ethics and social responsibility. (On this question see point e) of the previous section.) We repeat only that a fundamental role in the development of a new theory of the enterprise oriented to responsibility will, undoubtedly, be carried out by universities, the media and by business schools. We hope that these institutions teach that the predominance of the financial economy over the real economy is neither inevitable nor desirable. In other words, we hope that these mentioned will contribute to making the conviction prevail that investments in the production of goods and real services are preferable to investments made in financial operations with a view to making more money. This is a principle with deep historical roots but which still maintains a certain validity. All of this does not mean that financial speculation should be eliminated – since it appears important for the smooth operation of the market – but rather that it should be regulated in a transparent manner and be kept within reasonable limits.[96]

Notes

1. Zanda (2006), p. 48.
2. Castronovo (2007), p. 86.
3. Castronovo (2007), p. 87. On this point, see also Galbraith (1967), pp. 26ff.
4. Dore (2009), pp. 37–38. Dore points out that he was inspired in this view by the work of Khurana (2007).
5. Zanda (1974), p. 282.
6. It has been said that 'the activity of large corporations must be encouraged and defended until their contribution to free individuals from needs equals the reduced freedom from inducing them to cooperate in production and "shaping" their way of thinking and acting. When the freedom sacrificed exceeds that obtained, people need protection against the power of the large corporations, in order not to be caught in the cogs of the economic machine that they have contributed to create' (Zanda 1974, pp. 282–3).
7. Bureau of Economic Analysis (2004).
8. The capitalism of large corporations became relevant in the period between 1890 and 1910, above all in the United States. In this period, beginning from the states of New Jersey and Delaware, the temporal, spatial and operating obstacles that made mergers and acquisitions complex and that prevented the possession of shares in other companies were progressively eliminated. The economic panorama changed as never before. In the leading sectors, owing to an uncontainable wave of mergers and acquisitions, large listed corporations appeared and markets were characterized by the retreat of small and medium-size companies from free competition. Using Schumpeterian

terminology, the capitalistic system changed: from 'competitive capitalism' to a 'capitalism of trusts'.

9. Zanda (2006), p. 48.
10. Gallino (2005), pp. 98ff.
11. Galbraith (1967), p. 38.
12. The inflationary impulse produced by the oil crisis of 1973 was caused by the sudden decision of OPEC to increase the price of crude oil from $3 to $11 a barrel. Another important increase, from $13 to $28, was announced by OPEC in 1980 just before the Iranian revolution. On this point, see Heilbroner and Thurow (2008), p. 200.
13. Heilbroner and Thurow (2008), pp. 203–04.
14. Heilbroner and Thurow (2008), p. 199.
15. Until 1971, the trade balance of the USA, which reflects current transactions carried out by companies, individuals and public operators, reported a small surplus; subsequently negative balances were the rule from the beginning of the 1980s. This meant that Americans bought from foreign countries a larger amount of goods and services than they sold. The trade balance deficit was mainly due to the oil crisis triggered by OPEC and by the stagnation of productivity in manufacturing industry in the United States. The US trade balance deficit grew from $2.3 billion in 1980 to $116 billion in 1986. This caused a decrease in the value of the dollar, which lost 35 per cent in 1989. The deficit was reduced to $31 billion in 1990 and in the following year reached parity due to the financial resources received to cover the military expenses for the war against Iraq. Subsequently the negative trend returned and the value of the dollar has progressively fallen. The US balance of payments (related to the construction or purchase of plant and equipment and the purchase of shares, obligations and government bonds) during the 1970s, was very unbalanced, especially because American companies were expanding abroad. But at the beginning of the 1980s there was a radical change of direction, in association with the rigorous anti-inflationary monetary policy of the Federal Reserve, which raised interest rates on 3-month government bonds to more than 14 per cent. Foreign capital was drawn into the USA because of a fall in inflation and high interest rates. This capital influx prevented the immediate devaluation of the dollar, which should have lost value because of the trade deficit. In 1985 overvaluation of the dollar became unsustainable and the European central banks and Japan intervened to reduce the value of the dollar, which at the end of the 1980s, as said, lost 35 per cent of its value. On this subject, see Heilbroner and Thurow (2008), pp. 235ff.
16. Savona (1998), pp. 51ff.
17. Savona (1998), p. 19.
18. Increasing uncertainty on the values of interest and exchange rates and the remarkable development of international commerce stimulated insurance cover of the associated risks. This provoked unimaginable development of derivatives related to interest rates and foreign-exchange rates and prepared the way for the 'financialization' of the world economy, which reached its peak in 2008 and 2009, producing significant damage to the financial markets and the real economy.
19. Savona (1998), pp. 11–12.

20. In the United States, 'in 1980, consumer prices were growing by 13%, this means that, every five to six years, the cost of living tended to double! In 1982, the rate had been halved [. . .]. Ten years later, the annual rate of growth had fallen to 3%, a great improvement, which however did not reassure the public. In 1997, the consumer price index increased by only 2.2%, the lowest value since 1965' (Heilbroner and Thurow 2008, p. 199).
21. An insincere strategy of social responsibility aims at pure economic interest; it is carried out only within the limits of economic convenience. In contrast, a sincere strategy of social responsibility is inspired by ethical objectives; in some cases it impacts negatively on business income; but in the long run it usually influences the economic situation of the business favourably: in this case it becomes a happy combination of social concern and economic interest.
22. In our opinion, during the period of 'managerial capitalism', managers who were not pressed by the analytical control of owners could be inspired by higher ethical principles and social responsibility. Therefore we are convinced that during this period, some space was given to social concern and not only the cold, blind and inexorable goal of profit-maximization.
23. Smith, *An Inquiry into the Nature and Causes of the Wealth of Nations,* published in 1776.
24. Levitt (1958). Theodore Levitt (1925–2006) is one of the greatest experts in marketing management. He taught for 30 years at Harvard Business School, was Editor of the *Harvard Business Review* and he won the McKinsey Prize of the *HBR* four times.
25. Friedman (1962; 1970).
26. Joel Bakan, following an interview with Friedman, wrote: 'Friedman thinks that corporations are good for society (and that too much government is bad). He recoils, however, at the idea that corporations should try to do good for society. "A corporation is the property of its stockholders [. . .]. Its interests are the interests of its stockholders". [. . .]. There is but one "social responsibility" for corporate executives, Friedman believes: they must make as much money as possible for their shareholders. This is a moral imperative. Executives who choose social and environmental goals over profits – who try to act morally – are, in fact, immoral. There is, however, one instance when corporate social responsibility can be tolerated, according to Friedman – when it is insincere. The executive who treats social and environmental values as means to maximize shareholders' wealth – not as ends in themselves – commits no wrong. [. . .]. It's true, Friedman acknowledges, that this purely strategic view of social responsibilities reduces lofty ideals to "hypocritical window dressing". But hypocrisy is virtuous when it serves the bottom line. Moral virtue is immoral when it does not' (Bakan 2004, p. 34).
27. Gallino (2005), p. 99.
28. On this point Ronald Dore observes: 'In today's shareholder managerial capitalism the managers [. . .] are much less independent. They work under the close supervision of a board of directors that represents the interests of the shareholders and in which, frequently, a dominant shareholder is present. Among managers' motivations it is probable that the idea of social usefulness or the motivation of building up a long-lasting organization that honors

their memory are neutralized by the attraction of stock options, bonuses and by the constant threat of their immediate removal – all carefully planned and specified in long-negotiated contracts, in order to induce managers to satisfy the expectations of the shareholders. Expectations which, at present, in all probability may be summarized in increasing share value rather than stability. According to Khurana, managers have become "hired workers"' (Dore 2009, pp. 38 and 39).

29. Lazonick and O'Sullivan (2000).
30. Zanda (2006), pp. 49–50.
31. We will return to this point in sections 6.6 and 6.7.
32. Gallino states that, at the moment, a company is no longer conceived 'as an institution that creates profits producing goods and services, but rather as an entity capable of increasing company capital value (measured on the basis of price market), in several ways, among which the production of goods and services is only one of the possible options. Adopting this point of view, the increase in market value must naturally exceed the amount of profits obtainable by the production of goods and services. Therefore profit is no longer considered only as the surplus of revenues minus costs regarding goods and services, but as the surplus of market value at time t_2 in comparison with time t_1, where the difference between t_1 and t_2 can be also only a few days' (Gallino 2005, p. 100).
33. Fortuna (2009), pp. 530ff.
34. 'The ratio between earnings from stock options and wages indicates how high investors' confidence in the effectiveness of this incentive has been, over a long time, and how appreciated it has been by managers. In 2000, in the top 200 American corporations, the first exceeded the second by a ratio of 6.6 to 1 regarding the compensation of Chief Executive Officers. In figures, the average compensation per head was 11.3 million dollars, 375 times the average salary of employees. Of this sum 60% came from stock options, 18% from the annual bonus and 11% from preference shares, while only 9% was salary' (Gallino 2009, p. 116); the author quotes Pearl Meyer & Partners, *Trends 2001: Looking Forward and Back* (www.execpay.com/trends 2001.htm).
35. Dore (2009), pp. 39–40; the information comes from www.dailyreckoning. com.au/barclays-executive/2007/03/29.
36. Stock exchange values, in a complex economic and much more complex financial system, tend to free themselves from the values of business investments and to be determined on the basis of cloudy or optimistic forecasts of managers (and investors), which almost represent prophecies that everybody wants to come true; the stock exchange allows investors to chase, to imitate and to exceed each other in a process of value creation based more on desired expectations that on reliable information about future cash flows and risk. Prophecies often come true; but then the time comes when the trend reverses, giving rise to a series of negative forecasts on the future of companies, leading to the loss of share value. The behaviour of managers and the related effect on the price of shares are analysed in Oricchio (2010), chapters II and VI.
37. Fontana (2007), pp. 114ff.
38. Gallino (2005), p. 121.

39. Gallino (2005), p. 121. Here Gallino states that 'the economic interest of the manager has come to coincide with that of the investors, not with that of the company, which is conceived as a social and technical system in which the production factors are arranged in order to produce goods and services. The company ends up being considered as a contingent legal support, whose material substance is indeed irrelevant to the aim of creating value in the short term, sometimes, literally, from hour to hour, thanks to the infotelematic technologies that keep under observation all the stock markets of the world, and use them to carry out instantaneous operations'.

40. Gallino (2005), p. 128.

41. 'In the attempt to discipline managers so that they applied themselves to maximize value for shareholders, institutional investors, as well as the families of owners, have used various means. Dismissal without notice is frequently used. In 1992 and 1993 many groups of American institutional investors who were not satisfied with the financial performances of the companies in which they held a significant number of shares, formed an alliance in the respective shareholders' assemblies. They asked for and obtained the resignation of the CEOs and most of the members of the Board of Directors of large companies such as General Motors, IBM, American Express, Kodak, Westinghouse, Borden' (Gallino 2005, pp. 118–19). As Gallino observes (pp. 120ff.), in order to induce managers to maximize the value of their shares, the owners also used other instruments: threats of hostile takeover; concession of shares to managers in order to integrate their wages (stock grants) and especially stock options.

42. Much literature is available on the irresponsible corporation. There are thousands of articles by legal scholars, economists and business scholars. Among the works published on corporate irresponsibility the following are recommended: Friedland (1990); Wells (1993); Mitchell (2002); Stiglitz (2002); Tabb (2002); Bakan (2004); Barlow and Clarke (2004); Rusconi and Dorigatti (2004); Gallino (2005); Proulx (2005).

43. These corporations calculate, on the one hand, the costs deriving from business policies aimed at manipulating public opinion and from the eventual payment of penalties for incorrect behaviours and, on the other hand, the benefits resulting from irresponsible managerial action (certainly not inspired by ethics), which damage the interests of stakeholders (shareholders excluded).

44. This phenomenon is called by economists 'the mechanism of externalization of costs'. The logic of profit maximization imposes the use of every expedient so that third parties bear the burdens of a corporation's impact on the community, the environment, and so on.

45. See Bakan (2004), p. 88.

46. The legal structure of corporations, the exclusive satisfaction of shareholders' interests, and the short-term view, produce immoral behaviour. This point is developed by Mitchell (2002), pp. 3ff.

47. For an irresponsible corporation, compliance with the law is increasingly becoming a business decision. Reporting the opinion of Robert Monks, Joel Bakan writes: '"if the chance of getting caught and the penalty are less than it costs to comply, our people think of it as being just a business decision." Executives, when deciding whether to comply with or break a law, "behave rationally and . . . make cost effective decisions", [. . .] which means they ask,

"What's the penalty, what's the probability of being caught, how much does that add up to, and how much does it cost to comply and which is bigger?"' (Bakan 2004, p. 80).

48. When corporations lobby governments, their usual goal is to avoid regulation. Sometimes they seek to stop governments from introducing new or stronger regulations (as the auto industry did with the fuel efficiency standard); other times they pressure governments to repeal, weaken, or narrow the scope of existing regulations (as Enron did with the regulation of energy futures trading)' (Bakan 2004, p. 102).

49. 'The propensity to consume without taking care of long-term social costs is a natural, unavoidable consequence of the blind tendency to maximize profits. If it becomes the primary objective, it means that we forget the environment, health and sustainability and then the only legitimate question is: how can we buy and sell more goods in comparison with the past year, achieving a higher profit-rate? The fact that people really need this surplus of goods or the fact that this surplus allows them to achieve long-lasting effective benefits must be considered insignificant issues. The excessive propensity to maximize profit means losses in terms of quality of environment, consumers' health and long term sustainability' (Yunus 2008, p. 218).

50. General Electric in 2002 had a sales turnover of $134 billion; it had 70,000 recorded patents and it operated in many diversified sectors.

51. Bakan (2004), pp. 75ff.

52. Proulx (2005), pp. 77ff.

53. Proulx (2005), p. 81.

54. Proulx (2005), pp. 83–4.

55. Proulx (2005), p. 82.

56. Proulx (2005), p. 83.

57. Bakan (2004), pp. 1–2.

58. It is an organization that acts in the area of social responsibility only after a cold calculation of economic convenience, based on the determination of the difference between costs and benefits from violating or respecting laws that protect stakeholders and environment.

59. These policies are related to personnel, public relations, industrial relations, marketing, supply and so on.

60. In the opinion of E. Cavalieri, the behaviour of the irresponsible corporation (more and more speculative and less and less entrepreneurial) was one of the main causes of the economic-financial crisis that began at the end of 2008 (Cavalieri 2009, pp. 280–1).

61. Gallino (2005), p. 129.

62. On lobbying, Gallino writes: 'As for lobbying, already in 1996, a report of the leader of the Republican majority of the United States House of Representatives estimated that over 67,000 workers were regularly paid in the "lobbying sector" in Washington, which became the main private employer of the city. Thirty years before, there were less than 17,000. In other words, in 1964, there were 31 people for every member of Congress, who worked in order to influence governmental policies; in the mid 1990s lobbyists had gone up to 125 per [. . .] member.

For some time the European Union has been going in the same direction. In order to influence the decisions of the European Parliament, the

EU Commission and the Council of Ministers, there is a "lobbying sector" in Brussels of more than 3,000 stakeholders' representatives, including 200 large companies with their special offices. The whole sector employs more than 15,000 people full-time. It is possible that the corporations do not represent the majority of stakeholders either in Washington or in Brussels. Nevertheless they are the most influential group if we consider the resources they are able to mobilize, including services of important law firms' (Gallino 2005, pp. 16, 17).

63. The public debate on the social responsibility of the company is very wide and is enhanced by those enterprises that continue to require the improvement of business ethics. It is interesting to know what stakeholders think about social responsibility. An important work on this subject is Murru (2009).

64. Yunus (2008), p. 220.

65. Yunus (2008), p. 220.

66. Yunus (2008), p. 221.

67. On the risk of bypassing accounting rules, see Ianniello (2003), chapters IV and V.

68. Interesting contributions towards a reformulation of corporate social responsibility can be found in Alford and Compagnoni (2008).

69. Among these sources we undoubtedly have to consider religious teachings and, in particular, the Christian Social Doctrine, inspired by the principles of the 'common good' and the 'development of the human person'. On this point, see Alford and Naughton (2006).

70. 'By now it is well-established in literature that the company is a collection of many different elements, supported by a system of relations between people with interests that sometimes converge, other times contrast, but are always interdependent. This complex relational system has great importance in the current industrial, political and social context, where the protection and recognition of workers who, directly or indirectly, voluntarily or involuntarily, contribute to the development of companies play a fundamental role' (Moscarini 2008c, p. 183).

71. For an interesting formulation of the problem, see Sciarelli (2002; 2007); Moscarini (2007, pp. 39ff.; 2008c, p. 13 ff.; 2008a).

72. 'That does not mean the people who run corporations are inhuman. [. . .]. They must, however, serve the corporation's dehumanizing mandate. [. . .]. At the heart of that structure is a simple dynamic: a corporation "tends to be more profitable to the extent it can make other people pay the bills for its impact on society", as businessman Robert Monks describes it. "There's a terrible word that economists use for this called externalities"' (Bakan 2004, p. 70).

73. An original formulation of general criteria to inspire management in achieving company survival and value creation and distribution can be found in Stampacchia (2007), pp. 187ff. On the relationship between the assumption of social responsibility and economic-financial performance, see Sancetta (2007), pp. 22ff. Interesting empirical research on the effects of social responsibility on company results can be found in Becchetti et al. (2008), pp. 313–487.

74. Reich (2008), p. 197.

75. Reich (2008), p. 197.
76. Reich (2008), pp. 198ff.
77. Dore (2009), p. 19.
78. Gallino (2009), pp. 24, 28, 31.
79. Gallino (2009), p. 105.
80. Usually in business practice the rules established by those who hold power, concerning the maximization of profits (and the connected value of the shares), require that subsidiary companies attain a return on equity (ROE) of at least 15 per cent. This requirement has forced industrial companies to carry out desperate and often irresponsible searches for profit opportunities.
81. 'The derivatives in circulation, like traditional futures or complex derivatives like [. . .] *credit default swaps*, in mid 2008, amounted to 765 trillion dollars, 14 times the GDP of the world, considering their nominal value. Of these only 80 trillion were bought or sold on the stock exchange, while the remaining 680 and more were exchanged exclusively over the counter (OTC) without intermediation between the contractors [. . .]. But it should be specified that the market fair value of a derivative is usually much lower than its notional or nominal value. The first refers to the sums that can be earned or lost according to the course of underlying assets, the second represents the amount of the assets that would have to be exchanged at the end of the contract. The Bank of International Settlements estimates, for example, that, in mid-2008, all types of OTC derivatives were worth 20.4 trillion dollars on the market' (Gallino 2009, p. 33).
82. Obviously this has determined that a higher proportion of domestic income of the most developed countries has ended up under the control of financial operators.
83. 'If we consider investments made directly by pension funds, mutual funds and insurance, it is true that for each company in which they acquire shares, they amount to around 2–3% of the company capital available on the market. It seems very little to exercise real power of control in a company. In reality this percentage is anything but negligible. It can amount to investments of hundreds of millions of euros each; it also means that it is sufficient to have the agreement of around ten investors to make proposals to managers that they cannot refuse [. . .]. Also the leading banks and investment companies [. . .] each control hundreds of funds, which operate autonomously along prearranged lines for ordinary activity, but must conform as a group to the decisions of the controlling body whenever decisions go beyond ordinary activity. All of these investors pursue the same objective, the maximum return on capital invested, since this means the maximization of value for shareholders' (Gallino 2009, pp. 112 and 113).
84. Institutional investors – in the opinion of Gallino – have required a ROE of at least 15 per cent from the industrial and commercial companies in which they have invested. He specifies that: 'in economies that, like in Europe, have seen their GDP increase by 2% or a little more for long periods, and interest rates around 3–4%, to achieve similar rates of performance through the production of goods and services is practically impossible. Despite this, on average, companies have succeeded. Between 2004 and 2006, for example, companies in the Cac 40 stock market group, the main index of the

Paris stock exchange, declared an average ROE above 15%. Italian companies included in the Mibtel index had a similar performance. There are also some European companies that greatly exceeded this limit. At the top of this group is Deutsche Bank, which not only promised its shareholders a ROE of 25% at the beginning of 2005, but at the end of the year performed even better.' Gallino specifies that companies have managed to achieve a ROE of about 15%, as institutional investors requested. This goal was attained by systematic, speculative financialization of the company activity.

85. The awakening of the shareholders of large industrial corporations became visible from the beginning of the 1980s and, above all, the 1990s when pension funds, life insurance companies and mutual funds appeared on the economic and financial scene, together with other institutions: private equity funds; hedge funds; asset management companies; funds specializing in takeovers, in corporate restructuring and subsequent sale also after break-up and so on. These shareholders were not oriented to the long-term growth of the company they controlled, but mostly aimed to obtain immediate high profits by means of financial operations without any sincere assumption of social responsibility.

86. This theory has taken to the limit the 'contractual conception' of the company, according to which it can be represented as a system of contracts that can be modified over time. However all the contracts signed do not have the same importance: the most important is the contract between the owners (the principal) and the managers (the agents). These agents must give priority to the requests of the shareholders and secondly the expectations of the other stakeholders. The contractual theory requires that managers – in order to achieve the goals of company survival and development – try, as much as possible, to reconcile the various expectations of stakeholders and to develop a synergic combination of the multiple interests. In our opinion, the enterprise theory developed by Friedman and his followers has drastically 'forced' the contractual conception of the company by interpreting it in the sense that the 'agent' must inexorably pursue the maximization of profit, with his choices uninfluenced by social responsibility.

Regarding political orientation, it should be pointed out that governments – above all those of Great Britain and the United States, since the governments of Mrs Thatcher and President Reagan, have carried out a program of economic-financial 'deregulation' and stimulated the return of investors to govern large corporations, giving priority to satisfying the interests of risk capital owners.

87. 'It should be remembered that for some time the sharp distinction between commercial banks and investment banks has disappeared, as a result of two legislative innovations: the general deregulation of capital movements from 1974 in all OECD countries and, in particular, the abolition in 1999 in the USA of the Glass-Steagall Act that imposed their separation in 1933. EU countries adopted similar measures. This liberalization once more permitted commercial banks, with growing autonomy and absence of control, to take part in numerous other financial activities, including speculation, just like investment banks' (Gallino 2009, p. 29).

88. Dore (2009), p. 10. An indicator of the negotiating strength of the large banks with their respective governments is shown by the relationship

between the value of assets of the single credit company relative to the GDP of the nation in which the bank has its headquarters. For example, in 2007, in the UK this relationship for the Royal Bank of Scotland was 126 per cent; in France, for BNP PARIBAS it was 104 per cent; in the Netherlands, for ING, it was 290 per cent; in Switzerland, for UBS, it was 480 per cent; in Italy for UNICREDIT, it was 80 per cent. This negotiating strength of banks made the various governments suggest to the Standard Setters that they modify some accounting principles concerning non-liquid markets and to have a more flexible application of mark-to-market in favour of mark-to-model. Also, from the point of view of monetary policy in the USA, after interest rates reached zero, there was the partial and selective direct purchase of toxic assets in bank balances by the Federal Reserve. A similar policy (called 'quantitative easing') was used in the UK. On this argument, see Oricchio (2010), chapter VI.

89. Dore (2009), p. 24.
90. The amount of investments in toxic assets, now worthless, has not been reliably estimated. There are only hypotheses: astronomical figures are mentioned. Some say that there is probably a higher quantity than expected of 'bad credit' related to capital property bought by real estate companies.
91. Rossi (2008).
92. Dore (2009), p. 34.
93. Interesting considerations on the behaviour of institutional investors can be found in Cavalieri (2009), pp. 29ff.
94. The recent financial crisis is not connected with excessive investments carried out in the real economy, but is closely dependent on investments that banks and other financial institutions have carried out using the money of other people in order to obtain profits 'operating on paper' in the short term.
95. James Tobin's proposal is similar. He proposed levying a tax of about 0.5 per cent on all speculative transactions in foreign currency and then assigning the funds to help underdeveloped countries.
96. Dore (2009), pp. 91–4.

7
The Efficient-market Hypothesis (EMH) and Financial Crisis

Gianluca Oricchio

7.1 Originate-to-distribute and originate-and-hold: the challenge to the efficient-market hypothesis begins

The severity and amplitude of the recent global crisis provide convincing evidence that there is something fundamentally wrong with the prevailing theory on how financial markets work and with the approach to market regulation that has accompanied it. Understanding what has happened and what should be done to avoid such a catastrophic crisis in the future will require a new way of thinking about how markets work.

The key point analysed in this chapter is the *efficient-market hypothesis* (EMH) and its accounting corollary, the mark-to-market principle.

It is a thought commonly shared that the correct estimate of the pricing of credit risk has a central role in the proper operation of the banking and financial sector. This central position, from this writer's point of view, seems to have been recently undervalued in the common view.

Presumably, if there had been a better ability to price credit risk and a greater awareness among financial operators on these subjects, several errors would have been avoided. A consistent credit risk pricing is a key factor in the reduction of leverage during expansive monetary policy.

The re-pricing of credit risk seen recently in the financial markets following the so-called *subprime crisis* has highlighted interest in the *management of credit portfolios*. This attention is founded upon three different levels:

1) The role of central banks and effect of the different business models adopted in the banks (originate and distribute, originate and manage, and originate and hold) on monetary policy;

155

2) The function of credit risk market prices in giving a perspective on the real economy and on the lending market; and

3) The banks' ability to select for creditworthiness and to define a commercial price as close as possible to the risk-adjusted price, further to the introduction of the regulation on capital requirements.

It is interesting to remark how significantly the credit risk perception has changed during the financial crisis. Figure 7.1 illustrates the average credit risk in the period January 2005–May 2007 in which we can see how, at a European level, the corporate credit risk is higher than that of the banks, which, in its turn, is higher than that of the sovereign states.

Consequently, during the crisis, banks were perceived to be riskier than, or in line with, corporates (March–April 2006 and February–March 2010). Other than that, the public policies that sustained the financial system have made sovereign states take over the major part of the banks' risk, which has made the sovereign states' risk higher than that of the banks (January–March 2010); see Figure 7.2.

The banking business model has had a great impact on the leverage multiplier. There are three different banking business models based on the role of ACPM (Active Credit Portfolio Management) or Credit Treasury:

1) *Originate and distribute*: the credit risk is almost totally transferred to the market. The Credit Treasury Unit has the role of industrializing the process of credit origination, aiming at a sale to the investors;

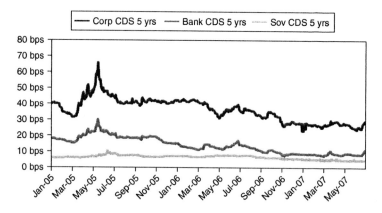

Figure 7.1   Credit spreads before the financial crisis
Note: Sovereign credit spread is an average of Germany, Italy, France, Portugal, Spain and Greece.
Source: Group Credit Treasury, Unicredit Group.

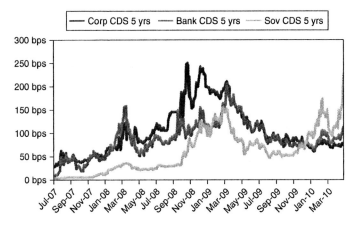

Figure 7.2 Credit spreads during the financial crisis

2) *Originate and hold*: the risk is almost entirely retained on the books. In this case, the Credit Treasury Unit pursues only the aim of boosting the pricing discipline of the Commercial Branch, charging the insurance price to the accounts of the managers; and

3) *Originate and manage*: the Credit Treasury Unit has a role that lies between the previous two. The aim is both to perform a pricing discipline in the Commercial Branch and to finalize deals transferring credit risk to the market, looking at capital relief, managing the economic capital, and minimizing the profit and loss (P&L) volatility of the bank.

The basic Credit Treasury Framework is illustrated in Figure 7.3.

Major international banks have adopted an *originate-to-distribute* business model: the balance sheet velocity in terms of capital rotation has been materially increased and, with a limited amount of equity book value, the banking system has originated a huge amount of credit. The combination of the originate-to-distribute business model with an expansive monetary policy has depressed credit risk premiums at a very low level. Return on capital has increased and banks' market capitalization has hit record levels. The equity risk premium was also depressed and the corporate share price reached new high levels as well. In this period the efficient-market hypothesis seemed to be the best theory of finance.

In the next sections some lessons learnt during the crisis are illustrated and new developments in theory of finance are considered, including the *adaptive market hypothesis* (AMH) and *positive accounting behaviour*. A need for a new theory of finance based on bounded rationality is then outlined.

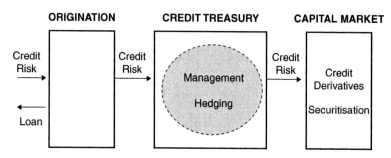

Figure 7.3   Credit Treasury high level business model
Source: Group Credit Treasury, Unicredit Group.

7.2   Two recent crises and the efficient-market hypothesis: lessons learnt

The two recent crises of the financial markets have re-proposed in a meaningful way the topic of the stock market valuation efficiency. Two questions are essential:

1) Are the 'bubbles' predictable and manageable?
2) Does the difference between fundamental analysis and market prices give information useful for better understanding the first question?

The two recent crises (the so-called 'dotcom boom' or 'bubble' at the beginning of the 2000s and the financial and banking crisis of 2008–10) have had many elements in common: both the 'bubbles' occurred in a period of expansive monetary policy, low interest rates, moderated inflation expectations and low unemployment rates.

In both these contexts equity risk and credit risk were materially undervalued.

From the perspective of *accounting information,* in the dotcom crisis many new creative accounting techniques were adopted by top managers in order to reduce the external perception of risk and reduce the gap between the quarterly EPS (earnings per share target on quarterly basis) and the effective result.[1]

The extension of accounting manipulation led to a 'crisis of ethics in Corporate America'; auditing companies that supported the misleading behaviour have been penalized (and one, Arthur Andersen, went out of business). After the financial institution crisis of 2008–10 auditing companies generally maintained a strong attitude in not colluding with management expectations of the flexibility in mark-to-market application.

Table 7.1 Cumulative losses and cumulative capital increases of main international quoted credit institutions in billions of euros (2009)

	Loss	Capital
Worldwide	771.9	661.9
Americas	532.2	385.9
Europe	216.1	239.9
Asia	23.6	36.1

Source: Bloomberg.

The crisis of the financial markets started in 2007 when a fall in investor confidence hit some asset classes (*asset-backed securities* – ABSs; *collateralized debt obligations* – CDOs, and their related derivatives) and spread to the interbank and equity markets.

As a result, with no market price for many financial instruments, some assets have been transferred from trading book to banking book, and *mark-to-market* (Statement of Financial Accounting Standards [SFAS] no. 157, Level 1) has been replaced with *mark-to-model*, which is far more discretionary (SFAS no. 157, Level 3). Nevertheless, the amount of losses has been huge: the high leverage in financial institutions has revealed non-sound equity capitalization.

Table 7.1 illustrates the accumulated entity of banking losses and banks' capital increases.

In Figure 7.4 we can see the amount of assets estimated on a mark-to-model basis as percentage of equity book value (the so-called *hard-to-value ratio*) for a selection of investment banks.

Many credit institutions have proceeded to limited writedowns in order not to erode in meaningful way the equity book value and this phenomenon has decreased the level of confidence between the banks. Swap spreads increased and there was no more liquidity in the interbank market.

In this situation, big banks have been described as '*zombie banks*': financial information was no longer reliable and credit risk was at the highest levels. The efficient-market hypothesis was creaking.

After the collapse of Lehman Brothers, governments and central banks adopted 'exceptional' or 'unorthodox' measures, such as:

- the concession of the status of 'commercial bank' to Goldman Sachs and Morgan Stanley in order to access Federal Reserve facilities and to 'sterilize' the risk of a of an imminent liquidity crisis;
- the Federal Reserve purchase of structured credit assets (renamed '*toxic assets*') from banking system (quantitative easing);

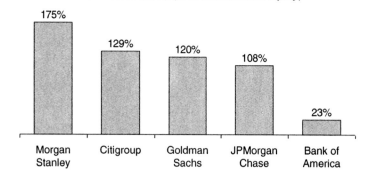

Figure 7.4   Hard-to-value assets (2009)
Source: Bloomberg.

- the Federal Reserve purchase of Treasury Bonds in order to finance government fiscal policy (quantitative easing);
- the pressure on the FASB and IASB in order to introduce elements of flexibility in the appraisal of financial instruments (and avoid more write-downs and write-offs).
- In a certain sense, it can be stated that accountancy principles have also been used (and employed) in order to mitigate the financial crisis, as well as monetary policy and fiscal policy.

7.3   The efficient-market hypothesis and accounting behaviour

The modern theory of finance is largely based on the efficient-market hypothesis (EMH). According to EMH, in its purest version, a market price is the best estimate of the fair value of the listed instrument. Based on this economic hypothesis several corporate finance and accounting principles follow:

- the stock market price, under certain conditions, is equal to the net present value of expected cash flows;
- the best model to estimate equity risk premium in the discount rate is the *capital asset pricing model* (CAPM) (for the companies to risk inherent credit, that is *investment grade*);
- a principle of coherence between cash flows and discount rate must be respected: levered cash flows must be discounted with a CAPM based on a ß *levered*; the financial debt cash flows must be

discounted with a proper credit risk spread; *unlevered* cash flows must be discounted with a rate representing the *weighted average cost of capital* (WACC);

- corporate accounting should be based on market prices and not on historical costs. When market prices are not available the key valuation principle is fair value.

In this framework the way in which the *management actions are translated and represented in accounting statements do not have to influence the market value of public companies*. Moreover, *accounting based on the matching principle is irrelevant* and *cash is king*.[2]

The choice between different accounting criteria become market-value-relevant if modification of tax cashflows are considered. From a general point of view, 'earnings are the result of the opinion of someone (or the "true and fair view") while the liquidity remains a fact'.[3]

EMH is based on several assumptions: the basic hypothesis is that financial operators act rationally. This relies in a more or less explicit way on the validity of the model of *unbounded rationality*[4] and on the notion of *economic man* ('homo economicus'): the latter has perfect knowledge of the solution-alternatives of any given problem; he is in a position to calibrate all the consequences associated with all behaviour-alternatives; he is able to estimate the utility function in cardinal terms; the choices made by *economic man* are necessarily optimal.

In contrast, we prefer to adopt a model of *bounded rationality*. According to this concept, the subject that makes the decisions is an *administrative man*: he does not know all the solution-alternatives of any given problem; he cannot calibrate all the consequences associated with all behaviour-alternatives; he does not know how to estimate the utility function in cardinal terms; he works within time constraints; his choices cannot be considered optimal, but merely satisfactory.

The modern theory of finance should be analysed in the light of a bounded rationality approach: the EMH could then be modified into an *adaptive market hypothesis* (AMH), where principles of evolutionary biology (competition, mutation, reproduction and natural selection) and human emotions are central to the understanding of rationality. Emotions are the basis for a reward-and-punishment system that facilitates the selection of advantageous behaviour.[5]

Several instances of empirical research (an example of which, adapted to the Italian context, is introduced in this chapter) demonstrate the 'informative superiority' of earnings in formulating forecasts on the future cash flow.

It is interesting to determine what in reality an investor looks for in accounting information. A recent survey[6] has shown that he asks for the following things, in order of importance:

1. Earnings: 51%
2. Revenues: 12%
3. Operating cash flow: 12%
4. Free cash flows: 10%
5. Pro-forma earnings: 12%
6. Other: 2%
7. Economic value added: 1%

In summary, investors are interested in earnings (62%), not cash flows (22%), and consequently the CEO and the CFO are interested in earnings.

This the reason why the main target of any company plan is expressed in terms of *earnings per share (EPS)*. The top managers' capability to meet the company plan target is verified on a quarterly basis by the publication of the *quarterly results*. In particular, every three months if the actual forward EPS is below expectations a *'negatives surprise'* is generated and the price of shares is negatively affected; if the actual forward EPS exceeds the expectations, a *'positive surprise'* is generated and the price of shares goes up. The ability to the management 'to respect' (and 'to possibly improve') the EPS target in the medium-long term is essential for building his credibility in the eyes of investors.

The performance appraisal generated by investors – and the related reaction of the financial markets – is based on EPS data: it means that 'numbers talk' and: i) the ability to achieve over time the EPS target (*EPS track record*); and ii) the ability to reach and to maintain an EPS level above comparable competitors (*EPS benchmarks*) are both essential to the success of the managerial performance.

Managers try to set the investors' EPS target expectations by means of management guidance: managers have a continuing relationship with investors (an organizational function called *investor relations*) and frequent meetings with them ('roadshows'). In this framework several researchers favour the *income smoothing hypothesis*; the attempt of the *management* to diminish the oscillations of net income around a *trend,* possibly an ancestor, would involve the attainment of the following objectives:

1) to pay to shareholders normal (regarding competitors) and usual (regarding the past) dividends;
2) to diminish the perception of the degree of business risk among *shareholders* and, more in general terms, *stakeholders*.

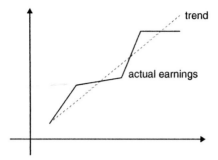

Figure 7.5 The smaller the earnings volatility, other conditions being equal, the higher the price of shares
(Small earnings volatility ⇒ low risk perception ⇒ low risk premiums ⇒ price of shares high).

In 1964, Gordon[7] formulated, among other things, the so-called *proposition 4* and *theorem 4* in relation to the income smoothing hypothesis:

- *proposition 4*: the variability of the yields represents an important measure of the economic-financial risk of an enterprise and is directly connected to the value of the price risk premium used in order to discount future earnings;
- *theorem 4*: the minimization of the variability of the expected result around a *trend* is a priority for top management. Using this, top management can increase the value of the enterprise (see Figures 7.5 and 7.6).

From 1964 to now, a great deal of research has demonstrated the validity of the income smoothing hypothesis. According to such studies, top management spreads the company's earnings over time by means of active discretionary accounting of profit and loss.[8] Subsequent practice has therefore confirmed the validity of Gordon's original hypothesis.

The link between earnings volatility, equity risk premiums and share prices is central in the CEO's decision-making process. The following simplified framework is useful for understanding 'optimal' corporate accounting behaviour.

We assume that share price is equal to future earnings present value and there is no economic premium for asset control or economic discount for minorities.

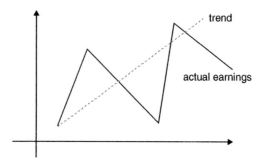

Figure 7.6   The higher the earnings volatility, other conditions being equal, the lower the price of shares
(High earnings volatility ⇒ high risk perception ⇒ high risk premium ⇒ price of shares low).

On this basis, the analytic relation between a 'share price variation' and a 'future earnings variation' is linear. In formula, it is:

$$\Delta W = \Delta R \; 1/ke$$

where:
  ΔW = share price variation;
  ΔR = future earnings variation;
  ke = cost of equity

The linear relation is illustrated in Figure 7.7.

If one assumes that the reduction in the level of future earnings is equal to 10 per cent, there is a negative variation in share price equal to 10 per cent.

Two further considerations need to be raised in relation to the simplified framework above:

1) the *credibility* of managerial announcements and actions; and
2) the separation between 'permanent' and 'non-permanent' future earnings variations.

Some managerial announcements are more credible than others and the impact on share prices is therefore higher. For instance, material personnel reductions, sale of non-core assets with capital gains and write-offs and related tax benefits are able to produce, other conditions being equal,

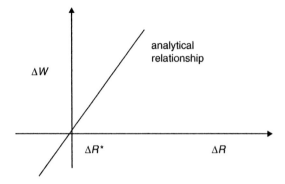

Figure 7.7 Linear relation between share price variation and future earnings variation, other conditions being equal, in a simplified framework

an increment in the share price that is usually much higher than the positive share price impact of, for example, managerial announcements related to new product development or revenue targets based on synergies. It is also important to separate the future earnings increase that can be considered 'permanent' from the future earnings increase that cannot be assumed to be so.

The combination of the credibility of managerial announcements and actions with the 'permanent/non-permanent' level of future earnings expectations produces a different shape in the linear relationship between share price and future earnings in the simplified framework. As we can see in Figure 7.8, the linear relationship is maintained only for a limited amount of future earnings variation (that is, the variation that is assumed to be permanent over time), while for a higher amount of future earnings (that is, the variation that is not considered permanent over time) the impact of the share price is less than proportional.

In a similar way, negative variations in the level of future earnings should be separated into 'permanent' and 'non-permanent' categories. The effect on market capitalization is different: the variations that are considered permanent have a linear negative impact on share price; the variations that are assumed to be non-permanent have a less negative impact on market capitalization (see Figure 7.9).

If we put together the impact of positive and negative variations in future earnings level on market capitalization, the empirical relation assumes an 'S-shape' (see Figure 7.10).

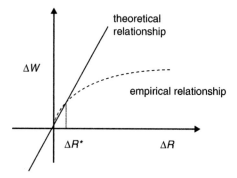

Figure 7.8   Future earnings increments that are considered to be permanent have a linear impact on share price; future earnings increments that are not considered permanent have less impact on share price

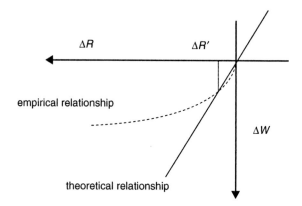

Figure 7.9   Future earnings negative variations that are considered to be permanent have a linear impact on share price; future earnings negative variations that are not considered permanent have less impact on share price

According to Figure 7.10, a *positive accounting interpretation* of the abovementioned relation can be proposed. To this extent, four different 'situations' can be identified in the following terms (see Table 7.2):

A 'positive accounting interpretation' means that top managers try to use their discretionary judgment in preparing financial statements in order to minimize the negative impact of bad news on market capitalization and try to maximize the positive impact of good news on share price. To this extent, 'Situation 3' is more preferable than

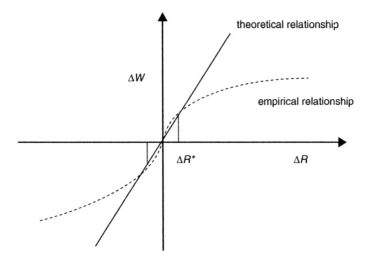

Figure 7.10 The theoretical relation vs. the empirical relation between the level of future earnings variations and the impact on market capitalization

Table 7.2 Four different 'situations'

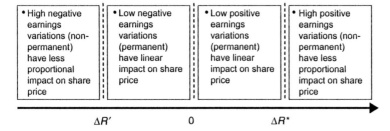

'Situation 4' in an ordinary business: the maximum positive variation of future earnings is transformed in market capitalization. On the other hand, in a negative scenario, 'Situation 1' is preferable to 'Situation 2': it is better not to give constant bad news to investors and, if it is necessary, to concentrate big write-offs or write-downs in a single quarterly report.

In other words, top managers of public companies try to drive investors' expectations and optimize market capitalization by communicating constant earnings improvements or, in a crisis scenario, consolidating losses in a single quarterly report.

Finally, two quotations to round off this account of the 'positive accounting interpretation':

1) '[W]hen making financial reporting choices, preparers of accounts may affect the construction of events in way in which to create, or destroy, value';[9]
2) 'In communicating reality accountants construct reality'.[10]

Notes

1. Berenson (2003).
2. Watts and Zimmerman (1990).
3. Smith (1995).
4. Simon (1982); Manca (1995).
5. Lo (2005).
6. Graham et al. (2005).
7. Gordon (1964).
8. Beidleman (1973); Barton (2001); Bartov et al. (2002); Graham et al. (2005); Skinner and Sloan (2002); Verrecchia (2001).
9. McKernan and O'Donnell (1998).
10. Part of the title of an article by Ruth Hines (1988).

8
Control of Intangible Resources and Corporate Management
Gianfranco Zanda

8.1 Preliminary remarks

In the last two decades of the 20th century, certain changes of great importance took place, which will almost certainly continue to influence the behaviour of large companies and affect the evolution of western society.

These marked the start of the Third Industrial Revolution,[1] which concerns the control of certain 'new knowledge' necessary for the management of firms of the future. In the opinion of Thurow, 'exactly how the game should be played is uncertain. The winners will be those who first figure out the nature of the wealth pyramid in a knowledge-based economy'. Success will be facilitated by strong propensity for change and innovation in the socio-economic and political contexts. On the contrary, it will be slowed down in those situations where freedom and creativity are limited, in which there is a strong resistance to change, in which new knowledge and innovation are repressed. The 'old' and traditional socio-economic institutions have in fact the reassuring quality of being known, tried, tested and proven to have produced good results in the past, but are now dated.[2]

A system of events, it is said, tends to attribute increasing importance to 'new knowledge' in society and in corporations[3] and therefore to those who possess this new knowledge or control it. This happens because this new knowledge seems to be indispensable for the management of modern companies. As Galbraith observes,[4] in general, power in an economic context belongs to the factor of production 'which is hardest to obtain or hardest to replace. In precise language it adheres to the one that has the greatest inelasticity of supply at the margin'. In our opinion, the 'new knowledge' in question is increasingly becoming

169

the 'strategic factor' of future production combinations. In fact, it is the scarcest factor of production and the most difficult to increase. It is therefore natural that power in companies and in society as a whole is associated with this factor.

To better understand the evolution that is taking place in the capitalist system, it is necessary to examine certain factors within the current socio-economic context. Studies in corporate economics cannot be separated from the context, which expresses the needs of people, their interests, the evolutionary directions of society, its wealth, aspirations and recurring economic crises. The current context, in rapid change, contains the embryo of the society that will come and that will express the future economic system.[5]

The factors that caused the change that is taking place and have increased the importance of the immaterial good – 'knowledge' – will now be discussed.

8.2   The new scientific and technological knowledge

The first factor is the development and use of new scientific and technological knowledge.

The new knowledge that appeared in the final years of the 20th century and that has gradually been establishing itself in the 21st century concerns, above all, the following sectors: biotechnology, information technology, artificial materials, microelectronics, robotics and telecommunications.[6]

These sectors of knowledge are capable of activating the production of very innovative and highly desirable services. These services are capable of satisfying both primary needs and the higher needs of the personality: self-esteem, respect from others and self-realization. The scientific and technological progress made in this field will, in all probability, succeed in eradicating many diseases, improve quality of life and physical fitness, lengthen youth and life expectancy; enormously improve intellectual capacity and the working capacity of people; create new foods with particular characteristics; permit immediate communication with people located anywhere in the world; and supply unimaginable cultural and spiritual gratification to individuals through entertainment, sensations, emotions, opportunities to develop knowledge skills, self-confidence and self-esteem. Most of this gratification, very probably, will take place through the so-called 'virtual world', which each human being can join (and even lose him/herself in) to play a role or build a network of social interaction, capable of reasonably gratifying conflicting motivations and the most hidden aspirations. It is likely that production, in terms of technology, will be completely revolutionized and companies will change enormously, in operational processes as well as in their system of management and in strategies to create value.

In this fantastic new world, constantly in evolution, the life of companies will not be easy. Undoubtedly it will be more complicated than at present. This is because of the generalized distribution of the multimedia network, which allows users to contact a great number of people located throughout a global market, almost completely overcoming geographic obstacles. It is also because of the great variability of the needs of consumers, which will make competition prompt and incisive. The success of companies will depend strongly on the speed with which potential change is perceived and on the promptness of response to the new and increasingly refined needs of consumers and users of goods and services.

8.3   The use of the multimedia network and market changes

In the distant past, the market was understood as the physical place in which people met to buy and sell manufactured goods, foods and livestock. There was, therefore, a clear geographic reference. With time, the concept of market came to connote a system of purchases and sales of goods and services. But the geographic reference still remained, even if, from time to time, its spatial extension was made explicit, to local, regional, national and international markets. Market transactions have always mainly involved the purchase and sale of the right of ownership of goods and to a lesser extent the purchase and sale of the services connected to the ownership of goods. In other words, transfers of ownership were more frequent than the contracts with which, through a payment, both material and immaterial services were exchanged.[7]

For some time, two main factors have been working together to change the concept of the market.

In the first place, the presence and generalized use of the multimedia network which has progressively caused a contraction of the market understood in the traditional sense. This traditional market is retreating and is being replaced by the internet, which allows instantaneous and easy business transactions (research, planning, production, sale, and so on) with participants located all over the world.[8] The internet also allows the immediate and systematic recovery of information about consumers, supplies, competitors and investment markets, in order to be able to make rational economic calculations. The talent of creative and innovative people, in this way, has had the opportunity to establish itself at a global level, overcoming geographic distance and promoting cultural exchange and understanding among the various cultures. In short, with time, the market, conceived of as a physical space within which transactions take place, now takes place in cyberspace. Real shops progressively abandon trading, while virtual ones begin to spread. In other words, economic activities and also social relationships are migrating towards the multimedia network. The problem of the use of the internet is extremely important and also worrying. In fact,

> while one fifth of the world's population is migrating to cyberspace and access relationships, the rest of humanity still is caught up in the world of physical scarcity [. . .]; more than half of the human race has never made a phone call. The gap between the possessed and the dispossessed is wide, but the gap between the connected and the disconnected is even wider. The world is fast developing into two distinct civilizations – those living inside the electronic gates of cyberspace and those living on the outside.[9]

The second factor involved in changing the characteristics of the traditional market is the change in the type of transactions that operators make. As we have said, transactions regarding transfer of the rights of ownership of material and immaterial goods are giving way to the access to services deriving from those rights, by the payment of a fee. In other words, it is increasingly frequent to find that the purchase of services supplied by a material or immaterial good takes place via a lease contract rather than a transfer of the rights of ownership of the good itself, and this is facilitated by the multimedia network, which allows access to the services deriving from property belonging to third parties.

Finally, not only has the physical market been absorbed by the internet, but internet transactions are less about transfer of property rights and increasingly about access to services deriving from property. As Rifkin states,

> companies and consumers are beginning to abandon the central reality of modern economic life – the market exchange of property between sellers and buyers. This doesn't mean property disappears in the coming Age of Access. Quite the contrary. Property continues to exist but is far less likely to be exchanged in markets. Instead, suppliers hold on to property in the new economy and lease, rent,

or charge an admission fee, subscription, or membership dues for its short-term use. The exchange of property between sellers and buyers – the most important feature of the modern market system – gives way to short-term access between servers and clients operating in a network relationship.[10]

8.4 The relationship between the market, the industrial system and innovative services. The arrival of the 'light' company based on access to internet services and outsourcing

Another change taking place in the modern economy is the continuous fall in the production of material goods compared to services. This tendency has been taking place in the more developed countries for about 40 years, but in the last 20 years this process has accelerated. Thus from industrial capitalism based on manufacturing there has been a change to capitalism based on services. This tendency has been caused by a series of factors that include: the arrival of innovative technologies (in the sectors of biotechnologies, information technology, artificial materials, microelectronics, robotics and telecommunications); flexibility of these technologies, which can be applied to satisfy a very large number of material, social and spiritual needs; the spectacular progress of the multimedia network that permits easy and immediate access to new technologies, as well as the development of various forms of collaboration between people and organizations that possess the new technologies; and the reduced importance of companies owning 'physical capital'.

For companies, the physical, technical and financial capital owned has become less important for two reasons. First and foremost, in the modern economy, the strategic element in the management of organizations is increasingly knowledge (intellectual capital) rather than technical and financial capital. Secondly, companies often prefer to sell and then rent or lease real estate, machines and equipment rather than make them weigh on the balance sheet as fixed assets, in order to become 'lighter', more flexible and more capable of adapting quickly and conveniently to variations in the external and internal environment. In some cases, companies even go so far as to create a so-called 'hollow corporation', which is a production organization that has made a complete transition from the ownership of assets to the renting (financial and operational leasing) of these goods. In this way, companies can reduce investments, limit risk and control their activities better. Through outsourcing contracts and strategic alliances with suppliers, competitors, research organizations and consumers, they even succeed in improving their income statement results. This requires that companies develop strategic management competences in order to deal properly with counterparties in relation to particular interests and to try to reconcile interests to realize reciprocal benefits. It is appropriate to point out the importance for modern companies of internal and external collaboration (national and, above all, international). In a globalized world, brought closer by the multimedia network, the most efficient organizations are probably those that are more open to change and to collaboration. This is because the creation of value is becoming so complex that it goes beyond the single company and its departments. In the more modern sectors, innovation and the creation of value – in the fields of design and planning, production and marketing – rely increasingly on specialized knowledge spread among many companies operating in a vast internal and external environment.[11] It is therefore indispensable to combine and merge the various specializations using collaboration, outsourcing and insourcing, always taking into consideration distinctive competences and shortcomings, and strong and weak points.[12] In this way, innovation and the creation of value are the consequence of the mixing of specialist skills (internal and external). Strategic management becomes therefore the capacity to develop synthesis and collaboration both within the company and with operational and research units outside the organization.[13]

Finally, we must examine how the possibility of using the intellectual and physical property of third parties by means of leasing reduces corporate risk. The reasons can be summarized as follows:

1) lower investments of fixed capital reduce fixed costs and this removes 'rigidity' from business and from the income statement;
2) technological progress is also very fast in the industrial equipment sector; therefore renting covers the firm against this risk;
3) the unpredictable nature of demand for services produced can be better faced with a cost structure that can be adapted to the dynamics of the market; the light, flexible and adaptable company can rapidly and adequately take advantage of the new opportunities that the market presents; this is very important in a new economy characterized by change and by the need to put in place, in the shortest possible time, strategies tailored to the patterns of demand, supply, scientific and technological progress and competitiveness factors that create differentiation advantages.

8.5 New services in the field of culture and the development of the 'experience' industry

The innovative services produced by the corporations of the modern economy are strongly connected to the application of the six technologies that have been previously mentioned. With time they will tend to differentiate themselves from those services currently being bought by consumers and other users (such as companies that, in turn, produce and sell goods and services).

These services affect health, physical and spiritual well-being, the length of life, the improvement of intellectual performance and, more generally, the vast field of culture.

Culture, in the broadest sense, is a strongly expanding sector and one on which the preferences of producers and consumers will probably concentrate, using the multimedia network. As Rifkin says,

> film, radio, television, the recording industry, global tourism, shopping malls, destination entertainment centers, themed cities, theme parks, fashion, cuisine, professional sports and games, gambling, wellness, and the simulated worlds and virtual realities of cyberspace are the front line commercial fields in an Age of Access.[14]

Rifkin maintains that an economic system based increasingly on culture (cultural capitalism) is developing and that it has reached the stage where culture has now become a commodity. The result is that the cultural sphere is losing its autonomy and is increasingly attracted by the economic sphere: many expressions of creativity, imagination, genius and inspiration by individuals, groups and communities are organized and commercialized in order to satisfy the cultural needs of customers with purchasing power and connected to the multimedia network.[15]

Apart from this, the market for culture has undoubtedly considerable potential for growth, in particular because in this field needs are practically unlimited and open to important diversification. These needs are of a higher order: self-esteem, prestige and self-realization. These motivations, practically, know no limit[16] and their gratification can be achieved by unlimited solutions.

It is therefore highly probable that the new economy based on culture will develop new business opportunities, which will offer information, entertainment, spiritual gratification, sensations and dreams. It is likely that this economy will create virtual worlds in which those using the multimedia network can undergo formative experiences or discover a human and social dimension (or an escape) in line with personal motivations. Such simulated environments contain certain dangers of a psychological and social nature.[17] However, it is likely that the sensations and the intense experiences characteristic of virtual worlds will strongly attract the attention of the majority of people and that the more time they spend in cybernetic environments, the more significant the related dangers become.

The above phenomena and, consequently, the future development of 'cultural production' are also stimulated by new forms of behaviour among the companies producing these new services and their beneficiaries. The organizations that produce very innovative cultural services are increasingly becoming 'theatre companies'. Their managers necessarily become creative characters, gifted with imagination and capable of communicating images, messages and sounds that create sensations, intense experiences, emotions and socialization processes. They will not be concerned any longer about what type of product to sell and what material goods people lack. Instead they ask: what intellectual gratification do people lack? What human experiences and what sensations do people want to try? On this point, James Ogilvey states that the progressive development of the 'market of experience' is a symptom of the fact that people do not desire the traditional goods of the industrial economy any longer:

> today's consumers don't ask themselves as often 'What do I want to have that I don't have, already'; they are asking instead, 'What do I want to *experience* that I *have not* experienced yet' [...]; the experience industry is all about trading in what makes the heart beat faster.[18]

Therefore managers of the corporations of the future that operate in the field of the experience industry must act according to new strategies and with innovative marketing instruments. They will aim at finding externally the most valid cultural resources available or produce internally those new cultural elements to be used to supply suitable cultural services to enable consumers to have new experiences, new sensations, through virtual worlds.

In some advanced cultural industries, the company – in Rifkin's opinion – will tend to become a huge theatre and the entire organization of the production of services will tend to be shaped according to the dictates of theatrical art. Creative managers must begin with the choice of the sensation to transmit, continue with the problem of casting (the choice of the actors that must play the various roles), with the elaboration of the material, the arrangement of the scenes, the specification of the acts in the operational process and the control of the economic feasibility of the initiative.[19] As well, the people involved in the production of innovative services in the 'sensation industry' will tend to play a new role within the company: from being involved in production, they will pass on to being creative and their role will increasingly be defined in terms of a game. In this context, companies

> are beginning to reinvent their organizational environments to make them more compatible with creativity and artistry – the corner-stones of cultural commerce, [so] the work environment is steadily being transformed into a play environment, reflecting the new emphasis on cultural performance and the marketing of lived experiences.[20]

In brief, a new model of employee is emerging within an original type of corporate organization. Because to create culture it is necessary to free the imagination and the impulse towards fantasy and transform work into play, the game *ethos* exists alongside the work *ethos*. Therefore, in Rifkin's opinion, *homo faber* (the typical protagonist of industrial capitalism) is operating in concert, at least for the moment, with *homo ludens*.[21]

This game *ethos* is spreading, not only among managers and workers who produce new cultural services, but also among the consumers who use such services.[22] The broad range of cultural activities in which the experience industry is organized now occupies an increasingly large portion of our lives. This industry, in order to provoke in individuals new emotions that 'make the heart beat faster', ensures that users who take part in the game pay a fee and play a role that is no longer exclusively passive. In cyberspace – as Rifkin observes[23] – the passive role of spectator increasingly gives way to the active role of the character actors and even the star. Each person who takes part in the game will live a concrete experience and, cocooned in an artificial electronic environment, will be able to create moments of great gratification for him- or herself.

***

At this point it must be emphasized that traditional activities will not disappear with the arrival of the new economic system; they will simply mark time and gradually be rivalled and overtaken by these innovative activities.

With the application of the six technologies mentioned above and with massive access to the multimedia network, it is highly probable that advanced cultural services will occupy first place in the economy in the long run; the other services connected to the six technologies will be in second place after which will come manufacturing of material goods, construction and agriculture.[24]

All sectors will be influenced in various ways by the six new technologies,[25] by the adoption of the multimedia network, which will allow access to the production and sale of goods and services, through leasing rather than through transfer of ownership and through the presence of flexible, internationalized companies in which 'knowledge' is the strategic factor determining their survival and economic success.

8.6 Changes in marketing in the emerging sectors of the modern economy

Thanks to the use of modern technologies, the production of 'innovative services' is beginning to prevail over that of material goods. Access to services, by means of financial and operational leasing contracts, has become an increasingly widespread practice compared to the purchase of the property rights to the goods that generate the services. In other words, ownership gives way to rental or to a similar contract. This is as true for consumer goods as it is for investment goods. In the more advanced nations (at the cutting edge of the new economy), consumers increasingly prefer to access their house, car, television, furniture, computer and domestic appliances through a subscription, leasing or a similar legal right and by paying a periodic fee or rent. The same behaviour is characteristic of industrial companies that make use of leasing and so avoid purchasing tangible assets (plant, buildings and so on) necessary for the production of goods and services. As stated earlier the 'hollow company' is characterized by a 'light' balance sheet, flexible organization, fast decision-making[26] and capacity to develop or be included in the networks and relationships that create opportunities for development and economic success.

The innovative company of the future will, in all probability, do everything to create a wide range of networks:

a) a network of suppliers for the materials and services connected to production, planning and the development of products;
b) a network of producers with whom to share management of production, outsourcing and eventual joint use of plant, machines, human

resources and sales channels, within the strategy aimed at making the company 'light';

c) a network of technological cooperation to manage new knowledge and exploitation of advanced technology in a rational manner;

d) a network of distributors and clients created in order to forge close and lasting business ties, and to share and reconcile needs and any conflicting interests.[27]

In this very different environment, new policies and marketing techniques are necessary. The fundamental orientation of marketing tends to change: it is no longer focused on the product, market share and the need to sell a particular product to global consumers, but on the need to create a lasting commercial relationship with the single consumer, to whom various products or services must be sold over time. Therefore the fundamental objective is to develop lasting relationships with the individual consumer and encourage her/him to purchase a wide range of products or services. Such commercial relationships are a fundamental intangible asset for firms and constitute the basis for creating value. According to the new orientation, it is no longer so necessary for companies to stimulate masses of consumers to purchase in order to increase total market share. It is more important to develop and put into practice corporate policy aimed at getting to know individual customers, binding them to the firm and its business and creating loyalty in order to build stable relationships that are reciprocally advantageous.[28] In this way, the company enters into the life of customers, supports them, follows them and, gradually, even becomes pervasive in their lives by sharing particular values and behaviours. The fundamental instrument in this process is the brand.[29] To achieve their purpose, marketing managers are supported by information technology, telecommunications and the multimedia network to study the behaviour of consumers, their aspirations and their purchasing power. From the data collected and analysed, they outline strategies to achieve lasting commercial relationships that will develop progressively. The leading companies, on the basis of specific economic studies and using sophisticated information technology and statistical instruments, are able to estimate each client's purchasing power in a year, in two years, in the medium term and in the long term. They can therefore calculate the economic and commercial value of single customers, in the short, medium and long term by discounting the future flows of expenses foreseen and using appropriate rates that take into account the evaluation risk; they can also determine the value of the 'relationship capital' related to the totality of customers. Highly trained managers can simulate the value of the 'relationship capital' resulting from the marketing strategy adopted in order to achieve a satisfactory level of profitability in the long term. In an environment of this type, corporate success and the connected creation of value are consequently linked to identifying the strategy that allows the company to maintain a relationship with the single consumer for their lifetime and induce them to dedicate more time, attention and money to the company and its products and services.

Finally, marketing tends to have three fundamental objectives:

1) to create mechanisms that develop lasting commercial relationships while the company manages the behaviour of clients;
2) to increase the so-called 'quota of the single client' (time, interest and money dedicated to the company);
3) to estimate in a systematic and continuous way the value of 'relationship capital' deriving from new marketing strategies based on the supply of goods and services that appear to customers innovative and 'unique' compared to those of competitors, therefore inducing them to think they cannot do without this product in the future.

The secret of the new marketing is, therefore, to maintain and continuously revitalize customer relationships in order to make the economic value of the company grow, above all, in the long term.

This marketing behaviour is becoming well established. This is well illustrated by a case reported by Peppers and Rogers.[30] It concerns a company that proposes to create lasting and profitable commercial relationships by following the 'relationship-based marketing' approach. For a fixed fee this company initially makes available to families all the nappies that they will need for their children during a particular period of time. In this case, the commercial relationship is based on a single-service contract. But the firm does not stop here. It remains in close contact with each family and, at a later stage, through a service or lease contract, supplies a series of new products and services: toys, baby food, medicines and clothes. Once the relationship becomes stable and satisfactory, the firm works to establish, strengthen and stimulate the relationship. So – with a fee, lease or other similar contract – the firm continues to supply clothes for the children when they grow up, new toys, books, stationery, school uniforms and, widening the relationship time horizon, holidays for the entire family, video games, compact discs and even financial services aimed at providing the means for them to study at university. Naturally the whole thing is carried out on the basis of a strategy to increase the economic value of the single customer and the 'relationship capital' of all its customers.

8.7 Intangible resources and knowledge as the strategic factor of corporate management

From the final two decades of the 20th century, the intangible factor of 'knowledge' has occupied centre-stage in the general economy and in companies for a range of reasons already mentioned and that we now summarize with some additional considerations.[31]

First of all, it is now indispensable to introduce specialized knowledge into corporations in one or more of the following fields: biotechnology, information technology, artificial materials, microelectronics, robotics and telecommunications. These areas of technical and scientific knowledge appear to be a determining factor in producing goods and, especially, highly innovative services capable of satisfying not only physiological and safety needs, but also social needs and the motivations of self-esteem, respect from others and self-fulfilment.[32] The scientific and technological knowledge necessary to maintain the large company at the highest level affects both production structures and corporate organization; the knowledge portfolio of firms can no longer be the exclusive patrimony of a single talented individual capable of promoting the evolution of the company. Such knowledge is, instead, 'created, continually renewed and improved upon by a group of specialized and properly organized individuals'.[33] While in the past it was normal that scientific and technological knowledge was introduced into organizations by employing staff or using consultants, in modern innovative companies – characterized by the use of the multimedia network – such knowledge, to a great extent, is acquired from the internet. This calls for the stipulation of agreements with firms and technical and scientific organizations and the development of a wide technical network that allows companies to jointly manage the problems of research, its cost, risk and use. Corporations that find themselves outside the network will be isolated and have difficulty in surviving, and developing and creating value. But rapid growth in scientific and technological progress will cause numerous problems even for those corporations that have access to the multimedia network. This is because the opportunity to acquire knowledge and information and form alliances at a global level also makes the technologies (even the most innovative) available to a great number of alert and careful entrepreneurs. So competition without limits will develop and victory will go to those who are more open to novelty, aspire to occupying the role of first mover, and to those that are more creative, imaginative and prompt in 'assembling' the various specialized competences to be used in the corporate business.[34] In conclusion, it can be foreseen that scientific and technological knowledge will tend to be increasingly important and will represent a great part of the intellectual capital[35] of production organizations operating in the more advanced sectors of the modern economy. It can also be foreseen that the activities of strategic management, indispensable to assembling, organizing and applying technical and scientific knowledge to production processes, will become increasingly important.[36]

In second place, firms operating in modern sectors need to acquire new marketing skills in order to control market trends and to adapt corporate management to them. The control of the environment, particularly consumers, users, suppliers and competitors, requires specialist skills in marketing, information technology, statistics and other technical areas. What is most important for the company is to develop lasting commercial relations with single clients and to sell them a series of products by means of fees or leasing contracts.[37] As with scientific and technological knowledge, it is not necessary to employ new staff to acquire the above competences in marketing; the multimedia network can be used to gain access to such competences. These skills, once systematically introduced into the organization, form part of the intellectual, intangible capital of the company. Obviously, the higher the quality of the marketing competences, the more effective the action of management will be in terms of development sustainability, economic and financial results and company value. Many future companies operating in the more advanced sectors will probably make little use of physical and financial capital; their true capital will largely be the capacity of managers to create and progressively develop lasting commercial relationships with clients. At present, in the USA and in Europe, corporations of this type exist which have built their fortunes on marketing understood in the modern sense, that is relationship-based marketing aiming at the systematic cultivation of customer loyalty in the longer term.

In third place, with the change in the structure of the market, with the production of services prevailing over the production of material goods, with the progressive use of leasing and with the spectacular development of the multimedia network, access relationships have become the fundamental paradigm with which to manage the success of the firm. In the society of the past, the economic difference between individuals was marked, above all, by the quantity of goods and money they had. With the advent of the internet, the relative importance of people is increasingly connected to the possibility of 'access to the Net': those who do not have this access are destined to be among the masses fighting strenuously to achieve or regain success. But access to the Net is also important for the firm, for it to obtain the technical knowledge and marketing information necessary for competent corporate management. Without doubt, specialized network knowledge is essential for the success of innovative modern companies. In future this will bring differential advantages in terms of competition and creation of value. Naturally, once this knowledge is introduced into the company, it will represent a significant part of both its intellectual capital as well as the value of its total economic capital.

In fourth place, the presence of numerous specialists with specific knowledge requires synergistic coordination to achieve the goals of the company. This process of harmonization is achieved

> by instituting functional systems of tasks, powers, responsibility, communication and motivation, by establishing norms of behavior, procedures and organs of coordination and control. Such functions are rather complex and delicate and require other specific capabilities to be put into practice, in particular the professional aptitudes possessed by certain individuals, the so-called organizers. The success of the company depends, to a considerable extent, on their efficient work.[38]

Naturally, these competences also represent a part of the intellectual capital of the company and of its total economic value.[39]

Finally, power and management in leading companies require increasing knowledge of strategic management, in order to outline the evolutionary path of the company system in a volatile and very complex environment.[40]

In future, strategic knowledge will be needed both to manage internal forces (centres of decision, control and operation) as well as to respond to the expectations of external forces (stakeholders, who are naturally interested in corporate behaviour and results).

This is why internal strategy to control the operation of the corporate system will need professional knowledge of the design of organizational structure. The same is true for: the development of an effective system of planning and control; the creation of an adequate information system to support decision-making, control and operations; and the training and motivation of human resources in order to align the interests of workers with the interests of the company as a whole.

The external management strategy will require, above all, the ability to study and utilize[41] the environmental forces that affect competition in the sectors in which the company operates[42]: the bargaining power of clients, suppliers, competitors, the threat of entry into the same sector by new competitors, the potential competition connected to the use of products and services that can replace those sold by the company.[43]

In addition, the external strategy will involve carrying out in-depth analysis to identify the points of strength and weakness of the company, in relation to the above-mentioned external forces and environmental threats. This strategy will require the capacity to develop, test and carry out a plan of strategic positioning in order to acquire competitive advantages by means of different strategies: 1) adaptive (or defensive); 2) coercive; 3) predictive of change in the environment or in the actions of competitors, or a combination of these.[44]

The choice of a positioning strategy will be effective:

a) if the points of strength regarding the company's own technical, financial and human resources are exploited in the best way;
b) if use is made of the weak points of the 'opposing external forces' (competitors, clients, suppliers, and so on);
c) if the areas of business that are most promising, those in which the competition can be faced with reasonable success and those to avoid, are identified;
d) if both the movements of the above-mentioned forces that influence competition as well as the changes in the general economy and of society are foreseen;
e) if managers play a creative role regarding technological innovation, products, marketing, organization and motivation of human resources.[45]

In these cases differential advantages can be gained over competitors along with success in creating a lasting relationship with customers.[46]

The creation for customers of an image of diversity and uniqueness of the firm and of its products and services, compared to those of present and potential competitors, is one of the main predictors of success of a positioning strategy.[47] Other important indicators are the economic value of the spending power of clients who are linked to the company, as well as corporate profitability.[48]

Finally, strategic management knowledge, obviously, constitutes an intangible asset of great importance for companies active in new economy industries.[49]

Notes

1. Thurow (2000), pp. 52ff.
2. According to Simon and Zatta (2008, p 102), 'strong resistance to change is the rule and not the exception. More than anything else, the history of humanity is the history of resistance to innovation and change'.
3. S. Zanda (2009), chapter II, section 6.
4. Galbraith (1967), p. 56.
5. 'For the first time since 1917, then, we live in a world in which property rights and free markets are viewed as fundamental principles, not grudging expedients; where the unpleasant aspects of a market system – inequality, unemployment, injustice – are accepted as facts of life. As in the Victorian era, capitalism is secure not only because of its successes – which, as we will see in a moment, have been very real – but because nobody has a plausible alternative.

   'This situation will not last forever. Surely there will be other ideologies, other dreams; and they will emerge sooner rather than later if the current economic crisis persists and deepens. But for now capitalism rules the world unchallenged' (Krugman 2009, p. 14).
6. Thurow (2000), prologue, p. xii.
7. Rifkin (2001), pp. 3ff.
8. Friedman (2007), p. 232.
9. Rifkin (2001), pp. 13–14.
10. Rifkin (2001), pp. 4–5.
11. On the ability of particular internet companies to consider strategic alliances as the fulcrum of value creation processes, see Massaroni and Ricotta (2009), pp. 3–29.
12. Friedman (2007), p. 449.
13. Friedman (2007), pp. 444ff.
14. Rifkin (2001), p. 140.
15. Rifkin (2001, p. 138) specifies: 'After thousands of years of existing in a semi-independent realm, occasionally touched by the market but never absorbed by it, culture – shared human experience – is now being drawn into the economic realm, thanks to the hold the new communications technologies are beginning to enjoy over day-to-day life. In a global economy increasingly dominated by a commercial electronic communications grid and every kind of cultural production and commodity, securing access to one's own lived experiences becomes as important as being propertied was in an era dominated by the production of industrial goods.' On the absorption of the cultural system into the commercial sphere, see, in particular, the following pages: 11–15, 137–67, 171–85.
16. Maslow (1943); McGregor (1966), chapters I and II.
17. Some people tend to transfer to or to maintain in the real world the behaviour that they exhibit in the virtual world. The virtual realities of cyberspace are a fantastic and temporarily rewarding atmosphere, but they do not solve the problems found in real life.
18. Ogilvey (1990), quoted by Rifkin (2001), p. 145.
19. Rifkin (2001), p. 164.
20. Rifkin (2001), pp. 164–5.

21. Rifkin (2001), p. 260. In particular, he points out the following: 'Now that we are moving from industrial to cultural capitalism, the work ethos is slowly giving way to the play ethos. Play is what people do when they create culture. [. . .]. The new era of capitalism brings play to the foreground of global commerce. The commodification of cultural experiences is, above all else, an effort to colonize play in all of its various dimensions and transform it into a purely salable form. Access, in turn, becomes a way to determine who is allowed to participate – to play – and who is not. The Dutch historian Johan Huizinga was among the first to recognize the importance of play in the making of society. He suggested that Homo ludens (man the player) be afforded equal status to Homo sapiens (man the reasoner) and Homo faber (man the maker) in defining the essence of what it means to be a human being. While other creatures play, human beings excel in the ludenic arts.' See also Rifkin (2001), pp. 12–15 and 163–7.
22. It is, as already noted, the experience industry sector, from the theatre to the cinema, from tourism to entertainment, from song to dance.
23. Rifkin (2001), pp. 170–1.
24. Rifkin (2001), pp. 166–7.
25. For example, biotechnology will create, among other things, remarkable innovations, generating plants and animals with modified characteristics. Robotics will modify the system of manufacturing, agricultural production and commercial distribution. Distribution will be reorganized using the new computer science and telecommunication technologies. The health service and wellness centres will be revolutionized by new applications of microelectronics and biotechnology.
26. In the current increasingly competitive context, the 'economies of speed' – which allow companies to adapt quickly to continuous environmental change and to take immediate advantage of opportunities and find remedies for risks and other negative phenomena – are becoming more and more important. They are now regarded as one of the main sources of business success. According to scholars and managers, they are progressively replacing economies of scale in the hierarchy of importance.
27. Rifkin (2001), p. 19, who quotes Castells (1996), vol. I, p. 191.
28. In the manufacturing economy of the past, the fundamental objective was the realization of sales, while the link with the single customer, through guarantees and free assistance post-sale, was only a possibility. Currently things are changing; in the advanced sectors of the New Economy, this relationship is progressively reversed. Many companies are even inclined to sell cheaply or to give away their products in order to establish a long-lasting commercial relationship with the single customer.
29. 'Buying the label puts one in the make-believe cultural world of shared values and meanings that the designers create. The fact that it is all just a come-on, a sophisticated marketing device, is of little consequence. Millions of people have shown their willingness to suspend disbelief and buy their way into these stylized environments. The designer clothes, appliances, and whatnots become costumes and backdrops for living out imagined lifestyles and experiences' (Rifkin 2001, p. 172).
30. Peppers and Rogers (1993), pp. 45–6, quoted by Rifkin (2001), p. 99.

31. Regarding 'intellectual capitalism', which is progressively asserting itself, characterized by the production of sophisticated and personalized services, see Prandstraller (2009), chapter II, paragraphs 2.6 and 2.7.
32. On the nature and hierarchy of these needs, see Maslow (1943; 1954); Zanda (1974), p. 263. See also Galbraith (2004), chapter V; Trequattrini (2008), pp. 794ff.
33. Zanda (1974), p. 263.
34. This phenomenon is a real process of 'commoditization' of technology. As Friedman observes, 'the higher the number of analogical processes that become digital, virtual, mobile and personal, the higher the number of activities and functions that are standardized, digitalized and made easier to manipulate and, therefore, more accessible to many' (Friedman 2007, p. 435).
35. As well, the abilities of strategic management represent an intangible asset. We will return to this subject in the following pages.
36. On problems arising from the outsourcing of processes that are not part of the core business, see Simon and Zatta (2008), pp. 204–5.
37. It is not therefore important to try too hard to stimulate customers to carry out single purchases. On the contrary it is important to develop marketing plans that, starting from the study of the behaviour and purchasing power of single customers, are able to enter the lives of clients and form lasting business relationships.
38. Zanda (1974), p. 264.
39. This theory represents the paradox of the modern advanced economies. The more we investigate natural, social and technological phenomena, the more we become specialized. Our advanced specialization makes us somewhat free, but potentially uncontrollable. This requires company specialists in organization to coordinate and harmonize the efforts of the single experts towards the general goals of the company. This control obviously – as specialist knowledge becomes increasingly esoteric – must be based less and less on fixed rules and procedures, which always compress the imagination and creativity of the single experts, and more and more on policies and guidelines that define and limit the decisional and operating processes of the specialists.
40. In this case, management is not intended as the 'management of the existing' based on the control of subordinates, but as the creative ability to develop solutions that produce satisfactory results using the specialist competences of professionals, who are stimulated by means of effective systems of leadership. In short, 'strategic management' is not limited to the supervision of subordinates (a small part of the managerial function), but is, above all, a creative intellectual activity relating to a system of decisions in the following areas: technology, marketing, products, competitiveness factors and policies of motivation and management of human resources.
41. Melis emphasizes that the firm acknowledges impulses and information from the environment as constraints and opportunities; moreover, that the firm assumes these 'also as external resources on which to base its own operations and growth' (Melis 1993, p. 12).
42. These forces are becoming more and more unpredictable; they are influenced by unusual, extreme, unthinkable and highly improbable factors and have

enormous economic, financial and human impact. Taleb writes: '[. . .] I will expose myself and assert, against many habits of thought, that the world is dominated by what is extreme, unknown and highly improbable, while we continue to deal with secondary aspects, to concentrate on what is known and repeated. This implies the necessity to use the extreme event as a starting point, and not as an exception to hide under the carpet. I also propose the more audacious (and more annoying) idea that, despite our progress and the increase of our knowledge [. . .] the future will be less and less predictable' (Taleb 2009, p. 21).

43. Porter (1979), p. 141.

44. On this subject Porter asserts: 'Once the corporate strategist has assessed the forces affecting competition in his industry and their underlying causes, he can identify his company's strengths and weaknesses. The crucial strengths and weaknesses from a strategic standpoint are the company's posture vis-à-vis the underlying causes of each force. Where does it stand against substitutes? Against the sources of entry barriers?

   Then the strategist can devise a plan of action that may include (1) positioning the company so that its capabilities provide the best defence against the competitive force; and/or (2) influencing the balance of the forces through strategic moves, thereby improving the company's position; and/or (3) anticipating shifts in the factors underlying the forces and responding to them, with the hope of exploiting change by choosing a strategy appropriate for the new competitive balance before opponents recognize it' (Porter 1979, p. 143).

45. 'The success of companies strongly depends on the ability of entrepreneurs to create conditions of technological and sociological disequilibrium. This gives firms the possibility to enjoy competitive advantages. Disequilibrium means change, overcoming the old, high-return and high-growth opportunities. Naturally it is necessary to take factual advantage of the disequilibrium conditions; entrepreneurs are strongly conditioned in this by the environment in which they operate' (Laghi 2001, p. 57).

46. This long-lasting relationship, as previously emphasized, is the most important intangible asset of the company and, naturally, of its economic capital.

47. In general terms, the success of a human activity is inversely proportional to its unpredictability and its possibility of imitation by a third party. On this point, see Taleb (2009), p. 13.

48. The level of profitability is connected not only with the strategic positioning that makes the company 'unique' and less imitable, but also with the level of operating efficiency that managers will be able to realize (low costs and high technical performance) and with the capacity to obtain higher prices in comparison with competitors. This last possibility is, undoubtedly, closely connected with the strategies of 'uniqueness' of the company.

49. On the methods of evaluation of intellectual capital, see Trequattrini (2008), pp. 155ff.

9
Ethical Foundations of Corporate Social Responsibility. The Contribution of Christian Social Thought

Helen Alford

9.1 The problematic link between ethics and CSR, and what the Christian social tradition can offer to help[1]

We need to start from a general understanding of what a business is. Businesses are made up of people and things (money, capital equipment, assets in general), and are organized according to certain legal forms and principles. Human ingenuity has arrived at this combination of elements in order to achieve certain goals. As such, business structures represent a combination of natural and artificial (or man-made) components; natural components include the people in the business and their work, whereas artificial components include the policies the business adopts, as well as the legal form it has. The business is therefore a complex form, neither purely natural nor purely artificial. A machine is purely artificial; it is an instrument, and is judged to be good if it is good *for* achieving the task for which it was made. A business is not so simple; it is created not only *for* something else, though its members are brought together for the sake of working together or putting in resources for a purpose, but in the process of doing so, its members begin to develop an intrinsic good between them, where 'good' here means the realization of the potential of those involved, or their development towards the fullest expression of their being. A business may begin with an idea for doing something in the mind of the entrepreneur, in a way not dissimilar to the idea of the machine in the mind of the inventor. But as the business comes into existence, it develops into more than an instrument, whereas the machine can never become anything other than an instrument. This is because human beings bring themselves to a business, and, as they work in it, they not only produce objective goods, products and services, but they also develop in themselves; we could say they 'produce themselves', in communion with the others with whom they work. Although we will say more about this later, this point should already be relatively clear; we have all experienced what we are talking about here, as it happens to each one of us working with others in an organization. We have various ways of describing this phenomenon, including phrases like 'gaining experience' or 'developing work-related skills'. All this can only happen in communion with the others, for no-one can 'gain experience' like this on their own. People working together are developing a good which they hold together, in common, as well as developing each one of themselves individually. Recognition of this phenomenon has prompted the development of the literature on 'core competences' in the firm, which are capacities of the business as a whole. They are not held individually, but are rather held in common between the members of the business. But to return to our summary: for now, the important point to note is that, according to this analysis, the business has both instrumental and intrinsic ends. It is not just a 'mere fiction', nor is it nothing more than an 'artificial construct' that is useful to us in achieving our ends, though it does have instrumental ends and does need to be efficient and effective about achieving those ends. Neither is it a living being in its own right with its own intrinsic ends, though since its active component is made up of human beings it does 'produce' intrinsic goods as part of its operation and its activity needs to be ordered towards the development of the intrinsic common good of society. The business is a complex reality that constitutes a category in its own right, one that we can most succinctly describe as a form of 'common good', with both instrumental and intrinsic aspects, as we will soon discuss further. Another way of thinking about the business in the same vein is to see it as a 'community of work'.

Most approaches to business ethics and to the question of Corporate Social Responsibility (CSR) only see the business as an instrument (like a machine), and therefore they do not recognize that it is also producing intrinsic goods as part of its normal operation, both at the level of the individual and at the level of the business as a whole (among its members or those that participate in its activity). The term that is often used is 'nexus of contracts', and, although this creates a more complex image in the mind's eye of what a business is than the image of the machine, it still keeps the image at the instrumental level. We make contracts because they are useful to us in achieving our goals (otherwise, we would not make them), and a 'nexus' of contracts is where many of them meet. We can begin to see why the dominant ethical traditions in the field of business ethics have difficulty with providing a strong ethical anchorage for CSR when we begin to see the drawbacks of their limited (and therefore faulty) understanding of the nature of a business.

Two examples will help us see what these drawbacks are. Writing in the Kantian tradition, Freeman and Gilbert propose that the only way to create an ethical business strategy is to adopt the 'personal projects enterprise strategy' (PPES) approach.[2] They argue that most approaches to strategy do not recognize that all the stakeholders of a business are free, autonomous beings who should be treated as ends in themselves. Rather, much strategic thinking is aimed at persuading stakeholders, if not manipulating them, into following a business strategy that serves the interests of a few. The only truly ethical business strategy, according to them, is to aim at realizing the personal projects of all the members or stakeholders of the business. Now it does not take a lot of thinking about this to realize that this is an impossible job on a practical level; how exactly is it to be done? This approach therefore is strong on recognizing the individual dignity of each stakeholder, but provides no way of synthesizing a decision for the good of the group as a whole. Here we can clearly see that it is the underlying individualism that is causing the problem.

A second example comes from the social contract tradition. Lorenzo Sacconi has developed one of the most advanced explanations of the ethical basis of CSR so far, starting with two social contracts.[3] The first one is a general one, agreed by all members of the business, which, while giving them all equal rights in the business, turns out to be impractical (in a way not dissimilar to the impracticality of Freeman and Gilbert's PPES). So on the basis of the first social contract, a second one is negotiated; in this one, decision-making powers are delegated to one group (managers) in order that the business can function, but the managers agree to make decisions on the basis of the principles underlying the two contracts so that everyone's rights are protected. As in the case of social contracts in general, no actual contract is negotiated; the idea of the contract is a useful concept for explaining the ethical basis of CSR. The final part of the argument deals with what makes the managers stick to the 'agreement' they have made – after all, if there were no consequences to breaking the notional contract, there could be a strong incentive for them to do so on occasion, for their own personal gain. Here, the reputational mechanism comes into play; the idea is that managers will not in fact behave opportunistically because they will know that it will damage the reputation of the business, and that this will make it harder for them to obtain funds, win customers and attract talent to work in the business. However, apart from the problem of the very abstract nature of the social contracts themselves, simple experience shows that the reputational mechanism is weak, if it works at all. Businesses have significant control over what information about them reaches the press, and NGOs are not necessarily present in all parts of the world to denounce violations of the 'social contract' when they occur. Most importantly of all, however, is that the whole approach makes being ethical an extrinsic activity; it is about keeping to rules and applying sanctions; it does not touch the inner dynamism of the human being. As research has showed, such mechanisms tend to 'crowd-out' intrinsic motivations for being socially responsible or ethical, and in the end make it more likely that non-socially responsible or non-ethical behaviour results.

As we have already hinted, the problem here for these mainstream approaches goes deeper. Their difficulty in visualizing the business in anything other than instrumental terms develops from a still more fundamental difficulty: a one-sided, individualistic view of the human being. This is a problem in general for an understanding of business, and therefore of business ethics and CSR. It is because the philosophical tradition preserved in Christian social thought can help us with these problems that what we have to offer here is of importance to the field of business ethics in general, and not just for Christians who want to live their faith coherently in the workplace.

The underlying problem for mainstream business ethics and CSR is an incomplete anthropology, one that blocks adequate recognition of the development of the people working *together with each other* within the business, and similarly does not recognize the possibility for intrinsic good to develop between the business and the wider society around it. An individualistic starting point cannot recognize real, intrinsic good *in the relationships between people*. On this point of weakness, a personalist anthropology, as developed within the tradition of Christian social thought, can provide some help. The personalist approach recognizes the importance of the individual aspect of the human being, and the advantages and gains that have been made by those who have developed theories of individualism. But it goes further than individualism to recognize another aspect of the human being, which, at least in the business sphere, turns out to be equally important and no less necessary to recognize if we are to solve some of the serious problems facing business ethics, and, in particular, facing CSR. For, as personalism recognizes, the relationships we have with each other are not only useful to us in achieving our individual ends; they are also intrinsically important to each one of us, for they are part of who we are. The human person is both an individual, with his own interests to pursue and who is largely in competition or in conflict with others, and, at the same time, a *being in relation* with others, where it is the shared goals and goods developed in pursuing those goals that are important, and one's behaviour is based on cooperation and solidarity. The human being is both of these things simultaneously, entirely and at all times both an individual and a being in relation (in the language of personalism, the 'being in relation' side of the human being is called 'person'). Understanding the fundamental duality at the basis of human existence, individual–person, is the first key recognition that needs to be made if we are get beyond the shortcomings of an individualistic approach.

Once this conceptual breakthrough has been made, we are able to recognize that through the relationships set up between people in a business, real, intrinsic human good can be created between them (they develop together), and that the business itself can be seen as a kind of common good among its members. This second recognition allows us to reach the key point in this discussion for the ethical underpinnings of CSR, and hence for business ethics. For on this understanding of business we can provide managers with a way of both recognizing individual interests and rights (perhaps through a stakeholder analysis) and a way of synthesizing (prioritizing) the satisfaction of these rights and interests in an ethical way, that is, on the basis of what promotes the common good that the actors involved have developed between them and from which they all benefit. This we will deal with in more detail in the last part of the chapter. We have seen that most mainstream approaches to the ethical basis of CSR either cannot do this at all (Freeman and Gilbert is an example), or they can only do it with very limited effect, using a mechanism that tends to 'crowd out' intrinsic reasons for being socially responsible. And yet it is essential to be able to do this if we are going to be able to provide an alternative to the dominant rule for decision-making – maximize shareholder wealth – with the instrumental use that it makes of CSR (in this approach, CSR becomes a device for building a good reputation, and no more than that). Although we should recognize that much progress has been made in the area of business ethics and CSR through the development of stakeholder thinking, either based on Kantianism or on the social contract, we also need to recognize that these approaches have got to a point where they are blocked in their development. They need the injection of a new dimension into their basic anthropology for them to be able to get beyond the impasse. Personalism could be the very approach that they need, for, as we said, it recognizes the gains made by individualism but also recognizes its limitations and proposes a way forward.

As a set of philosophical ideas, the personalist approach to business and CSR is accessible to people in general, even if the thinking on which it is based has been preserved within the Christian tradition. Since it is also entirely compatible with Christian theology, it also represents an approach to business ethics and CSR that helps Christians live out their Christian commitment as business people. It does both things by building an understanding of the business itself which starts from two complementary points: the idea of the human being as both individual and person, and the idea of the common good.

9.2   The idea of the human being as both individual and person

If we are going to get beyond some of the problems in the dominant ethical approaches to business and ethics and CSR, we need a more complex anthropology than these approaches allow, something like a personalist anthropology. In such an approach, the human being is seen as both an individual and a person. The nearest analogy we could make to this theory elsewhere would be the theory of the 'wave-particle duality' of light. There are some experiments with light that can only be explained by physicists if they think of light as if it were a discrete particle of energy (a quantum or photon), while there are other experiments that can only be explained if light is considered to be a wave. At least on current understanding, we cannot get to a more simple explanation of light; we have to live with this duality where we sometimes think of it as a particle and sometimes as a wave. The personalist theory is somewhat like this, for it is helpful to us in explaining human behaviour in relation to groups if we can think of a human being as both individuated (a bit like the particle explanation of light) and as in relation with others, as a person (somewhat like the wave explanation).

Recognizing a duality in the human being, as both individual and person, can help us answer questions that we need to answer in order to give CSR a stronger ethical foundation.[4] One of these questions, posed by Jacques Maritain, among the foremost personalist thinkers of the 20th century, is: 'Does society exist for each one of us, or does each one of us exist for society?'[5] In our case, the society being spoken of could be the business (*società/société* in Italian and French are the words used for 'business'), or the business in relation to wider society, and the reply to it is directly relevant to resolving the problem that Freeman and Gilbert face: how to respect each stakeholder as an end in themselves while making a decision for the good of all (for the society)? Recognizing the duality 'individual–person', therefore, helps us handle the 'duality', if we may call it that, 'human being–society'. On the other hand, if we are not clear about the terms individual and person, we find it hard to answer these questions satisfactorily, as Freeman and Gilbert's problem indicates. Furthermore, this is a distinction that crosses cultures and religions; Maritain, for instance, points out that it is also found in Eastern religions and philosophies, such as Hinduism.[6]

The human being is at the same time both an 'individual' and a 'person': '[o]ur whole being is an individual by reason of that in us which derives from matter, and a person by reason of that in us which derives from spirit'.[7] Or, to put it another way, each of us is 'in his entirety an individual and in his entirety a person'.[8] It is pretty clear from basic observation that each one of us is a physical individual (conjoined twins notwithstanding) and, thanks to the development of biological science, we have a name for the species to which we belong, of which we each represent an individual member: *homo sapiens sapiens*. At the same time, however, the personalist theory holds that we are also 'persons'. What does the term 'person' mean here? Ratzinger gives a history of the development of the term.[9] It was probably coined in Latin by Tertullian, one of the early Church Fathers, working from the Greek word *prosopon* which referred to the masks that players in the theatre used. Tertullian, like others, was struggling with what was a central problem for early Christianity: how could God be both one and three at the same time? In the end the formula they reached was that of 'one substance, three persons'. In reference to the idea of the Trinity, therefore, the idea of person is purely one of relation: the 'persons' of the Trinity are not constituted by separate 'substances' but by their relation with each other. Gradually, the consequences of this idea were worked out for human beings, for by linking the idea of personhood in God to the Genesis text describing human beings as made in the 'image and likeness of God', the idea of person came to be associated with human beings as well. Personhood, then, is relationship and finds itself in relationship, since God, of whom the person forms an image, exists as three persons in constant self-giving to each other. A phenomenological viewpoint would corroborate the idea that the person becomes him or herself in relationship with others.[10] According to this theory, then, each one of us is a person, with an intellectual and spiritual life that 'naturally' seeks out relations with others (and is open to the transcendent).

The genesis of the word 'person' is without doubt Christian, but it recognizes something about the human being that we do not have to be

Christians or believers to recognize. Growing empirical evidence shows that, while our relationships can be useful to us in achieving individual goals, it is a mistake to see them only in this way – indeed, it may block our recognition of relationship as the primary *locus* of our development and fulfilment. This latter point is something that the personalist position would predict. Empirical research is indeed showing more and more that it is in our relationships that we become more whole, that is, we find our fulfilment in our relationships.[11] In the personalist approach, relationships are not to be seen only or even primarily on the model of contracts (although sometimes contracts may be involved), nor are they only or primarily about rivalry and competition (though both may sometimes be involved in them). These models refer to our relations to others as individuals, not as persons. On the personal level, however, relationships are *part of who we are*. Empirical evidence continues to support the view that relationships are intrinsically important to us. We know from practical experience that human beings cannot develop fully without other human beings, especially as regards language and rational thought. But even when we have reached maturity, we continue to need relationships with others for social esteem[12] or to be happy at all.[13] Increasingly, evidence from the economic and social sciences is showing that it is *in the relationships themselves that people find fulfilment*, not that relationships are useful to them in achieving their own personal projects. Indeed, our individuality is an essential basis for our fulfilment, but it is as persons in relations with others that we reach that fulfilment, that we can develop as far as possible. Through these 'natural', or we might even say 'inevitable', relationships, human beings may grow into full freedom and maturity or they may be prevented from thus developing.

Human development thus depends not only on respecting rights (that is, on not interfering in people's areas of freedom) but also on growing through acting and living together, especially through working together, and on creating common goods between us as a result, goods which cannot just be 'parcelled up' and allocated to one person or another according to some kind of stakeholder calculus. These 'common goods' exist only in the relationship, or in the communion between people, or they do not exist at all. Since businesses are created for coordinating human work towards achieving certain objectives, they result in the creation of a 'community of work' where good (human development, including social development) is created through the working relationships that people develop with each other in the course of their work together. As we noted in the summary, this kind of good within the firm is recognized in the business literature in ideas like the 'core competences' of a business, which are properties of a business as a whole and functions of the relationships between its members, rather than of the individuals alone.[14] If the same individuals were split up from each other and went to work elsewhere, they would bring all sorts of skills and talents to their new tasks, but the competences that they shared between them would be lost. Similarly, the idea of social capital, widely used today in economic, sociological and business parlance, is incorporating the importance of relationships into economic discourse.[15]

Since we are always and at the same time both an individual and a person, we relate to others on both these levels too. On this point, Maritain says that, as persons, we relate:

> [. . .] because of [our] very perfections [. . .] and [our] inner urge to the communications of knowledge and love which require relationship with other persons. In its radical generosity, the human person tends to overflow into social communications in response to the law of superabundance inscribed in the depths of being, life, intelligence and love [. . .].

As individuals, rather, we relate to each other:

> [. . .] because of [our] needs or deficiencies, which derive from [our] material individuality.[16]

That we relate to others both as individuals and as persons is going to be a key point in our analysis of ethics and CSR. As persons, we relate to others out of an inner urge to do so – it can be from love, from the desire to communicate or to grow in knowledge, and it can also be for the sake of cooperating with another for a shared goal, perhaps as an act of solidarity. As individuals, we relate to others for the sake of satisfying our material needs; we are therefore, at least potentially, in competition and even conflict with each other. Consumable goods can only be consumed by one or another person, and can only be 'shared' with others by dividing them up (so either I get all and you get none, or we both get less than the full amount). Similarly, capital goods are usually owned by one person/group or another, and so there is also competition for these goods (goods can, of course, be held in common, if a proper legal basis is set up for doing so). So on the personal level, we relate in a mutually supportive, non-competitive way, while on the individual level, we are competing with each other. Note, however, that while our material needs may be met (it is not necessarily easy to identify when this holds, but at least in theory it is possible), our urge to relate to others on the personal level is not so limited, and may continue to grow and deepen. Furthermore, saying that being in relation with others is an intrinsic part of human nature is not the same as stating that human beings are naturally altruists, or that they are 'kind' or other-centred. In a personalist vision one can choose to be egoistic. What cannot be chosen is whether or not being-in-relation is fundamental to being human.

This leads us on to a further aspect of this duality. Although as individuals we are physically separated from others, our individuality arises from our being part of a species. And in so far as we are each a part of something, our individual good and fulfilment is subordinate to that of the whole. This rule applies to all animal species: the survival of the group (ultimately the species as a whole) is more important than the survival of any individual member. As persons, however, and in the particular set of relations we have, we are unique – we are wholes in our own right. It is as if we each constituted our own species. It is on this basis that we must recognize human beings as ends in themselves, as each uniquely valuable (for a Christian, there is the added element that each person is in the 'image and likeness' of God). As individuals, then, we are parts, and our good is subordinate to that of the group; as persons, we are wholes, ends in ourselves, and we derive support from the group in reaching our own fulfilment, which as we said, develops in the relationship with others. We can summarize this in the following table:

Table 9.1   The individual–person duality

Each human being is:	In itself:	In relation to others:
Entirely a Person	A whole, complete	Overflowing into relationships, desires communion with others
Entirely an Individual	Incomplete, a part of a human group (ultimately of the species)	Is materially individuated, relates to others because of its lacks, its neediness

If we apply this to some practical business examples, we can begin to get some useful insights. On the question of pay and distribution of benefits, for instance, the human being will receive a part of what has been produced. On one level this is inevitable, since the only way profit or other economic gain can be shared is by splitting it up into parts and allocating the various parts to different people or groups (and the individuals involved are in competition between each other with regard to the allocation of this good between them). It is also so because the worker or shareholder or other stakeholder has been a 'part' of the whole system that has produced this gain. At the same time, where people have been deeply engaged in the production of this gain (as in the case of those working within the firm), so that much of their time and effort is committed to achieving this goal, treating these people as wholes through the pay they receive becomes important. This kind of thinking is behind the 'just wage' or 'living wage' idea – the human being needs to live (or to gain a significant part of their living) from what he or she is earning in the firm, and so they also need to be considered as 'wholes' in themselves, not just parts of the business that created the economic gain. Another example would be training for employees. On the one hand, the training has to be useful to the firm so that the employee becomes more productive, and in that sense he or she is being treated as a part of the whole production system. At the same time, each worker is a whole, a person in his or her own right, and the training also needs to be seen in view of the contribution that it will make to the development of the person as a whole.

Perhaps the most interesting example, however, is how this can help us understand what is happening during the ordinary everyday operation of the business. Through working together, people contribute to the overall output of the firm – they are parts of that system – and they obtain the financial means to live and to pursue their ends more widely through that work. At the same time, they are growing as persons, in their working relationships with others. This second, 'subjective' product, which is the 'output' of that working and growing together and which is constituted both by the relationships and by they themselves as persons in relation with each other, provides that shared basis (culture, way of doing things, community) on which the pursuit of objective output can be effectively based. So there is a mutual relationship between the development of the objective, economic output and the development of the subjective output, between the people participating in the common activity of the business. As we know, people can be coerced by contracts and legal means to produce, but we also know that they do not produce anything like as well as they would do if they were in a situation where they were valued and the relationships of which they are a part supported them in their work.

As a result of this image of the human being as a duality, both individual and person, Maritain is able to give an answer to the question on the relation between the society and the person:

> [. . .] we can draw two conclusions. The first concerns the mutual relations of person and society. To characterize these relations we might make use of the following formulae: just as the person requires society both on account of its abundance or as a person, and on account of its poverty or as an individual, so the common good, by its very essence, directs itself to the persons as persons and directs the persons as individuals to itself. [. . .]. The second conclusion concerns the state of tension and conflict which is inherent in human society. Social life is naturally ordained [. . .] to the good and freedom of the person. And yet there is in this very same social life a natural tendency to enslave and diminish the person in the measure that society considers the person as a part and a mere material individual [. . .]. The person as person insists on serving the community and the common good freely. It insists on this while tending toward its own fullness [. . .]. The person as an individual is necessarily bound, by constraint if need be, to serve the community and the common good, since it is excelled by them as the part by the whole.[17]

So there are three things said here on the relation between society and the person:

1) As individuals, our good depends on the good of the community (in this case, the business) in which we participate, and our personal goals and desires need to be subordinated to those of the group; as persons, the business exists to support each one of us in reaching our fulfilment. Both of these things are true at the same time, since human beings are both individuals and persons at the same time. So there is a relationship of 'reciprocal implication and mutual subordination' between the good of each human member of the community and the good of the community as a whole – their common good.[18] We will say more about this common good in the next section of this chapter.
2) Not surprisingly, we experience some tension between these two aspects of human existence and the relationships we have with others on these two levels. This experience can be both negative (as when we are treated as individuals/parts too often) and positive (as when the desire on the part of decision-makers to treat human beings as ends in

themselves causes them to strive for better working conditions, better distribution of resources and so on). This tension can be quite clearly felt in the business. In the negative sense, we can often experience the feeling of being used, even manipulated, in the workplace – certainly not treated as ends in ourselves. The chances for us to make decisions may be limited; we are useful instruments for getting things done, and that is about all. Our opinions may be canvassed, but we know very well that they are not likely to have much impact on what happens. In short, we experience being treated as parts rather than as wholes. While there is a real sense that we are 'part' of the organizations in which we work, one of the results of this reflection is that those managing a socially responsible company will try to use this tension positively. They will try to treat those working within it as wholes as much as is possible, even though they must simultaneously manage the contribution that employees make to the performance of the business as a whole, of which they are 'a part'. Both things are true at the same time: at work, we are both a *part* of something bigger than us, and our good needs to be subordinated to the good of the whole, as well as being a whole, to which the good of the output of the business is directed. There is an inevitable tension here, and it is part of good, socially responsible management to deal with that tension and to manage it properly. Maritain points out that one of the results of this tension is a slow but real progress through history towards treating human beings as persons, as wholes, even at the political or economic level. A case could be made to show that this is behind the gradual development of democracy at the political level; we could say that the gradual improvement of working conditions, of reduction in pollution – indeed, of the possibility of considering an intrinsic rather than a merely instrumental CSR, are other signs of this.

3) As individuals, we may be required or even constrained to serve the communities (including the work communities) of which we are a part, which is the other side of the coin of saying that our good on the individual level depends on the good of the whole. As persons, we can offer willing service, that is, service that does not diminish our identity, but is rather an expression of our full possession of ourselves which we then freely choose to put at the service of others. Again, it is possible to see both these forms of activity/service at work in the business.

We said earlier that thinking of the human being as a duality, as an 'individual–person', would help us answer the question: 'Does society exist for each one of us, or does each one of us exist for society?', and that answering this question would to be crucial to finding a solid ethical grounding for CSR. We have spent some time working out a helpful way of looking at the human being, or at 'each one of us', as Maritain's question puts it. Now we need to develop a similarly helpful understanding of 'society', one that makes sense within the same philosophical framework as does the duality of the human being. Once we have these two pieces in place, we have the basis for answering the question and for dealing with the ethical foundations of CSR. Just as the idea of 'person' was key in the first part of this chapter, the idea of the 'common good' is going to be similarly crucial in building up our concept of a group (whether society as a whole, a business, or whatever), one that is compatible with the understanding of the human being we have been developing.

9.3   The idea of society as a common good with both foundational and excellent dimensions

In modern philosophical approaches, society as a whole, or any group of human beings held together by sharing something between them (identity, goals, affective bonds and so on), has usually either been seen as a kind of living being in its own right, or, quite the opposite, as nothing other than the sum of the individuals that make it up. From the personalist point of view, both of these are extremes and set up a number of obstacles against understanding society more deeply (as well as dangers for society itself). Instead, the personalist position sees society as a kind of common good with two basic dimensions, rather like the two dimensions of the human person. These are the 'foundational common goods', like shared infrastructure, shared systems (the legislative system, for instance) and shared policies, and the 'excellent common goods', like shared values, sharing in a good life together, and the human development of the group as a whole, the development of each person in communion with others. Foundational common goods, like the foundations of a house, are good *for* something else, that is, good foundations on which to build something that is intrinsically good. And excellent common goods are just those intrinsically good things that we aim to build together, using the foundational goods as the means for doing so. But before going further, let us say more about the general idea of the common good.

The definition of the common good that we use here emerges from the Aristotelian-Thomistic tradition, and has been carried forward into our own day through the tradition of Catholic social thought.[19] In this tradition, what is 'good', or 'a good'? It is directly connected with life – life itself is good, and the development of a living being towards its fullest expression is also good. The argument unfolds in two steps; firstly, living beings, like human beings, have the capacity to develop – they are beings with 'potential', always with new possibilities for development that are never fully expressed but towards the full expression of which they can direct their activity. Secondly, it is through action that this development takes place – we grow and develop through what we do. Action and growing into the fullness of being are inextricably linked. Acting 'ethically' or 'in a socially responsible manner' is, therefore, to act towards the full development of the human beings involved in and affected by the action.[20]

Where does this leave us in terms of the common good? Insofar as we are talking about something 'good', we are talking about something that supports and adds to the development of those who are part of the group, those to whom the good is common (which can be a family, a local community, the whole of the human race, or – especially important for us here – a business or a business in communication with its environment). How can this good be common? Only totalitarian theories can hold that the group is some kind of living being in itself of which human beings are only parts (like the hand is a part of the human body) and for whom the parts, the human beings, can be sacrificed without too much ado. According to such theories, there is only the good of the group, in which, in some way, each human member of that group participates. Individualistic theories also have a problem with this idea, since they do not have any way of seeing that there could be a good that could really exist in any way other than at the level of the individual human being. The idea of the common good in these theories, such as utilitarianism, is not much more than a convenient shorthand for referring to the sum of the goods of each individual member of the group. If we want to get to a practical and useful idea of the common good, we have to avoid these two extremes.[21]

The last quote from Maritain above can help us see the way forward. For just as the idea of the duality of the human being allowed us to take the first step beyond the limits of an individualist ethic in understanding what is going on in the business, so the recognition of an equivalent duality between the good of each member of the business and the good shared between all its members, its common good, allows us to complete our basic understanding of the nature of the business, opening the way for us to recognize an ethically rooted CSR (as we will see in the final section of this chapter). As Maritain says in that quote, as individuals, our good is oriented towards and subordinate to the good of the community of work (the common good of the business), whereas as persons, we are in no way subordinate to that good, and rather it supports our development. All 'common goods', at whatever level of society (family, local community, national community, global community) or of whatever kind of society we are talking about (a business, a voluntary organization, a state, and so on), arise out of common, shared activity, just as the good of each human being (that is, his or her development towards full maturity) arises through his or her activity. 'The' common good is ultimately the result of shared relationships and shared activity across the widest possible group of human beings, much of which is shared between us not because we have worked directly on it, but because it 'overflows' from its source out to others (we could say it has positive externalities). It includes goods we have received 'from creation' (from God), as well as from previous generations. It is a heritage, a gift and a task to be achieved.

Since much of my activity is carried out with others, there is going to be a close link between what is good for me and what is good for others around me, and from this we can deduce that there is going to be a close link between the good of each human being and the common good, but that they are not the same. The common good is not just the sum of individual goods, nor is it the only real good in which each individual participates. As we already mentioned, there is a relationship of 'mutual implication and reciprocal subordination' between the good of each one of us and the common good.[22] In a certain sense, the common good provides the 'humus' or the context within which personal or private good can be developed, but it is also only through the development of persons that the common good may be created and be strengthened. 'The' common good is something created and shared in by *all* members of the community but at the same time it underpins and permits their perfection and growth.

If the common good is everything that enables and promotes good human life or as Maritain puts it, 'communion in good living', then it cannot be defined in static terms. In fact, it represents an achievement and a goal to continue to try to achieve ever more fully with regard to the fullest human development of the members of the group that participate in this good.[23] On the other hand, we may distinguish five main aspects within it, as presented in contemporary literature, that will help us grasp its meaning better.[24] Three of them can be included in the category of 'foundational common good' that we discussed above, and two in the category of the 'excellent common goods'. Foundational common goods include the modern idea of 'public goods', such as parks, transport infrastructure, security services and so on.[25] A second group includes air, water and similar natural goods where governments are not so much providing them as protecting them. A third group includes internal and external policies, effective organizational and production structures, safe working conditions, many of which are immaterial in their operation but which help us achieve our common goals. All of these are used without being diminished by each person who works there, and they benefit both the community of work as a whole and each of its 'constituent wholes' (that is, the human persons working in it). A final group of goods we could include here are not so much common in themselves, but nevertheless they constitute part of the 'foundations' of the common good: these are the goods and services produced and traded in the marketplace.[26] Two forms of excellent common good discussed in the literature include other goods of an immaterial nature that are just good in themselves, such as relations within a human community, including those in a business community; what is often referred to as social capital. The second type of excellent common good often discussed includes moral values and virtues, all that enhances human life and flourishing, such as solidarity, freedom, peace, justice, respect for human life and so on.

Is there anything that can be held in common but which could not be recognized as being part of a common good? Certainly. It is possible to have 'common bads' as well as common goods.[27] For instance, we can make bad judgments about what is good in the sense defined here. This means that we can make mistakes about what contributes to the development of human beings. History is full of examples where mistakes of this kind have been made, and we know from our own lives that we often choose to do things which afterwards we regret, or later see to have been a distraction from doing something really fulfilling or just a waste of time. Thus, it is important to add another criterion here: for the common good to be genuine, it must be *really* good, not just apparently so. This criteria, while it may be difficult to apply in many cases, is still essential to include, since it allows us to exclude the kind of 'good' that holds together rogue organizations, terrorist groups and mafia-style 'communities', as well as excluding those that otherwise acceptable groups may engage from time to time in acts which could be *useful* for them at the time, but which are not *really* good (such as exploiting the weak position of poor workers).

Since the common good is the result of the activity of particular human beings in particular historical contexts, and of the output and activity of their forebears that has come down to them, it is always historically conditioned, and its interpretation depends on the cultural and social context under consideration. The historical singularity of every realized common good is particularly clear in the modern world, with so many possibilities thanks to the complex technological and institutional resources at hand, and so many cultures and religions in contact with each other. In such a context, it is more often than not a complex process to arrive at a genuine idea of the common good. This is where dialogue and a common, shared search for the good takes centre stage. The discursive ethics of thinkers like K.-O. Apel could provide an input here. In its terms we may say that the idea of the common good belongs to the ideal community of communication, and is among or, better, embraces already recognized moral norms (such as justice, solidarity and co-responsibility). The humus of the common good is essential for the dialogue between stakeholders of the company and for the resolution of the conflicts that arise in an enterprise in everyday real business life, for it provides a necessary solid shared foundation rooted in the nature of the human person, in his flourishing and developing, embedded in a certain framework of culture and history, all of which run deeper than in the power relations and individual, relativist interests of stakeholder theory.

How do tensions, differences of opinion, competition and even conflict find their place within the common good of a business? Conflictual situations are an undeniable part of business life, including the competition between people for a promotion (for, in the end, if I get the job, someone else doesn't), or increasing the company's share in the marketplace, inevitably leaving less room for other companies. How would a Thomistic personalist perspective, then, treat this tension present, for example, in the allocation of foundational goods between different stakeholders of a company?

Fortunately, particularization of interests and diversification of activities is itself an element of the common good. As anyone knows who has lived in societies where competition in the economic realm was condemned, competition is an essential mechanism in producing effective economic results. If people need to compete for a promotion, other things being equal (which, of course, they may not be), it is likely that they will work harder and do more to develop their skills and gain experience than they would have done without this incentive. Similarly, if businesses have to compete with each other, it is more likely that they will improve their products and services, aiming to serve their customers more effectively so as to ensure a continued customer base. This discussion takes us back to the individual dimension of the human being, where we are fundamentally in competition with each other for material resources. So competition is not in principle opposed to the common good; indeed, quite the opposite. What is opposed to it, or at least to the personalist understanding of the common good, is to see the common good as *only* produced by competitive relationships – this would be equivalent to saying that human beings are only individuals, and not also persons.

The point that we seek to underline here is that the common good embraces and even requires the coexistence of cooperation and competition for the development of the human person. In fact, this is just the re-discovery of the old idea of 'civic economy' developed during the 1700s in Italy, which is also echoed in the works of Adam Smith when he observes that narrow self-interest could never be sufficient for the good functioning of the market.[28] In fact, as some scholars argue, Smith's thinking has been oversimplified and impoverished by his followers who rid it of any relational fabric, such as 'sympathy' or 'fellow-feeling'.[29] Such a partial reading could probably explain why the 'invisible hand' metaphor (mentioned just once in *The Wealth of Nations*) is cited much more widely in modern literature than is Smith's condemnation of limited-liability companies, which in his opinion may 'do more harm than good'.[30]

The way in which particular goals and ends can be pursued as part of the common good makes us think of another mechanism necessary for realizing a shared, common good in a pluralistic individualistic society – the principle of subsidiarity. Its negative aspect (the duty of non-interference) usually is easily accepted: the human search for self-determination is rooted in the modern mentality. Its positive aspect (the duty of intervention), which is usually less spoken of, finds its unique justification in the common good principle understood as the promotion of human development. What subsidiarity basically says is that human flourishing is to be found in the opportunity to act on one's own initiative (the negative aspect of subsidiarity) but also in the light of common goals (the positive aspect).

9.4 CSR and the personalist approach: can the latter give the former a more solid ethical footing?

We argued in the opening to this chapter that what we had to say here was important not only for Christians, but also for anyone interested in the ethical basis of CSR (which is another way of saying, for anyone interested in the long-term future of CSR. If its ethical basis is weak, it is likely to be instrumentalized to profit-maximizing goals, to lose its meaning and value, and as a result, to be quietly forgotten). At this point, we need to show this more fully. We need to show as clearly as we can how CSR can be well-rooted in its ethical basis using a personalist philosophy. We have already shown that it is only weakly rooted ethically if we use a Kantian or social contract approach; can the personalist approach really do better?

The personalist approach begins its method of digging CSR into its ethical roots with the recognition that the stakeholders, who need to be respected in a socially responsible decision, are not just individuals with individual interests. They are also persons, who, through their participation in the activity of the business, are in relation with each other. These relationships are not only useful in the achievement of individual goals; they are also part of the stakeholders qua persons, and in relating to each other (especially in working together) the stakeholders achieve goals that they share in common and develop intrinsic good between themselves, which is shared between them.

Each of the stakeholders wants to obtain some private personal gain from the firm (at least financially, and probably also in other ways: progression up the hierarchy, a sense of self-worth and so on), and in so far as this is so, they are in competition with each other. However, they can only enter into competition with each other on the basis of the healthy development of the business as a whole – on the basis of the good they hold in common, which is the business itself. This is the first half of the argument. Here, we see the stakeholders as parts of a whole, which is, as we said, how individuals relate to a group. An individual is part of a bigger group, and its good is subordinate to, or dependent on, the good of the whole. If the argument stopped here, and we said that the socially responsible decision was the one that was in the interest of the common good in this sense only, Freeman and Gilbert, among others, could rightly accuse us of instrumentalizing the stakeholders, while giving a kind of quasi-living status to the business as a whole. But this is only half the argument.

For, at the same time, the stakeholders also relate to the business as wholes to a whole, as ends-in-their-own-right to a community of beings that are all ends-in-their-own-right. On this level, they are in communion with each other through their relationships, and are developing a common good between them that is good in itself, not just good for something else. Making a decision on the basis of the promotion of the common good on this level is precisely to make a decision for the good of each one, since the good held between each one here is for each of them personally as well as being for all of them.

What does this mean in terms of the day-to-day decision-making of managers in a business? In the case of the 'maximize shareholder wealth (MSW)' decision-making rule, it is relatively clear in theory what a manager should decide to do – whatever maximizes owner value. This is often extremely difficult to do in practice, that is, it can be very difficult to know in a particular set of concrete circumstances what will maximize shareholder wealth, but at least in theory, the manager has a fairly clear idea of what he or she should do. The existence of the large system of business schools and management education in the western world is witness, however, to how difficult this is to put into practice and how much help managers need in doing so. If we are to put CSR into the DNA of the company, we need to be able to give managers an equally simple rule, at least at the theoretical level, that they can try to apply in their decisions. We cannot leave them with the theoretical impasse with which Freeman and Gilbert have left them. And although it will probably still be very difficult for them to know concretely what such a rule should guide them to do in a particular set of circumstances, that is no less the case for the MSW rule. In our case, the rule could be something like 'aim to develop the common good of all stakeholders to the greatest degree possible'. Given the approach to the common good we have developed above, this recognizes all stakeholders as ends in themselves (wholes, persons), as the stakeholder approach would require, but also gives us a way of synthesizing a decision that is in the interest of each one of them and of the business as a whole, from which they all benefit.

What these decisions will look like practically depends on the concrete circumstances of particular businesses and firms. For the time being, we think that we have shown on a theoretical level at least, that we can make socially responsible decisions that are ethically grounded and which are practical to make, without crowding out intrinsic motivation, using a personalist anthropology as the general approach.

Notes

1. The author is grateful to Barbara Sena and Yuliya Shcherbinina for many insights contributed to previous papers that have contributed materially to this chapter. All errors are the author's own.
2. Freeman and Gilbert (1988).
3. Sacconi (2006).
4. The relational paradigm is becoming more important in economic thinking in general today. See, for instance, the idea of the 'individual-in-relation'

promoted by the feminist economist Julie Nelson (2005) or the writings of Zamagni (2005; 2006).

5. Maritain (1948), p. 1.
6. Maritain (1948), p. 24.
7. Maritain (1948), p. 33.
8. Maritain (1948), p. 40.
9. Ratzinger (1990).
10. Wojtyla (1979).
11. See Gui and Sugden (2005), for instance.
12. Hargreaves Heap (2005).
13. Bruni and Porta (2005).
14. Prahalad and Hamel (1990).
15. The idea of social capital emerged out of a re-evaluation of *homo oeconomicus* as the fundamental anthropological basis of modern economic theory. This has occurred as the business world has gradually become aware that the human being is a complex being, both rational and, at the same time, expressive and communicative. Whether understood as networks of civic associations (Putnam 1993 and 2000, Putnam, Feldstein and Cohen, 2003), or as values and unofficial norms that allow reciprocal help (Fukuyama 1995), or as a relational structure between two or more persons (Coleman 1990), the notion of social capital implies an interpersonal relational background of cooperation, solidarity and reciprocity which is fundamental for successful business. The very adjective 'social' implies that this kind of capital cannot be produced by a single isolated individual but is the fruit of the relations between interconnected persons. And it is 'capital' for it makes possible the achievement of certain objectives which would be unattainable in its absence.
16. Maritain (1948), pp. 37–8.
17. Maritain (1948), pp. 66–7.
18. Maritain (1948), p. 46.
19. Alford and Naughton (2001); Melé (2002).
20. We can also quite easily incorporate the need to act in accord with the nature of the environment around us, towards the development of the support system for life as a whole, into this scheme.
21. Sulmasy (2001).
22. Maritain (1948), p. 46. Another way of looking at this relationship is to take the analogy of friendship. When two friends are together, they 'naturally' act in such a way as to develop the good of their friendship. This means, for instance, that they look for things to do which are good for both of them, the needs of neither one dominating over the other, but where they can both find fulfilment. In a way, the friendship itself is an analogy to the common good. The friendship exists 'between' the friends – if they were separated from each other, the good of their friendship could not continue, since it cannot be parcelled up into two pieces, one for each of them. It either exists between them or it does not exist at all. Analogically speaking, the common good exists between people – it is something shared or it is not there at all. Both in the case of friendship and of the common good, we can talk about the idea of a 'third viewpoint' (Finnis 1980), which is not that of either of the friends alone or of any member of the group participating in

the common good, but is their shared, common viewpoint – the point from which they see what is good for both or all of them.

23. As Maritain puts it: 'The common good is something ethically good. Included in it, as an essential element, is the maximum possible development, here and now, of the persons making up the united multitude to the end of forming a people, organised not by force alone, but by justice. Historical conditions and the still inferior development of humanity make difficult the full achievement of the end of social life. But the end to which it tends is to procure the common good of the multitude in such a way that the concrete person gains the greatest possible measure, compatible with the good of the whole, of real independence from the servitude of nature. The economic guarantees of labour and capital, political rights, the moral virtues and the culture of the mind, all contribute to the realisation of this independence' (Maritain 1948, pp. 38–9).

24. De George (2004).

25. Alford (2005).

26. Alford and Naughton (2006).

27. 'Public bads' is a term used to indicate the opposite of public goods in the book *Global Public Goods: International Cooperation in the 21st Century* (Kaul et al. 1999).

28. Non-European cultures provide us with a similar insight where the very word 'economy' (*Kei Zai* in Japanese or *Ching-Chi* in Chinese) means 'governing in harmony to bring about the well-being of the people'. See Lu (1999).

29. Bruni and Zamagni (2004); Sparkes (2004).

30. Cited in Sparkes (2004), p. 11.

10
Patterns of Management and Their Influence on Business Behaviour
Silvia Solimene

10.1 Preliminary remarks

In Chapter 6, section 6, it was said that in the present age it appears indispensable to stimulate the 'awakening of conscience' of managers, in order to develop strategies of really sincere social responsibility that seriously consider the values, objectives and motivation of the various stakeholders. It has also been underlined that the 'utility function' of the manager of the future should not be based on the blind maximization of profit in the interest of the majority shareholders, but should be multidimensional, permeated by higher principles of ethics and aimed at social relations and the protection of environmental resources. All of this should be in the interest of the common good (in particular of the company, its survival and development) and of protection of the various stakeholders. In particular, the manager of the future should take care of and protect the people who work inside the company. They are a strategic factor to be recognized and developed both for the success of the organization and for the satisfaction of the needs of individuals.

In relation to the above, in the present chapter we will analyse the influence of leadership on the productivity of employees, on their satisfaction and on the coordination of the company system, that is, on harmonization and the direction of the behaviour of the various members of the organization.

After illustrating the features of traditional models of management, we develop an analysis aimed at defining leadership styles that realize, in the medium to long term, high productivity, high satisfaction of human needs and considerable coordination of company functions at the same time – all in conformity with the higher principles of ethics.

Effective leadership tends, in first place, to use intelligence, creativity, imagination and people's commitment in company activity. In particular, effective leadership has the objective of improving the quality of those who work in organizations and to stimulate them to consider their own efforts as the means by which to realize both their own personal interests and the objectives of the organization. In second place, good leadership settles conflicts of interest, stimulates the merger between the interests of people with those of the company, develops reciprocal trust, empathy and collaboration; all of this is reflected in the coordination of people's behaviour and of the various company centres, without resorting to control, threats, authority or material incentives.[1]

Effective leadership creates value through the development of cooperation and the gratification of the motivations of subordinates. To realize these objectives, it relies, as previously said, not so much on obedience or analytical control, but above all on the development of reciprocal trust, decentralization of decisions, self-control and acknowledgement of the professionalism of employees (human capital). Rather than build hierarchical organizational structures, good leaders are interested in the development of the people who work inside their organizations, and in the recognition of their capabilities and their proposals, in order to permit, through reciprocal integration of resources in the value creation processes, the growth in the value of all employees.[2]

In our attempt to research effective *leadership* models from the management and coordination points of view, we will try to merge contributions from various disciplines. This, in our opinion, permits the creation of a *framework* that offers a realistic and more complete view of the phenomena that influence behaviour, satisfaction, productivity and the coordination of people. In fact, it is stimulating to consider in a systematic way the internal elements, the dynamic relationships between them and the relationships between the company and the external environment. The systemic approach also transcends specialist theorization adopted by economists, sociologists, psychologists and organizational scholars, who on their own are not able to analyse, as a whole, the phenomenon of people management. In particular, this approach helps to integrate studies, research and analysis carried out by authors from different scientific backgrounds synergistically and to use principles, methodologies and results regarding different disciplinary areas fruitfully. Finally it helps to verify theory and experience, thus reducing to a unity the various points of views on the subject.[3]

Above all, in the field of leadership, scholars and managers are required to concentrate their efforts very seriously. At present, the physical sciences and technology are applied and developed very well in the various sectors of the economy and in companies. On the other hand, scholars and managers have not yet learned well how to apply the human sciences, and in particular management studies, to managing productive organizations in a satisfying way. In management, company policies are based on theories that are still being formed; often outmoded conceptions prevail and management models which are unable to bring about both the satisfaction of employees and improvements in their productivity are still applied. Unfortunately, many managers believe that the capacity to guide organizations is formed only with experience, and consequently everyone tends to consider himself an expert on the subject. Fortunately these beliefs are disappearing, even if very slowly, with time. Now the generalized opinion is spreading according to which the managers of the future will increasingly govern organizations according to scientific rules and not arrogantly, using intuition and experience. They will increasingly learn these rules at school, at university and in management schools. The quality of leadership does not depend only on the innate quality of people. Therefore, real leaders are not born, but develop through study, practical application, confrontation with others and above all under the guidance of a master;[4] obviously personal talent and innate qualities help.[5] According to Nye Jr, innate qualities are mixed with educational principles, even if, currently education has far greater importance than that attributed to it by traditional management theory.[6]

It seems equally appropriate to note that the validity of any leadership system depends considerably on how far top managers commit themselves to introduce effective management models.[7] More specifically,

the leadership model adopted by higher level managers strongly influences the management style of lower level managers (middle and supervisory management). This is confirmed by the research of Bowers, Likert and Seashore, who clearly demonstrate that managers find difficulty applying management tools [. . .] that are in conflict with the principles and practices approved by their supervisors. In other words, it is now an experimentally verified fact that the style of 'top managers' tends to influence the leadership model of lower level managers; the latter, in fact, have little probability of introducing 'personal variants', because the company climate, incentives and training supplied by the organization strongly condition their behaviour.[8]

10.2 Organizational entropy and leadership models

Companies are complex social organizations. The creation of a cohesive group of people which acts constantly bearing in mind the general objectives of the company is a laborious task. This is because man within an organization does not act like a machine. He has needs and particular behaviours. He does not conform automatically to the rules of the organization and, because he often possesses decisional discretion, he is hard to control.

This makes managerial activity aimed at aligning the behaviour of individuals with the interests of the organization and general objectives extremely complex.

Companies are, however, open systems insofar as they exchange energy, information and materials with the external environment. This environment is characterized, especially in the most modern operational industries, by strong dynamism that poses serious problems for management.

Under pressure of stimuli, conditioning and internal and external influences, it is difficult to realize general objectives. There is a strong tendency to positive entropy , that is, to break-up, to disorder and lack of coordination. But this phenomenon can be opposed by the management process, inspired by the leadership model adopted. In particular, the quality of decision-making processes, of execution and control depend on:

- the organizational structure adopted to specialize and coordinate the processes of decision, execution and control;
- the motivation, objectives and professional capacities of people who fill the various organizational roles;
- the leadership models adopted by managers. These models constitute, as said before, a 'variable of a higher order' that affects and moulds the organizational structure and the operation of the company system.[9]

Leadership is a key factor in the *management* process, along with planning, organization and control. Planning, based on available skills and knowledge, establishes the objectives to realize and the functions to achieve them. The organization supplies the necessary structural support and the information system to put into practice the decisions, action and necessary controls to create rational and coordinated behaviour. Control verifies the compliance of actions with plans and, in relation to internal and external information, provides systematic correction of company behaviour to keep it continuously oriented towards the most convenient general goals of the firm. Leadership, finally, 'fills' the company organizational structure with capable, motivated people and stimulates individuals, in various organizational roles, to supply the highest contribution of mental and physical energy in carrying out assigned tasks related to decision, control, organization and executive operations.

Effective leadership is founded on rethinking the relationships between company and employees. The traditional point of view according to which personnel is a 'production factor' to be stimulated almost mechanically in order to realize company objectives should be abandoned. Relationships are should be conceived that regard employees almost as voluntary investors.

> Just as shareholders invest financial capital in a company in the expectation of both income and capital growth, similarly employees invest their human capital in a company, with exactly the same expectations. The company's responsibility to employees, therefore, is both to ensure competitive remuneration and to continuously add value to them by enhancing their repertoire of useful knowledge and skills. The employees' obligation, in this new relationship, is to continuously learn, in order to protect and improve their human capital, and to use their expertise and their entrepreneurial capabilities to create new value and thereby improve the company's competitiveness and performance.[10]

In conclusion we reaffirm that the effectiveness of company behaviour, in terms of decisions, operational activity, organizational structure, controls and coordination, significantly depend on the leadership models adopted.

As seen previously, the company system can be divided into various subsystems, and each in turn can be broken down into lower-level units. In order that the behaviour of the entire system and of its parts is rational, in other words aiming stably to realize the general objectives, it is indispensable to introduce a hierarchy of objectives (strategic, tactical and operational) and functions (management means to reach these objectives). This hierarchy of ends and means is imposed and continually regulated by a limited group of people who hold the supreme governing power in the company. This group:

a) *takes the strategic decisions*: definition of the company's mission, specification of general objectives, identification of strategies to achieve objectives (choice of products and services to produce and sell; choice of markets in which to operate; choice of technologies to adopt; choice of competitiveness factors and choice of the use of human resources and materials);

b) *controls the operations of the company system*, both introducing a hierarchy of objectives, of decisions, of bodies and of command (through the use of formal authority), and using non-authoritarian influences based above all on competence, charisma and acceptance by subordinates.[11]

The problem of effective and efficient company behaviour can be summarized by affirming that leadership (above all that practised at the top of an organization) must develop a force of attraction and coordination among the various members of the organization. In other words, leadership must develop an orientation, harmonization and activation force to be applied to the various human resources present in the organization.

This situation can be represented by Figure 10.1.

In practice, the strategic resolutions adopted by the group that holds the power influence the company's behaviour at a global level: they represent guidelines and premises for decisions of a lower level. These latter, in turn, represent a mandatory orientation for the decisions taken by the bodies responsible for the units in which company subsystems can be organized.

The adequate functioning of the company system requires the coherence of ends and means and therefore respect for the ends–means hierarchy.[12] Managers at the various levels, in order to harmonize subordinates' behaviour, must develop a relevant 'power of attraction' that stimulates subordinates to work in conformity with organizational interests.

To create this force of attraction/harmonization it is possible to use both formal authority and non-authoritarian influences (which create acceptance of the role of manager by subordinates). Modern productive organizations increasingly rely on this second tool, even if lines of formal authority are preserved because they constitute the supporting structure necessary for the company's operation.

Formal authority, both hierarchical and functional, is assigned to managers by the organization: it represents the right to command and use human resources and materials in order to reach certain objectives; it includes the obligation of subordinates to accept orders received as the basis for their own behaviour, without the possibility of objecting, or

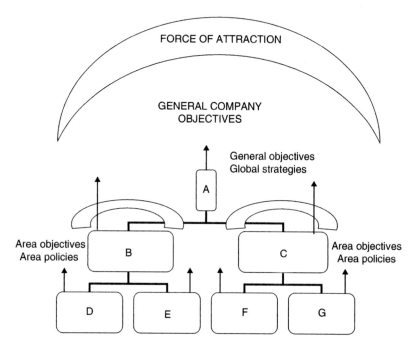

Figure 10.1   Effective and efficient company behaviour

criticizing.[13] Formal authority represents the 'backbone' of the organization. To be effective it must be clearly defined and used transparently
and, above all, with fairness, avoiding favouritism and discrimination.
Formal authority must not be used systematically by managers, but
only in exceptional cases. As will be seen below, traditional Taylorian
management theory, still today extolled in literature and pursued in
practice, is inspired by the principle according to which the management
of people, in order that they be effective, must be founded on authority
and the control of behaviour. This theory also emphasizes that the level
of authority, in concrete terms, must be equal to the responsibilities to
be faced; which means that, when tasks are arduous and complex and
whenever a situation is difficult to control (due to internal and external phenomena, or the personal incapacity of managers), the level of
authority must be increased. The logic of this assumption is justified
by the following reasoning. A manager who guides an organizational
unit is responsible for the activity and results of his employees. He must

therefore be able to impose certain behaviours and continuously monitor and tailor the work in order to realize organizational objectives. If this right to command and control is limited or eliminated, the operation of the unit the manager is responsible for will not be satisfactory, insofar as employees (according to the traditional theory) tend to behave in ways that do not correspond to the interests of the company.

Traditional management styles founded on the assumption of authority and analytical control are in crisis, above all in the most developed countries where the problem of motivating people has changed and companies have to resort less to authority and more to the creation of organizational conditions capable of developing consensus and the willing acceptance of managers' direction by their subordinates.

10.3 The traditional approach to leadership

In the course of time, in the most developed nations, a system of phenomena has been continuously developing that has imposed a profound change in the methods of company management and in the principles that inspire them:

> Conventional management models are no longer valid to manage modern productive organizations efficiently. They were conceived a long time ago, in very different conditions from those of modern society and with different objectives. In fact, they were developed in an environmental context in which: science and technology were relatively stable; markets had little dynamism; the production economy concerned above all material goods whose prices were rather linked to the present; company management was practised by one or very few people and unlike what happens today, little use was made of the deep knowledge of various groups of specialists; decision-making structures and company information systems were relatively simple [. . .]; most employees were blue-collar workers; the prevalent motivation of workers concerned physiological needs and security: the mass of employees were assailed by the fear of losing their jobs and the connected means of support.[14]

In conformity with the logic of '*task management*', the manager decided and the subordinates worked; the manager *centralized* the decision-making process because he possessed – at least was supposed so – all the skills to produce rational decisions; the function of the average manager consisted in increasing the productivity of personnel and stimulating it – using rewards and sanctions – to respond punctually to the orders received; organizations were characterized by respect for the hierarchical principle and phenomena that got in the way of this authority-subordination mechanism were infrequent and scarcely relevant;[15] management, generally, was programmed and controlled in a Taylorian sense and there was no space for the application at work of people's intelligence, creativity and imagination. The centralization of decision-making and control provoked, therefore, enormous underemployment of the most important company resource: the knowledge base of human capital.

Management models based on the conditions described, despite being still today followed by a large number of companies, do not respond to the need to govern modern organizations rationally, especially large ones with the latest technology and operating in extremely dynamic sectors.[16]

The process of change has created crisis for conventional systems of management, because it has modified some basic conditions. The progress of science and technology is relevant, rapid and widespread and is provoking changes in productive processes, organizational structure and decision-making systems at an increasing rate. The needs of technology, the instability and unpredictability of markets, the activities of the competition, and the increasingly incisive and pervasive intervention of public bodies in the economy contribute to make company management more complex and require management to be based on specialist knowledge in many different fields.[17] This knowledge is very common among a multitude of bodies variously located in the organization.[18]

The phenomena outlined above make past management systems, based on the hypothesis that 'knowledge' is concentrated at the top of organizations, inadequate. But there is more. In western industrialized society, people are now liberated from physiological needs and are moved by social motivations, for 'respect' and 'self-realization'. It should also be remembered that in our society the hierarchical principle and its connected mechanism of authority-subordination are slowly being 'threatened' by a series of economic, social and political phenomena. In fact, considerable economic well-being, the relative ease of finding alternative employment, legislative and union guarantees and many other factors make contemporary employees less 'tied' to a job and more inclined to assert the limitations of authority.[19] In conclusion, traditional systems have fallen into crisis, particularly in the most dynamic organizations, that is, in those mostly affected by these factors.

The need to adapt effectively to change in companies and in society as a whole requires substantial modifications to management systems. It is no longer possible to continue with superficial adaptation, which has, in brief, the effect of preserving the principles, policies and traditional methods of managing personnel and organizational structures. Instead, an effective revision of management philosophy, and in particular of the function of leadership, are essential.[20]

At this point it seems opportune to analyse more deeply some characteristics of traditional management models in order to better understand their deficiencies.

Traditional Taylorian management is inspired by assumptions concerning the behaviour of employees (McGregor's 'Theory X'[21]), which has a strong impact on organizations, operational rules and company plans. These assumptions can be summarized as follows:

- the average human being does not love work; he is lazy and indolent; he pretends to work and has the innate tendency to 'drag his feet' and 'slow things down';
- the average human being neglects the company's interests; he is hostile to change and seeks the gratification of his own personal needs and self-realization outside the company;
- the average human being prefers to be directed and commanded and does not aspire to accept responsibility;
- intelligence, imagination and creativity are not very common among people: the average human being is therefore not very intelligent, creative or enterprising.

The manager who works on the basis of these assumptions has, as a consequence, little trust in the intellectual and physical capabilities of employees. He therefore considers it indispensable to *programme in detail* the tasks of subordinates and to continuously control their execution. Thus decisions are centralized; demonstrations of authority are developed; control is perfected. The traditional manager thinks it is necessary to impose certain behaviours aimed at 'rendering human nature more docile' and at forcing people to respond effectively to the prescriptions of organizational roles.

In McGregor's opinion,[22] *managerial systems* based on the centralization of decision-making authority and control tend to guide the employees' behaviour towards the objectives of the organization through a broad range of policies, limited at the extremes by two well-defined motivational approaches:

1) *a hard management style*: requires centralization of decision-making, the systematic use of authority, analytical control, and the use of

threats and sanctions. Those who do not show docile respect for management commands are punished. In his opinion, the traditional hard management approach can be summarized with the phrase: '*if they don't want to do it, make them do it*';

2) *a soft management style:* still relies on the centralization of decision-making and authority, but makes use of a motivational system with rewards and concessions. This approach is based on the assumption that by being good, open and helpful towards employees, they will conform willingly to orders and to directives from hierarchical superiors out of loyalty and gratitude. It can be seen that the 'docility' of workers appears an indispensable prerequisite for the successful operation of the organizational system: like the hard approach, it is believed that a company's business would go well if only employees were inclined – even with rewards – to follow commands received, to do what *management wants*.

There are difficulties in the 'hard' approach. Force breeds counterforces: restriction of output, antagonism, militant unionism, subtle but effective sabotage of management objectives. This approach is especially difficult during times of full employment. There are also difficulties in the 'soft' approach. It leads frequently to the abdication of management to harmony, perhaps, but also to indifferent performance. People take advantage of the soft approach. They continually expect more, but they give less and less. Currently, the popular theme is 'firm but fair'. This is an attempt to gain the advantages of both the hard and the soft approaches. It is reminiscent of Teddy Roosevelt's 'speak softly and carry a big stick'.[23]

But neither the hard nor soft management models work when put to the test: in the medium to long term neither simultaneously develops high levels of productivity and high satisfaction of employees. They can work for some time; but with time, they create serious problems that reduce productivity and satisfaction and develop discord and frustration in the human organization, above all because the capacity and knowledge of employees are not recognized at work (in their specific company roles).[24] Also, if the control systems adopted, on the one hand, ensure significant *compliance* with tasks, objectives and orders received, on the other hand, they reduce or even prevent creativity and 'entrepreneurship' among employees.

The assumptions based on authority and control on which traditional Taylorian-inspired theories rest do not conform to reality. In particular, their hypotheses about 'human nature' ('Theory X') are very probably incorrect and in any case have not been scientifically demonstrated. The most enlightened scholars on the subject of organizational behaviour, and especially McGregor and Likert, are convinced that the negative attitudes of individuals towards work are a product of particular organizational structures and certain management policies inspired by assumptions from Theory X.[25]

Generally in present-day society the less satisfied needs – which constitute therefore the fundamental stimuli of human behaviour – are 'social', 'respect' and 'self-realization'. Therefore,

> we recognize readily enough that a man suffering from a severe dietary deficiency is sick. The deprivation of physiological needs has behavioural consequences. The same is true – although less well recognized – of deprivation of higher-level needs. The man whose needs for safety, association, independence or status are thwarted is sick just as surely as is he who has rickets. And his sickness will have behavioural consequences. We will be mistaken if we attribute his resultant passivity, his hostility, his refusal to accept responsibility to his inherent 'human nature'. These forms of behaviour are *symptoms* of illness – of deprivation of his social and egoistic needs.[26]

If management wants to gratify needs of a higher order, it cannot use a strategy of personnel management based on the rigid predetermination of employees' behaviour, on analytical control and on punishment and rewards 'extrinsic to work'. This strategy creates the basis for incompatibility between the higher needs of workers and requirements of organizational roles and prepares the ground on which conflict, arrogance, passivity of personnel and the tendency to require ever more money to satisfy in some way the motivations not fulfilled by work flourish. Obviously, dissatisfaction is soon accompanied by lowered rates of productivity. In other words, traditional management models are not suitable for motivating employees, because they satisfy needs (physiological and security) which are now reasonably gratified and therefore no longer a strong influence on the behaviour of personnel. If management wants to stimulate the cooperation of employees and at the same time reach both high levels of satisfaction and high rates of productivity it must devise a type of personnel management strategy that, while responding to the interests of the company, is also able to gratify the higher needs of employees in their work.

10.4 Towards new management models

According to traditional management theory, authority is the main tool for guiding and coordinating people: it is considered the source of company power and control.

Classical organization theory recognizes the following means–ends sequence: functions derive from objectives; tasks derive from functions; responsibilities derive from tasks; authority is assigned to deal with responsibilities and from this, power and the ability to influence others' behaviour follow. As previously mentioned, according to traditional theory, it is necessary to respect the principle of 'parity between responsibility and authority' in order to attribute to a manager sufficient power to permit him to impose his will on employees.[27]

Previously it was stated that the presumption that a manager can control the performance of his department through the use of authority alone is unfounded. No manager can deal with his peculiar responsibility using only formal authority; his power to manage the department of which he is head depends, apart from authority, above all on the influence he will know how to exert over employees; but influence is closely connected to the appreciation, acceptance, esteem and respect of his subordinates. These values cannot be conferred to the manager through a formal administrative act: they are values that have to be internalized with effort and with behaviour aimed at inspiring a climate of reciprocal trust and practical collaboration.

Illustrious scholars[28] contest the assumption that increased formal authority is followed necessarily and automatically by an increased level of power. On the contrary, it is probable that the opposite happens; that with the increase of formal authority, power decreases.

In reality, the level of power depends both on the extent of formal authority and on the acceptance of influence by subordinates. The latter is the more important element. Modern leadership is largely based on an acceptance which derives from the development of a correspondence of 'loving senses' between employees and managers; in the creation of an identification process of employees with their leaders, their roles and their company. In this case, the direction and harmonization of subordinates' behaviour are substantially spontaneous and shared. More precisely, on this hypothesis, leadership exerts an influence on people's behaviour without exploiting manipulatory effects; in other words, 'power' is founded on conscious acceptance of the influence of managers.

Accepting this, the question arises: how can acceptance be developed in employees?

10.5 Effective models of management: basic assumptions

In this section we illustrate the assumptions behind the creation of effective leadership systems and the process by which they can develop.

1) General requirements

- the manager replaces threats, fear and terror, with love, friendship, help and availability; punishment with sympathetic understanding; inexorable justice with repeatable, constructive forgiveness;
- the manager (especially if belonging to *top management*) has to stimulate and achieve change, innovation, research and the exploration of innovative pathways. In particular, he has to be a vivid source of inspiration and imagination (*vision*) of what the company should become in future and which routes it should take to arrive at its goal. Every effective leader has to make a great commitment and dedicate much time to developing and applying creativity; to this end, they must be able to delegate and organize their work in order to have time to develop original visions/business ideas that have an economic meaning and that stimulate change and innovation. Creativity, research and innovation must be actively pursued not only by the leader but also by his staff, who will have to receive adequate information about the *vision*, strategies and priorities defined by the leader[29] and be appropriately trained, integrated, oriented and stimulated. Every manager who aspires to become an effective leader must be inclined to help employees and colleagues so that they can apply and express their potential capabilities in their work;
- in relation to the above, the manager's role is not to exercise authority to 'make others do certain things', but rather to create structural and operating conditions that permit the design of roles and organizational relationships that satisfy both company interests and those of the people who work for the company. An effective management model should realize what Bakke and Argyris[30] call the 'fusion process'.

2) Qualities of the effective leader

According to research carried out at the University of Michigan, an effective leader has the following characteristics:

- the manager has to be competent and act with equity and transparency;

- the leader is a creator of hope, indispensable to facing life with courage, determination and wisdom;
- the manager has to be interested in employees' well-being, their professional and career development and the improvement of their economic situation;
- the manager has to develop participation in decision-making, be supportive and establish high performance objectives (in line with company interests).[31]

3) Assumptions that inspire the manager's thought and action

As McGregor observes, the assumptions of the type of management theory that uses authority and control ('Theory X') are unreal and misleading. In particular, as previously stated, its hypotheses about human nature are very probably wrong and have not been scientifically demonstrated.

If we observe the operational reality, everything seems to confirm that employees behave at work according to 'Theory X'. Then is this theory based on valid assumptions? Not at all. As we have previously seen, social scientists are now convinced that negative attitudes of individuals towards work are not a consequence of human nature but are rather the effect of particular organizational structures and certain management policies, based on assumptions that develop these attitudes: when someone has been managed for many years, or always, according to certain styles that stimulate passivity, discourage the acceptance of responsibility and prevent the application and recognition of creative energies at work, one can expect that expectations, mental behaviour and work behaviours will reflect past experiences.[32]

McGregor makes interesting proposals regarding personnel management, aimed at realizing both high morale and high productivity. He calls this new management approach 'Theory Y'.[33]

Unlike traditional assumptions about workers' behaviour in productive organizations, 'Theory Y' states the following:

- the average human being can love his work, and is neither lazy nor indolent; efforts made at work are equally natural during spare time and play;
- the average human being is not insensitive to company needs. If conditions are favourable he is capable of independent decision-making, self-control and personal responsibility;
- ingenuity, imagination and creativity are common characteristics and are at present underused;

- the average human being aspires to a role with which he can identify and which is capable of satisfying his motivations;
- the average human being needs help, training, understanding and encouragement (support).

The management philosophy inspired by these assumptions aims at developing individual talent, energy and creative potential at work and satisfying the main human motivations, establishing meaningful tasks, stimulating participation in company problem-solving and making people feel that their work is important and appreciated by everybody in the organization. This philosophy stresses, above all, 'intrinsic compensation', self-discipline and self-direction rather than authority and external control of behaviour, and treats subordinates as adult beings, able to direct themselves. It also recognizes that professional ability, intelligence, readiness to assume responsibility and the will to pursue company objectives are elements present in the personality of human beings and that it is not necessary to resort to coercion to direct human action to achieve conformity with the company's interest. The fundamental task of management is therefore to create the conditions necessary to achieve collaboration so that everyone can satisfy their motivations within roles in the organization.[34] For this purpose what is needed is a management strategy based on real motivating factors: success, recognition of success, work in itself, responsibility and advancement.[35] These factors are closely linked to the characteristics of assigned duties: they refer to the task to be performed and, more specifically, the content of the work; consequently, they are able to increase both the satisfaction and productivity of individuals.

The foregoing implies that management will have full trust in the capacities of employees, that it allows them to express their ideas freely,[36] that it genuinely uses delegation, that it makes use of staff inspection or supervision services with both long-sightedness and caution, that it removes pervasive controls and makes accessible the intrinsic rewards of work, that it encourages participation at every level, and that it involves employees actively, stimulating them to self-direct and self-evaluate and set themselves operational goals to be checked at certain deadlines.

4) The manager commits to the values cited and pursues them consistently

The effective leader 'practices what he preaches'. Actuality must follow declarations of intent. In other words, there must be a strict coherence between declared values and the system of behaviours adopted in practice. Only with this correspondence can there be created a shared organizational culture, a system of values that have a clear meaning and importance for everybody.

***

Whenever there exist the conditions described in points 1), 2), 3) and 4), it is reasonable to expect the following significant consequences:

- reciprocal trust;
- decentralization of decision-making;
- limited use of authority;
- much space given to group decisions and supervision;[37]
- controls strongly inspired by self-discipline;
- recognition of employees' capacities in their company roles;
- support given to employees;
- high performance objectives and high 'supportiveness' of *managers*;
- high productivity, creativity and innovation;
- employee satisfaction;
- reduction of conflict and simplicity of coordination of company activities.

But the consequences mentioned above generate, in turn, the following phenomena:

- the manager is regarded as the element that links company interests with the interests of subordinates: he is perceived as the person that pursues the common good and development of people. It must be underlined that people share certain values, ideals and objectives not only because of their attraction or because of intrinsic goodness, but also because these are pursued and 'incarnated' by a leader they appreciate and identify with;
- the manager is perceived by employees and peers as an instrument of 'growth', a source of help and satisfaction for their motivations;
- employees develop sharing and identification with their roles, objectives and company policies.

Finally, in relation to the above, the following outcomes develop:

- acceptance by employees of the influence of managers;
- the 'force of attraction' linking managers, roles, objectives and company policies. This force produces harmony, integration, equilibrium and coordination of company activity.

10.6 Research, recruiting, training, personnel development and their influence on the company system

The function of leadership includes also the following two groups of management tasks:

1) research, recruiting, training and personnel development;
2) organizational change, the basis of company survival, development and success.

In relation to the first point, it can be observed that research, recruiting, training and human resources development are fundamental means for improving the quality of decisions, operations and company control and for realizing the effective coordination of behaviours of the various members of the organization.

There is no doubt that if it were possible to hire personnel already technically and psychologically prepared to respond to the requirements of organizational roles, there would be no need to use either formal authority or any type of influence based on *soft power* linked with participatory management models as a stimulus and coordination tool. Moreover, there would be no need to resort to formal authority and/or other non-authoritarian influences if people in the organization were perfectly trained and personally and professionally developed and able to respond, without deviant behaviours, to the prescriptions of their task descriptions. This does not normally happen, but the aspiration of managers to realize this objective, even if only partially satisfied, can produce considerable positive effects on the coordination of people and of company departments. From this it follows that these functions are particularly under the control of managers.

In modern companies operating in dynamic sectors and with advanced technologies, the type of 'personality' usually required in management positions is an adaptable one: there is a preference for the person who, presented with an internal or external stimulus, is able to create a response that 'adapts' to the situation. This requires the gathering of information, its elaboration and the development of action inspired by a 'utility function' that devotes ample attention to the higher interests of the company. However, for mainly operational roles human resources are often preferred who have interiorized during their training process behaviour programs marked by a 'fixed response'. These individuals are psychologically and technically inclined to correctly execute the prescriptions of the organization and commands given by managers, without the possibility of personal interpretation of or criticism towards orders or directives received.

Training influences people's behaviour from a technical and psychological point of view. On the one hand, it prepares employees to perform certain tasks according to technical rules related to the organizational roles;[38] on the other hand, it influences the employees' personality and their predisposition towards interiorizing the values of the company, to identify with it and consider primarily the general interests of the organization in the execution of their work.[39]

Finally, it is worth repeating that research, recruiting and training are fundamental elements in coordinating employees' behaviours and the departments that form the company system. These are more effective the more they contribute to developing the 'force of attraction' of leaders and they make the goal of orientation and harmonization of the company system easier.

Concerning organizational change, it is important to say that the effective leader is the catalyst of this phenomenon. This is true for all levels of management, but in particular for top management who form the central management and control unit and contribute disproportionally to creating the company climate. The capable leader stimulates creativity and innovation and knows how to trigger and drive change; in other words, he is able to develop the vision of how the company will be in future and the strategies necessary to reach the goal. Therefore, an effective leader is not only a powerful force of attraction and a driver of the coordination of people. He is not only a dynamo that maintains enthusiasm and motivation to achieve the organization's goals, but also and above all is a source of imagination, of ideas, a creator of convincing and widely distributed stories about the future of the company in the external environment (that is to say a creator of original visions of strategic behaviour). In brief, the capable leader is a change agent, particularly in the society of the present, pervaded as it is by uncertainty and continuous change.

But change clashes with substantial internal and external forces that generate obstacles, conflict and resistance. It is now accepted that individuals who operate in organizations often have the tendency to look at change with suspicion because of fear of losing privileges, of being disadvantaged, being forced to move house, or because of caste spirit or fear of not being able to cope with the future.[40] The duration of resistance to change is linked to the time and effort necessary to change people's values, expectations, work habits and technical and managerial skills. Often change takes a long time and this depends on the personality and culture of individuals, the conditioning force of company culture,[41] the type of work carried out, the quality of training, the management models experienced in the past and the characteristics of present management models. Referring to this final point, it is useful to observe with Drucker[42] that managers

> use more time to undo the past than any other activity: what exists today is necessarily the product of yesterday. [. . .] People that form organizations, mostly developed in the company of the past. Their attitudes, expectations and concepts of value were formed in a previous time; they therefore tend to apply lessons from the past to the present. In fact, every company considers what happened in the past as normal, with a strong inclination to reject as abnormal anything that does not adapt to the model.

However, as McGregor[43] and Zander argue, resistance to change is not a natural phenomenon, intrinsic to human nature, but is fundamentally the consequence of the ways people were organized in the past and of the management styles they were subject to for a long time. It is in any case a normal phenomenon typical mainly of companies (the vast majority) that adopt conventional management systems (Theory X). From this it can clearly be deduced that the real quality of the leader can be measured by the success with which problems related to the effective introduction and management of change have been systematically[44] dealt with and solved.

It has been said that the objective of change is the modification of values, habits, beliefs and operational and management structures. It is therefore necessary to manage transition from one state to another with a clear, attractive vision, meaningful for employees and with a commitment that develops participation, harmonization and continuous impetus towards the desired results.

The ways in which transition happens are systematic; therefore they can be adequately programmed and controlled.

The process, which can take place over a longer or shorter time, goes through the following phases:

a) 'evaporation' of old values, beliefs, habits and structure;
b) preparation and execution of a change plan;
c) learning, interiorization and consolidation of acquired new mindset.

The speeding up of the process of change is stimulated by the participation of organization members. This involvement improves problem analysis, communications, learning and the process of sharing new values, habits, convictions and structures. For this reason good leaders start the change process by attracting people's attention to the need for change, on the means of realizing it and on the commitment required from all participants. Later, the members of the organization are arranged in homogeneous groups according to hierarchical level and heterogeneous groups according to function and are encouraged to offer opinions and information on their personal experience and to identify company problems and changes to introduce, while also indicating the priorities to respect in the transition period. Subsequently, the same participants are put in homogeneous groups according to operational functions and are encouraged to analyse the likely impact of the changes on specific company functions. At this point the leaders responsible for the process, on the basis of information received from the group work, prepare a systematic action plan outlining clear objectives and the management options to follow. Finally, the plan is put into practice and managers follow its realization, maintaining impetus and emotional commitment towards its objectives and developing new energies to keep people committed and oriented to the pre-established change strategies. It is essential to maintain this impetus since many companies do not complete change processes because the emotional stimulus peters out.[45]

10.7 Final considerations

Traditional doctrine (still dominant) has exalted, mythologized and stimulated the development of decisive, independent, tough, inflexible, centralizing managers able to achieve the objective of 'making others do certain things' and realize the maximization of share values from the short-term point of view.[46] This doctrine (also the academic one) justifies the unbridled and unreasonable race to maximize profits by making reference to the needs of the market and the invisible and impersonal hand that forces managers into 'due' behaviours that are therefore considered effective and even 'moral'. It should not be forgotten that Milton Friedman,[47] the father of current managerial philosophy, maintains that the only social and legal responsibility of managers is to maximize profits and that every other behaviour (every other ethical, human and social consideration) is dangerous and even immoral.

Traditional theory is, in substance, based on a determinism according to which the impersonal forces of the market require (at the cost of an inefficient economic system) managerial behaviours aimed at maximizing profits supported by a 'hard' management style that does not leave any space for ethical considerations: *business is business*. Unfortunately, as Goshal rightly observes, the deterministic theory outlined above is the fundamental cause for the rise to company management positions of managers inspired by hard philosophies (McGregor's X Theory).

The most significant point to underline, as Goshal observes, is that this deterministic theory tends to absolve managers from all moral obligations. Considering that responsibilities are based substantially on reason and moral principles, this theory tends to free managers from feelings of responsibility for their actions.[48] This causal determinism goes too far and diminishes the import of the ethical, moral and social dimensions of managers' strategic decisions; it is presented by its adherents as an absolute necessity to be respected if the economic system is to function effectively and efficiently. Managerial behaviour inspired by it is presented as scientific, inevitable and convenient and, in this deterministic view, to be admired.

Most recent criticism pointing to the progressive dehumanization and growing tension in the world of work therefore explains and unfortunately justifies it by reference to the dominant impact of economic competition and by the pressing influence of financial institutions, of capitalist families and single capitalists on *managers* of industrial and commercial enterprises. This strong pressure therefore has the effect of promoting and rewarding ruthless managers, determined that, with an iron fist, they can impose progressively growing profit objectives on companies (expressed in terms of return on equity of 15–20 per cent). Naturally this type of *manager* accepts the pressures, receiving, as a welcome reward, financial compensation which goes beyond every reasonable limit and has the effect of feeding their sense of power and omnipotence and preventing the awakening of their conscience, made drowsy by the inebriating effect of the availability of large sums of money.

Traditional managerial theory has had its day. In our opinion, it creates negative consequences not only from the point of view of the creation of value, but also in terms of its social and human aspects. Managers are not guided automatically and necessarily by the often irresponsible objectives of finance; they are really influenced by internal and external forces, among which the strength of the capital markets needs to be noted. However, managers have ample margins of autonomy; they decide what to produce, which markets to satisfy, the business model, the technology to adopt, the organization to install, the management styles to adopt, the level of efficiency to reach and the economic viability objectives to pursue. In this context managers take important strategic decisions that aim to prepare the company system for the future. If they take important decisions, they must therefore assume related responsibilities and if certain decisions impact on *stakeholder* interests, they must reconcile the diverse needs, try to make them compatible and, therefore, analyse and coordinate them; in every case, they must assume responsibility and not consider themselves blameless, and must avoid being inspired by the traditional deterministic theory that holds that managers' behaviour is inevitably determined by market forces (above all the financial markets), at the cost of ineffectiveness and inefficiency.

Thus managers of the future should be more courageous when they have to take important decisions that aim to revitalize their firm's creative force, the sense of community inside the company and the ability of organizations to create wealth. To do this,

> managers absolutely need a new theory, and a good theory in the sense that it would not only provide an adequate basis for executing the economic dimension of their role but would also give a moral foundation to the profession that amoral principles of the present theory have cancelled.[49]

Notes

1. Nye Jr (2008).
2. Goshal and Moran (2005), p. 17.
3. Lussato (1972), p. 102; Ashby (1958), pp. 1–6; Klir (1968); Simon (1965), pp. 63–76.
4. Ericsson et al. (2007), p. 1.
5. Malik has the opposite opinion. See Malik (2010), p. 18.
6. Nye Jr (2008), chapter I.
7. Argyris (1973).
8. Zanda (1984), p. 264.
9. Blake and Mouton (1969); Herzberg (1966; 1987); Gelinier (1968), pp. 8ff.; Likert (1961; 1967); Zanda (1979), pp. 156ff.; (1984), chapters III, IV, V; (2006), pp. 85ff.
10. Goshal and Moran (2005), p. 16.
11. Zanda (2006), pp. 157ff. On the authority-operation in organizations, see Caselli (1965), pp. 64ff.
12. Granger (1964), pp. 63–74; Litterer (1965), pp. 139ff.; Simon (1958).
13. Simon (1958), pp. 125ff.
14. Zanda (1984), pp. 69–70.
15. Zanda (1984), p. 70.
16. Zanda (1984), p. 70.

17. On creation, development and diffusion of knowledge, see Marchi and Marasca (2009), pp. 33–89.
18. Zanda (1984), p. 72.
19. Zanda (1984), p. 73.
20. Zanda (1984), p. 74.
21. McGregor (1960), part I; (1966), part I.
22. McGregor (1966), pp. 5ff.
23. McGregor (1966), pp. 6–7.
24. Likert (1959; 1967); Likert and Seashore (1963); McGregor (1966), pp. 14ff.
25. 'The findings which are beginning to emerge from the social sciences challenge this whole set of beliefs about man and human nature and about the task of management. The evidence is far form conclusive, certainly, but it is suggestive. It comes from the laboratory, the clinic, the school-room, the home, and even to a limited extent from industry itself. The social scientist does not deny that human behaviour in industrial organization today is approximately what management perceives it to be. He has, in fact, observed it and studied it fairly extensively. But he is pretty sure that this behaviour is *not* a consequence of man's inherent nature. It is a consequence rather of the nature of industrial organizations, of management philosophy, policy, and practice. The conventional approach of Theory X is based on mistaken notions of what is cause and what is effect' (McGregor 1966, p. 7).
26. McGregor (1966), p. 12.
27. The principle of correspondence between responsibility and authority constitutes one of the pillars on which classical organization theory works. This states that the responsibility of any manager for the behaviour of his subordinates is absolute; moreover it states that no manager can be held responsible for the performance of his department if he does not have the necessary authority to plan, organize and control employees' activity.
28. Berelson and Steiner (1964); Drucker (1954; 1964); Likert (1961; 1967); Likert and Seashore (1963); McGregor (1960; 1966); Prahalad (2010); Simon (1958); Tannenbaum et al. (1977).
29. 'Failing to communicate your vision and priorities has direct costs to you in terms of time and business effectiveness. It's hard to delegate if your people don't have a good sense of the big picture; hence you end up doing more work yourself' (Kaplan 2007, p. 5).
30. Bakke and Argyris (1954); Bakke (1950; 1953).
31. Likert (1967).
32. McGregor (1966), part I, sections 1, 2 and 3.
33. McGregor (1960), part I, chapter IV and part II.
34. McGregor (1960, part I, chapter IV; 1966, part IV, section 13).
35. Herzberg et al. (1959); Herzberg (1966; 1987).
36. Amabile and Khaire (2008), p. 50.
37. The adoption of group decision-making and supervision processes does not reduce the manager's responsibility: he can influence the composition of the group and has the task of guiding it to operate efficiently. The participatory manager rejects the principle that management has to be based on the exercise of authority. He will not succumb to the temptation to use this tool systematically; he will use it only in exceptional cases.

38. Simon writes: 'Nevertheless the role of training in administration is perhaps best understood by viewing it as one of several alternative means for communicating decisional premises to organization members. If, for example, a particular job in an organization requires certain legal knowledge, (a) a lawyer may be appointed to the position; (b) instructions and manuals may be provided to the person selected, with careful supervision of his work; or (c) he may be trained after selection. All these are, in a sense, training procedures, but in (a) the organization depends upon pre-service training, in (b) upon day-to-day supervision as a training device, in (c) upon formal training' (Simon 1958, p. 169).

39. 'Training, as a mode of influence upon decisions, has its greatest value in those situations where the exercise of formal authority through commands proves difficult. The difficulty may lie in the need for prompt action, in spatial dispersion of the organization, or in the complexity of the subject matter of decisions which defies summarization in rules and regulations. Training permits a higher degree of decentralization of the decision-making process by bringing the necessary competence into the very lowest levels of the organizational hierarchy' (Simon 1958, pp. 170–1).

40. Gelinier (1968); Zanda (1984), pp. 246ff.; Zander (1950).

41. Lussato observes: 'the conduct of an individual depends fundamentally on his past and his personal qualities, when the social group he belongs to is tolerant and little organized and the individual is characterized by a broad culture and a high level of creativity (simple social culture, complex individual structure). Conversely, when a person with not so marked qualities is introduced to a very hierarchical society where relations are complex and structured (tradition, adaptation to the culture, conformism and community of interests) and where ideological, religious or cultural pressure is homogeneous and effective, the behavior of the person will depend more on his role and social status than on his preferences and personal characteristics' (Lussato 1972, pp. 99–100).

42. Drucker (1973), pp. 31–2.

43. McGregor (1966), pp. 134ff.

44. Katz (1974).

45. Beckard (1975).

46. Mintzberg sharply observes: 'Decades of short-term management, in the United States especially, have inflated the importance of CEOs and reduced others in the corporation to fungible commodities – human resources to be "downsized" at the drop of a share price. The result: mindless, reckless behaviour that has brought the global economy to its knees' (Mintzberg 2009).

47. Friedman (1970).

48. Goshal and Moran (2005), p. 13.

49. Goshal and Moran (2005), pp. 4–5.

11
Summary and Closing Remarks

Gianfranco Zanda

We have now come to the conclusions of our research.

We started from the consideration, now widely accepted in scientific circles, that historically, power in companies and in society has been exercised by those who possessed the scarcest and most difficult factor of production to obtain. It is also an accepted fact that, in the course of time, a change in the importance of the factors of production resulted in a corresponding 'shift' in power from one factor to another.

In our work, we initially analysed the ways power was used in firms and in society by landowners, in the period from the Greek city-state to the First Industrial Revolution.

We then went on to consider the progressive decline of power connected to the ownership of land and the establishment of the superiority of capital. The problems of production, consumption and management in companies and in society during the First and Second Industrial Revolutions were treated in depth.

Later, we analysed the development of 'managerial capitalism', with its basis in the application of science and professionalism to managerial functions. The phenomenon of the 'managerial revolution', which brought about the separation between ownership and control in large corporations, was examined.

The question of the 'utility function' of managers of 'mature corporations' and its impact on the behaviour of these companies and on economic and social well-being were dealt with. Particular attention was paid to the propensity of managers to pursue goals related to social responsibility.

In this analysis, we have considered an important transformation that took place between the mid-1960s and the end of the 1980s within the capitalist system. The event in question was the establishment of 'financial shareholding managerial capitalism' characterized by the return to power of the representatives of shareholders (especially institutional investors) and the conditions imposed on professional managers. In this period, there was an important concentration of capital in the hands of pension funds, speculative funds, investment banks and insurance companies. Considerable pressures were put on the managers of large industrial corporations to adopt strategies aimed at maximizing profits and the value of shares in the short term. Such strategies were applied using financial engineering operations that were increasingly speculative in nature and less and less entrepreneurial. In this period, the 'institutional theory', which considers large companies almost as public institutions, in which managers also pursue social responsibility goals, lost its appeal. On the contrary, the theory according to which managers have a single duty gained enormous acceptance. This duty was maximizing profit and the value of shares; behaviour other than this is considered reprehensible, immoral and contrary to the law. The inevitable outcome of this situation was the arrival on the socio-economic scene from the beginning of the 1990s of the large irresponsible corporation. This type of corporation operated on the basis of a culture not inspired by the higher principles of ethics and which actually prevented managers from taking into consideration the needs, values and interests of the various groups of stakeholders that were not controlling shareholders.

In Chapter 6, measures that could be adopted to face up to the large irresponsible corporation were suggested. In the same chapter, the predominance of the financial economy over the real economy was analysed in depth. We also analysed the irresponsible behaviour of global finance and its relationship with the recent economic and financial crisis, and suggested the most appropriate measures to deal with the more worrying aspects of these phenomena.

In Chapter 8, we analysed certain fundamental questions that, in our opinion, will increasingly influence the behaviour of large companies and the whole of society in the future. In particular, we examined the causes and effects of the following events:

a) the advent of what Thurow defines as the 'Third Industrial Revolution'; this is the development and application of new knowledge in the following fields: biotechnology, information technology, artificial materials, microelectronics, robotics and telecommunications;
b) generalized and systematic use of the digital multimedia network;

c) change in the types of transactions that take place in the market: negotiations are less about the transfer of property rights on material goods that supply services and increasingly on accessing these services through leasing contracts;

d) development of the 'culture industry', which is a very promising sector for enterprises oriented towards innovation;

e) creation and application of new strategies and techniques in 'relationship marketing', oriented not so much towards promoting the product, increasing market share and the single act of purchase and sale, but towards creating stable commercial relations with the individual client that grow progressively over time.

At the end of Chapter 8, we concluded that the phenomena listed above now make it necessary for companies in innovative sectors to acquire a system of specialized knowledge in various fields: technology, marketing, supply and so on. These developments require companies to have skills in organization and strategic management to coordinate the specialized knowledge synergistically.

Intangible resources in general and knowledge in particular have become the strategic factor on which the survival, development and success of modern companies operating in leading sectors depend.[1]

At this point, we ask how this situation can affect the top management structure of large companies and the quality of their decisions. We ask how far and according to what procedure the 'revolution' that has taken place within the 'system of knowledge' can affect the present system of 'financial shareholding managerial capitalism'.

These are our conclusions.

- In our opinion, the top management of large modern corporations increasingly tends to be a small coalition of creative specialists with knowledge in the field of one or more innovative technologies, in management of the multimedia network, in the development of relationship-based marketing and in the application of appropriate principles of organization. The coalition will also include some experts in strategic management, who will carry out entrepreneurial functions of researching the new, breaking with traditional structures and facing up to organizational inertia; above all, it will be these strategists who will, with creativity and imagination, project the company into the environment and will guide it in the competitive process. The leading firm[2] will be well on its way to success with all these competences. It is therefore probable that the present 'shareholding managerial capitalism' is marking time and will progressively give way to an 'intellectual managerial capitalism', in which power is associated with the availability of specialized knowledge rather than with the possession of shares.[3]

- The need to control this knowledge will probably tend to increase the degree of autonomy of managers with respect to capital holders and stimulate change in the 'utility function' of managers themselves, leaving more room for the quest for increased 'social legitimization' of corporate activity. In summary, it is probable that the following events will occur in sequence: an increase in the level of knowledge necessary to manage companies; an increase in autonomy and room for manoeuvre of managers; and the development of the propensity to believe that the maximization of profit and share value are not the absolute and exclusive goals of companies. From this perspective, therefore, the 'utility function' of top managers will tend to be very similar to that of the traditional managerial capitalism that dominated between 1930 and 1970.

- Managers with greater autonomy will find themselves operating in very promising markets, especially that of culture. Culture is a sector in strong expansion, especially because in this field the needs of users are practically unlimited. Innovative companies could expand to offer entertainment, training, spiritual gratification, sensations, dreams and also virtual worlds which, through the digital multimedia network, will provide highly satisfying cultural experiences. The above will influence the behaviour of managers who will no longer be under pressure from the suffocating search for the business opportunities necessary to achieve the level of profitability and share value demanded by capital investors. In the presence of very promising markets in strong expansion, it will probably be easier to achieve satisfactory profitability and share prices for shareholders and also maintain the 'valuation ratio' and 'leverage' within safe limits. All this will also allow more space for expansion and the adoption of socially responsible policies.

- As well, the new marketing strategies may have a particular effect on the choices of managers. Relationship-based marketing is, above all, oriented towards developing stable commercial relationships and aspiring to create and progressively increase the 'relational capital' of the company, which would therefore become the object of continuous monitoring and evaluation. The search for stable relationships, which progressively increase over time, tends to move the time perspective for decision-making forward. In this way, the serious limits that characterize current financial shareholding capitalism, which operates with a short-term or even very short-term view can be overcome. The future company will, therefore, be considered an institution destined to last in time and not as a collection of uncoordinated operations often carried out without considering the principle of 'corporate continuity' (going concern), which must guide every responsible manager.

- The systematic use of the multimedia network will play an important role in the quality of the decisions of managers and both positive and negative effects can be predicted. On the one hand, using the internet makes it possible to immediately obtain a great deal of information that will improve the rationality of decisions and controls; it also allows acquisition of knowledge from outside the firm that is indispensible to management. Finally, it makes it possible to carry out exchange operations in a rapid and efficient way. On the other hand, immediate access to the digital network and therefore to markets, together with the great availability of information, stimulate the tendency to arbitrage and speculative operations. In our opinion, the positive effects of ready access to the internet greatly exceed the negative ones. In addition the negative possibilities can be limited when managers consider the company a permanent institution and not a legal packaging dedicated to maximizing profit in the short term and within which a series of uncoordinated and speculative operations are carried out.

- Thus it can be seen that the necessary pre-conditions are being developed to return the 'utility function' of managers of large innovative companies to that which characterized 'managerial capitalism'. In brief, the model of managerial behaviour that is gradually emerging involves the following:[4]
  1. the goals of the company are closely connected to the motivational system of top managers; these managers enjoy great autonomy compared with stakeholders;
  2. the primary motivation of managers is safety. This need is satisfied by assigning to the company the goal of realizing an adequate level of income (and not the maximum) to permit the payment to shareholders of a normal and usual dividend, to finance indispensable investments and to maintain the valuation ratio and leverage at a safe level; safety is guaranteed by maintaining the increase rate of company size within the physical and intellectual capabilities of managers and taking into account their ability to integrate new management forces while maintaining control of the company;

3. the higher motivations (social, self-esteem, respect of others and self-fulfillment) are gratified by pursuing and realizing a system of goals that are summarized as follows:[5]
   - dimensional growth of the company;
   - increase in the rate of profitability;
   - pursuit of social responsibility goals towards clients, employees, suppliers, local communities and also the natural environment.

The philosophy underlying the above model rests on a long-term view of management and considers the company an 'open' socio-economic institution, whose results are strictly linked to the satisfaction of clients, the satisfaction and quality of its human capital and, more generally, to the social legitimization that it has been able to gain. Such a philosophy, aims, in the long term, on the one hand, to create conditions and internal resources that trigger an 'explosion' of productivity, creativity and innovation and, on the other hand, to stimulate synergetic relationships with stakeholders. The goals of profitability, increase in company size and social responsibility – according to this philosophy, which we fully support – are not incompatible.[6] In other words, economic performance, if considered in the framework of a long-term strategy, is not in conflict with social interaction and entrepreneurial conduct inspired by ethics,[7] which sees reality not only with the eyes but also with the heart. These arguments were covered in Chapters 9 and 10.

- Considering the current situation, it seems plausible to maintain that 'financial shareholding managerial capitalism' is still in a dominant position and continues to control the operation of the more important companies in the most significant economic sectors. Therefore, we have not yet reached the decline of this system, but we are at a moment in which the foundations of the conditions to produce a new cultural, economic, social and political order can be briefly glimpsed. Future evolution of this system can be foreseen only with the help of a lot of imagination. We are optimistic that a new, more mature capitalism, which we will call 'intellectual managerial capitalism' is being formed. It is a system in which knowledge is the strategic factor for company success, in which top managers tend to be autonomous with regard to the interests of capital and free to pursue balanced goals of profitability, growth and social responsibility[8] through behaviour inspired by the higher principles of ethics and the realization of the common good and personal development. This system is also characterized by the intervention of public authorities as a driving and regulatory force. It seems that a capitalist system will continue to exist and to generate dynamism, in the sense 'that the essence of the capitalist order is to create change and that this continuous change necessarily implies the transformation of every aspect of social, political and economic life'.[9] This system favours the accumulation of capital and economic growth and requires that companies attain economic balance, which is the capacity to continuously develop a volume of earnings that will cover all costs and remunerate, at an appropriate level, the factor of production at their base, which is normally risk capital.

- It must be clearly stated that the great problem of capitalism and the market economy today, as in the past, is shaping their mission statements in a way to achieve a better tomorrow. Capitalism and the market economy should be wisely guided with the purpose of simultaneously achieving at least three objectives: increasing rational and complete use of the available production resources; progressive realization of an equitable distribution of wealth; full establishment of democracy; and protection of human rights. In approaching such a great problem, we should continuously bear in mind that economic development does not automatically go hand in hand with political and social rights or, more generally, with ethics. It is therefore indispensable to develop strong initiatives to create adequate rules to put the mechanisms of the economy at the service of the highest values, at national and international level. This is a very difficult and complex task because projects of a socio-economic nature are highly conditioned by political orientations, which, in turn, vary from nation to nation and therefore differ according to the principles and standards underpinning each socio-economic system. There are important divergences relating to the measures and procedures to adopt and the regulatory activity of public authorities. The task is also intricate because it is not easy to influence and coordinate the political 'sentiments' of individuals and groups effectively, especially at international level.

Notes

1. 'The twenty-first century will serve as background for the so-called "knowledge-based society". Knowledge will become the scarcest resource. Moreover, it will represent the decisive weapon from a competitive point of view. These developments will have an incredible impact on business culture. The value of knowledge will increase; to acquire new knowledge and to update the old, in the sense of "life-long" training, will absorb a considerable amount of time and work. [. . .]. Hierarchies will become less stable. The willingness to share

knowledge must become an element of business culture' (Simon and Zatta 2008, pp. 241–2).

In the last few years, there have been clear signs of the pre-eminence of knowledge. The efficiency of the management of enterprises is more and more closely connected with the availability of knowledge from which a new culture and a new way to create value in enterprises and society will probably emerge.

2. We repeat that the advent of enterprises in which intangible assets and knowledge are fundamental, will not bring about the disappearance of traditional economic activities. In our opinion, the application of the new advanced technologies, the use of relational marketing, the massive use of the multimedia network, and so on, will produce, in the long run, remarkable changes in the hierarchy of economy sectors: it is probable that the first place will be occupied by companies that produce services in the fields of culture and experience using the latest technologies; then will follow firms that produce goods and services using the above-mentioned innovative technologies; then there will be organizations that produce physical goods and traditional services; and lastly there will be the construction industry and agricultural firms. With time all the fields will use the new technologies, the internet and advanced management models.

3. 'Today a new kind of relationship between shareholders and management is emerging. Shareholders have the last word in the shareholders' meeting, but it is management that defines the road to take' (Simon and Zatta 2008, p. 221).

4. For more details, see sections 6, 7, 8 and 9 of Chapter 5.

5. The relationship between motivation and objectives is very complex and cannot, in our opinion, be defined in a rigid and analytical way by means of a mathematical formula, unless we want to carry out an academic exercise with unreliable results. The actual behaviour of managers (and their decisions) reflects particular environmental situations, their specific culture, their personality, their personal history, results achieved in the past, their level of ambition, and so on. Therefore, forecasting the behaviour of managers is an extremely complicated activity and, in any case, it is not immune to the law of probability.

6. Copeland (1994), p. 103.

7. Moscarini (2008b).

8. We are convinced that our optimistic forecasts will come true insofar as the following conditions are adequately satisfied: 1) the system of the real economy and that of the financial economy must be regulated in a transparent way at national and international levels; moreover, it is necessary to adopt appropriate incentives in order to stimulate market operators to behave virtuously; 2) efficient control ensuring respect for these rules must be carried out ; 3) it is necessary to maintain or create conditions of freedom, in order to stimulate the development of suitable counterbalances to face possible irresponsible or too-aggressive company strategies; 4) self-regulation provisions must be encouraged, including ethical codes and agreements between enterprises to ensure respect for the rights of stakeholders; 5) a cultural environment must be created with the aim of developing a new theory of the firm founded on ethics and social responsibility.

9. Heilbroner and Thurow (2008), p. 250.

Bibliography

AA.VV. (1964) *Les écrivains témoins du peuple* (Paris: J'ai Lu).

Ackoff, R. L. and Eckman, D. P. (1961) 'Systems, Organizations, and Interdisciplinary Research', in D. P. Eckman (ed.), *Systems: Research and Design* (New York: John Wiley & Sons).

Alford, H. (2005) 'Equitable Global Wealth Distribution: A Global Public Good and a Building Block for the Global Common Good', in H. Alford, C. Clark, S. A. Cortright and M. Naughton (eds), *Rediscovering Abundance: Interdisciplinary Essays on Wealth, Income and Their Distribution in the Catholic Social Tradition* (Notre Dame: University of Notre Dame Press).

Alford, H. J. and M. J. Naughton (2006) *Managing as if Faith Mattered. Christian Social Principles in the Modern Organization* (Notre Dame: University of Notre Dame Press).

Alford, H. J. and F. Compagnoni (2008) *Fondare la responsabilità sociale d'impresa* (Roma: Città Nuova Editrice).

Amabile, T. M. and M. Khaire (2008) 'Creativity and the Role of the Leader', *Growth*, Vol. 36, No. 3, October–December; also in *Harvard Business Review*, May, pp. 86–96.

Angela, A. (2007) *Una giornata nell'antica Roma. Vita quotidiana, segreti e curiosità* (Milano: Mondadori).

Ansoff, H. I. (1965) *Corporate Strategy: An Analytic Approach to Business Policy for Growth and Expansion* (New York: McGraw-Hill).

Argyris, C. (1973) 'The CEO's Behavior: Key to Organizational Development', *Harvard Business Review*, March–April, pp. 55–64.

Aristotle (1953), *Opere*, vol. IX (Roma-Bari: Laterza).

Ashby, W. R. (1958) 'General Systems Theory as a New Discipline', *General System*, 3, pp. 1–6.

Ashton, T. S. (1948) *Industrial Revolution 1760–1830* (London: Home University Library).

Bakan, J. (2004) *The Corporation. The Pathological Pursuit of Profit and Power* (London: Constable & Robinson).

Bakke, E. W. (1950) *Bounds of Organization* (New York: Harper & Brothers).

Bakke, E. W. (1953) *The Fusion Process*, Labor and Management Center (New Haven: Yale University Press).

Bakke, E. W. and C. Argyris (1954) *Organization, Structure and Dynamics* (New Haven: Yale University Press).

Barbero, A. (2006) *Carlo Magno. Un padre dell'Europa* (Roma-Bari: Laterza).

Barile, S. (2006) *L'impresa come sistema. Contributi sull'Approccio Sistemico Vitale (ASV)* (Torino: Giappichelli).

Barlow, M. and T. Clarke (2004) *La battaglia contro il furto mondiale dell'acqua* (Casalecchio: Arianna Editrice).

Barnabé, K. (2007), *Styles de direction, techniques de gestion et responsabilité des dirigeants d'entreprises*, Tesi di dottorato, Facoltà di Scienze Sociali, Pontificia Università Gregoriana (Marly: Imprimerie Marchal).

Barnard, C. I. (1938) *The Functions of the Executive* (Cambridge, MA: Harvard University Press).

Barnard, C. I. (1949) *Organization and Management* (Cambridge, MA: Harvard University Press).

Barton, J. (2001) 'Does the Use of Financial Derivatives Affect Earnings Management Decisions?', *The Accounting Review*, Vol. 76, No. 1, pp. 1–26.

Bartov, E., D. Givoly and C. Hayn (2002) 'The Rewards To Meeting or Beating Earnings Expectations', *Journal of Accounting and Economics*, Vol. 33, No. 2, pp. 173–204.

Baumol, W. J. (1959) *Business Behavior, Value and Growth* (New York: Macmillan).

Baumol, W. J. (1962) 'On the Theory of the Expansion of the Firm', *American Economic Review*, Vol. 52 (December), pp. 1078–87.

Beaud, M. (1997) *Le basculement du monde, de la terre, des hommes et du capitalisme* (Paris : La Découverte).

Becchetti, L., S. Di Giacomo and D. Pinnacchio (2008) 'L'effetto della responsabilità sociale sulla produttività e sull'efficienza delle imprese. Un'analisi empirica su un campione di imprese americane', in H. J. Alford and F. Compagnoni (eds), *Fondare la responsabilità sociale d'impresa* (Roma: Città Nuova Editrice).

Beckard, R. (1975) *Le développment des organisations, stratégies et modèles* (Paris: Dalloz).

Beer, S. (1967) *Cybernetics and Management* (New York: John Wiley & Sons).

Beidleman, C. R. (1973) 'Income Smoothing; the Role of Management', *The Accounting Review*, Vol. 48, No. 4, pp. 653–67.

Bendix, R. (1956) *Work and Authority in Industry: Managerial Ideologies in the Course of Industrialization* (New York: John Wiley & Sons).

Berelson, B. and G. A. Steiner (1964) *Human Behavior: An Inventory of Scientific Findings* (New York: Harcourt).

Berenson, A. (2003) *The Number: Why Companies Lied and the Stock Market Crashed* (Sydney: Simon & Schuster).

Berle, A. A. Jr and G. C. Means (1932) *The Modern Corporation and Private Property* (New York: Macmillan; revised edn [1968] New York: Harcourt, Brace & World, Inc.; Italian translation [1966)], *Società per azioni e proprietà privata* (Torino: Einaudi).

Berle, A. A. Jr, (1970) Preface to E. S. Mason, *La grande impresa nella società moderna* (Milano: Angeli).

Bertini, U. (1975) 'L'azienda come sistema cibernetico', in AA.VV., *Studi di Ragioneria, Organizzazione e Tecnica Economica. Scritti in Memoria del Prof. Riparbelli* (Pisa: Cursi).

Blake, R. R. and J. S. Mouton (1964) *The Managerial Grid* (Houston: Gulf Publishing Company).

Blake, R. R. and J. S. Mouton (1969) *Gli stili di direzione* (Milano: Etas Kompass).

Bloch, M. (1949) *La società feudale* (Torino: Einaudi).

Bloch, M. (2004) *Lavoro e tecnica nel Medioevo* (Roma-Bari: Laterza).

Boas, M. (1973) *Il Rinascimento scientifico* (Milano: Feltrinelli) (first published in 1962).

Boulding, K. E. (1953) *The Organizational Revolution* (New York: Harper & Brothers).

Boulding, K. E. (1956) 'General Systems Theory, the Skeleton of a Science', *Science Management*, Vol. 2, No. 3, pp. 127–39.

Braudel, F. and E. Labrousse (1980) *Histoire économique et sociale de la France*, vol. I (Paris: PUF).

Brown, P. (1971) *Il mondo tardoantico. Da Marco Aurelio a Maometto* (Torino: Einaudi).

Bruni, Luigino and Pier Luigi Porta (eds) (2005) *Economics and Happiness: Framing the Analysis* (Oxford: Oxford University Press).

Bruni, L. and S. Zamagni (2004) *Economia civile: efficienza, equità, felicità pubblica* (Bologna: Il Mulino).

Bucharin, N. (1966) *L'economia mondiale e l'imperialismo* (Roma: Samonà e Savelli).

Bureau of Economic Analysis (2004) *National Income and Product Accounts* (Washington, DC: US Bureau of Economic Analysis).

Burnham, J. (1941) *The Managerial Revolution: What Is Happening in the World* (New York: The John Day Company; Italian translation [1946], *La rivoluzione dei tecnici*, Milano: Mondadori).

Campbell, J. P., M. D. Dunnette, E. E. Lawler III and K. E. Weick Jr (1970) *Managerial Behavior, Performance and Effectiveness* (New York: McGraw-Hill Book Company).

Canziani, A. (1984) *La strategia aziendale* (Milano: Giuffrè).

Capaldo, P. (1965) *La programmazione aziendale* (Milano: Giuffrè).

Capaldo, P. (2008), *L'azienda*, part I (Roma, provisional edition).

Caramiello, C. (1965) *L'indagine prospettiva nel campo aziendale* (Pisa: Cursi).

Carcopino, E. (1947) *La vita quotidiana a Roma all'apogeo dell'impero*, 2nd ed. (Bari: Laterza).

Caselli, L. (1965) *Aspetti di organizzazione aziendale* (Genova: Bozzi).

Caselli, L. (1966) *Teoria dell'organizzazione e processi decisionali nell'impresa* (Torino: Giappichelli).

Castells, M. (1996) *The Information Age: Economy, Society and Culture*, Vol. I, *The Rise of the Network Society* (Cambridge, MA: Blackwell Publishers).

Castronovo, V. (2007) *Le rivoluzioni del capitalismo* (Roma-Bari: Laterza).

Catturi, G. (1989) *Teorie contabili e scenari economico aziendali* (Padova: Cedam).

Catturi G. and P. Di Toro (1999) *Interessi, motivazioni e valori degli 'attori' aziendali* (Padova: Cedam).

Cavalieri E. (2009) 'Una riflessione sulle cause e sulle responsabilità della crisi globale', *Rivista Italiana di Ragioneria e di Economia Aziendale*, Anno CIX, May–June.

Cavalieri, M. (2009) *Finalità e governance nelle imprese. Considerazioni critiche sulle modalità di creazione del valore* (Torino: Giappichelli).

Caves, R. A. (1970) *Economia industriale* (Bologna: Il Mulino).

Chandler, A. D. (1977) *The Visible Hand: The Managerial Revolution in American Business* (Cambridge, MA: Belknap Press; Italian translation [1992], *La mano visibile. La rivoluzione manageriale nell'economia americana*, Milano: Angeli).

Churchman, C. W. (1971) *Filosofia e scienza dei sistemi* (Milano: Istituto Librario Internazionale).

Cipolla, C. M. (1980) *Storia economica dell'Europa pre-industriale* (Bologna: Il Mulino).

Cipolla, C. M. (2003) *Storia facile dell'economia italiana dal medioevo ad oggi* (Milano: Mondadori).

Cipolla, C. M. (2005) *Uomini, tecniche, economie* (Milano: Feltrinelli).

Coda, V. (1967) *Proprietà, lavoro e potere di governo nell'impresa* (Milano: Giuffrè).

Coda, V. (1988) *L'orientamento strategico dell'impresa* (Torino: UTET).

Coleman, J. (1990) *Foundations of Social Theory* (Cambridge: University Press).

Copeland, T. E. (1994) 'Why Value Value?', *The McKinsey Quarterly*, No. 4.

Corzo, M. A. (1994) *Fondazione Memmo – The Getty Conservation Institute, Nefertari luce d'Egitto* (Roma: Leonardo Arte/Baioni Stampa).

Crouzet, M. (1953–56) *Histoire générale des civilizations*, vol. IV (Paris: PUF).

D'Alessio, L. (1980) *La direzione del personale di vendita* (Napoli: Massimo).

Davis, R. C. (1958) *Fondamenti di alta direzione* (Milano: Edizioni di Comunità).

de Montchrestien, A. (1616) *Traité de l'economie politique*, quoted in H. Denis (1965) *Histoire de la pensée economique* (Paris: Presses Universitaire de France).

De George, R. (2004) 'The Invisible Hand and Thinness of the Common Good', in Bernard Hodgson (ed.) *The Invisible Hand and the Common Good* (New York: Springer), pp. 38–47.

Delogu, P. (2001) *Il passaggio dall'antichità al medioevo*, in A. Vauchez (ed.), *Storia di Roma dall'antichità ad oggi. Roma medievale* (Bari: Laterza), special edition for Banca di Roma.

Deyon, P. (1969) *Le mercantilisme* (Paris: Flammarion).

Dore, R. R. (2009) *Finanza pigliatutto* (Bologna: Il Mulino).

Drucker, P. F. (1954) *The Practice of Management* (New York: Harper & Brothers).

Drucker, P. F. (1964) *Concept of the Corporation* (New York: The John Day Company).

Drucker, P. F. (1972) *L'organizzazione e la direzione della grande impresa* (Milano: Angeli).

Drucker, P. F. (1973) *La professione del dirigente* (Milano: Etas Kompass).

Duby, G. (1962) *L'économie rurale et la vie des campagnes dans l'Occident médieval* (Paris: Aubier Montaigne).

Emerson, H. (1913) *The Twelve Principles of Efficiency* (New York: The Engineering Magazine Co.).

Ericsson, K. A., M. J. Prietula and E. T. Cokely (2007) 'The Making of an Expert', *Harvard Business* Review, July–August: available online at: http://hbr.org/2007/07/the-making-of-an-expert/ar/1

Etzioni, A. (1961) A *Comparative Analysis of Complex Organization* (Glencoe: The Free Press).

Etzioni, A. (1967) *Sociologia dell'organizzazione* (Bologna: Il Mulino).

Fanfani, A. (1961) *Storia economica, Parte Prima, Antichità – Medioevo –Età Moderna* (Torino: UTET).

Fayol, H. (1956) *Administration industrielle et générale* (Paris: Dunod) (extract from the *Bulletin de la Société de l'Industrie Minérale*, 1916).

Finley, M. I. (2008) *L'economia degli antichi e dei moderni* (Roma-Bari: Laterza).

Finnis, J. (1980) *Natural Law and Natural Rights* (Oxford: Clarendon Press).

Fontana, S. (2007) *La valutazione dell'azienda mediante la contingent claim analysis* (Roma: Ascolino).

Fortuna, Franco (1975) 'Sviluppo della teoria economica dell'impresa e problemi di organizzazione', in *Studi di Ragioneria, Organizzazione e Tecnica Economica. Scritti in Memoria del Prof. A. Ribarbelli* (Pisa: Cursi).

Fortuna, Fabio (2009) 'Crisi finanziaria, management e comunicazione esterna d'impresa: alcune considerazioni', *Rivista Italiana di Ragioneria e di Economia Aziendale*, Nos. 9–10, September–October.

Freeman, R. E. and D. R. Gilbert Jr (1988) *Corporate Strategy and the Search for Ethics* (Englewood Cliffs: Prentice Hall).

Friedland, M. L. (1990) *Securing Compliance: Seven Case Studies* (Toronto: University of Toronto Press).

Friedman, M. (1962) *Capitalism and Freedom* (Chicago: University of Chicago Press).

Friedman, M. (1970) 'The Social Responsibility of Business Is To Increase Its Profits', *The New York Times*, 13 September.

Friedman, T. L. (2007) *Il mondo è piatto. Breve storia del ventunesimo secolo* (Milano: Mondadori).

Fuhrmann, H. (2004) *Guida al Medioevo* (Roma-Bari: Laterza).

Fukuyama, F. (1995) *Trust* (New York: Free Press).

Galassi, G. (1968) *Concentrazione e cooperazione interaziendale* (Milano: Giuffrè).

Galbraith, J. K. (1967) *The New Industrial State* (London: Hamish Hamilton).

Galbraith, J. K. (1987) *Economics in Perspective. A Critical History* (Boston: Houghton Mifflin).

Galbraith, J. K. (2004) *The Economics of Innocent Fraud* (Boston: Houghton Mifflin).

Gallino, L. (2005) *L'impresa irresponsabile* (Torino: Einaudi).

Gallino, L. (2009) *Con i soldi degli altri. Il capitalismo per procura contro l'economia* (Torino: Einaudi).

Gantt, H. (1911) *Work, Wages and Profits* (New York: The Engineering Magazine Co.)

Gaudemet, J. (1979) *La formation du droit seculier e du droit de l'église aux IV et V siècles* (Paris: Sirey).

Gelinier, O. (1968) 'Direction participative par objectifs', *Hommes et Techniques, Revue mensuelle*, No. 281, Paris.

Gilbreth, F. B. and L. Moller Gilbreth (1917) *Applied Motion Study* (New York: Harper & Brothers).

Gilbreth F. B. and L. Moller Gilbreth (1919) *Fatigue Study* (New York: Harper & Brothers).

Goetz, B. E. (1949) *Management Planning and Control* (New York: McGraw-Hill Book Company).

Goldin, C. and R. Margo (1992) 'The Great Compression: the Wage Structure in the United States at Mid-Century', *Quarterly Journal of Economics*, Vol. 107, pp. 1–34.

Golinelli, G. M. (2000) *L'approccio sistemico al governo dell'impresa. L'impresa vitale*, book I (Padova: Cedam).

Gordon, M. J. (1964) 'Postulates, Principles and Research in Accounting', *The Accounting Review*, 39 (April), pp. 251–63.

Gordon, R. A. (1940) *The Distribution of Ownership in the 200 Largest Nonfinancial Corporations*, Temporary National Economic Committee Monograph No. 29 (Washington, DC: TNEC).

Gordon, R. A. (1945) *Business Leadership in the Large Corporation* (Washington, DC: Brookings Institution).

Goshal, S. and P. Moran (2005) 'Toward a Good Theory of Management', in J. Birkinshaw and G. Piramal (eds), *Sumantra Goshal on Management* (New York: Prentice-Hall/Financial Times).

Graham, J. R., C. R. Harvey and S. Rajgopal (2005) 'The Economic Implications of Corporate Financial Reporting', *Journal of Accounting and Economics*, Vol. 40, No. 1–3, pp. 3–73.

Granger, C. H. (1964) 'The Hierarchy of Objectives', *Harvard Business Review*, May–June.

Gray, A. (1948) *The Development of Economic Doctrine* (London: Longmans, Green).

Green, C. (1972) 'The Satisfaction–Performance Controversy', *Business Horizons*, October.

Gui, B. and R. Sugden (2005) *Economics and Social Interaction: Accounting for Interpersonal Relations* (Cambridge: Cambridge University Press).

Hall, A. R. (1976) *La rivoluzione scientifica* (Milano: Feltrinelli). Originally published in 1954.

Hargreaves Heap, S. (2005) 'The Mutual Validation of Ends', in B. Gui, and R. Sugden (eds), *Economics and Social Interaction: Accounting for Interpersonal Relations* (Cambridge: Cambridge University Press).

Heaton, H. (1948) *Economic History of Europe* (New York: Harper & Brothers).

Heilbroner, R. L. and L. C. Thurow (2008) *Capire l'economia. Come funziona l'economia e come sta cambiando il mondo* (Milano: Il Sole 24 Ore).

Herzberg, F. (1966) *Work and the Nature of Man* (Cleveland: The World Publishing Company).

Herzberg, F. (1987) 'One More Time: How Do You Motivate Employees?', *Harvard Business Review*, September–October.

Herzberg, F., B. Mausner and S. Snyderman (1959) *The Motivation to Work* (New York: John Wiley and Sons).

Hilferding, R. (1961) *Il capitale finanziario* (Torino: Feltrinelli).

Hines, R. D. (1988) 'Financial Accounting: In Communicating Reality We Construct Reality', *Accounting, Organizations and Society*, Vol. 13, No. 3, pp. 251–61.

Hobbes, T. (1651) *Leviathan: or the Matter, Forme and Power of a Common Wealth Ecclesiasticall and Civil*; Italian translation, *Il Leviatano: o la materia, la forma e il potere di uno Stato ecclesiastico e civile* (Roma-Bari: Laterza, 1989).

Hofer, C. W. and D. Schendel (1978) *Strategy Formulation: Analytical Concepts* (St Paul: West Publishing Co.).

Huant, A. (1960) *L'entreprise, unité cybernetique vivante* (Paris: Éditions de l'Entreprise Moderne).

Hull, C. L. (1943) *Principles of Behavior* (New York: Appleton Century).

Ianniello, G. (2003) *Come si formano e si 'eludono' le regole contabili. Il caso Enron e dintorni* (Padova: Cedam).

Jones, A. H. M. (1974–1981) *Il tardo impero romano*, 3 vols (Milano: Il Saggiatore).

Kaplan, R S. (2007) 'What to Ask the Person in the Mirror', *Harvard Business Review*, January.

Katz, R. L. (1974) 'Skills of an Effective Administrator', *Harvard Business Review*, September–October.

Kaul, I., I. Grunberg and M. A. Stern (1999) *Global Public Goods: International Cooperation in the 21st Century* (New York: UNDP).

Khurana, R. (2007) *From Higher Aims to Hired Hands: The Social Transformation of American Business Schools and the Unfulfilled Promise of a Management as a Profession* (Princeton: Princeton University Press).

Kindleberger, C. P. (1982) *La grande depressione nel mondo, 1929–1939* (Milano: Etas Kampass).

Klir, G. J. (1968) *An Approach to General Systems Theory* (Princeton: Van Nostrand).

Koontz, H. and C. O'Donnell (1959) *Principles of Management* (New York: McGraw-Hill Book Company).

Krugman, P. (2007) *The Conscience of a Liberal* (New York: W. W. Norton & Company).

Krugman, P. (2009) *The Return of Depression Economics and The Crisis of 2008* (New York: W. W. Norton & Company).

Lacchini, M. (1988) *Strategia aziendale. Elementi di teoria* (Torino: Giappichelli).

Laghi, E. (2001) *Potere di controllo e misurazione del valore nelle aziende della new economy* (Roma: Centro Stampa De Vittoria).

Landsberger, H. A. (1958) *Hawthorne Revisited: a Plea for an Open City*, New York State School of Industrial and Labor Relations, Ithaca, Cornell University.

Larner, R. J. (1966) 'The 200 Largest Non-financial Corporations', *American Economic Review*, Vol. LVI, No. 4, part I, September.

Lazonick, W. and M. O'Sullivan (2000) 'Maximizing Shareholder Value: a New Ideology for Corporate Governance', *Economy and Society*, vol. 29, No. 1, pp. 13–35.

Le Goff, J. (2007a) *Il Medioevo* (Roma-Bari: Laterza).

Le Goff, J. (2007b) *L'uomo medievale* (Roma-Bari: Laterza).

Le Prestre de Vauban, H. S. (1707) *Project d'une dîme royale*, in AA.VV. (1964), *Les écrivains témoins du people* (Paris: J'ai Lu).

Learned, P. and A. T. Sproat (1966) *Organization Theory and Policy* (Homewood: R. D. Irwin, Inc).

Leavitt, H. J. (1958) *Managerial Psychology* (Chicago: The University of Chicago Press).

Leroy Beaulieu, P. (1891) *De la colonization chez les peuples moderns* (Paris: Guillaumin).

Lessico Universale Italiano, *Enciclopedia Italiana Treccani* (Roma: Istituto Poligrafico dello Stato).

Levitt, T. (1958) 'The Danger of Social Responsibility', *Harvard Business Review*, September–October.

Lewin K. (1935) *A Dynamic Theory of Personality* (New York: McGraw-Hill Book Company).

Lewin, K. (1936) *Principles of Topological Psychology* (New York: McGraw-Hill Book Company).

Lewin, K. (1951) *Field Theories in Social Science* (New York: Harper & Row).

Likert, R. (1959) 'Motivational Approach to Management Development', *Harvard Business Review*, July–August, pp. 35–82.

Likert, R. (1961) *New Patterns of Management* (New York: McGraw-Hill Book Company).

Likert, R. (1967) *The Human Organization: Its Management and Value* (New York: McGraw-Hill Book Company).

Likert, R. and S. E. Seashore (1963) 'Making Cost Control Work', *Harvard Business Review*, Vol. 46, No. 6, p. 96.

Lilley, S. (1980) *Rivoluzione industriale e progresso tecnico (1700–1914)*, in C. Cipolla (ed.), *Storia economica d'Europa*, vol. 3 (Torino: Utet), pp. 169–221.

Litterer, J. A. (1965) *The Analysis of Organizations* (New York: John Wiley and Sons).

Lo, A. (2005) 'Reconciling Efficient Markets with Behavioral Finance. The Adaptive Markets Hypothesis', *Journal of Investment Consulting*, Vol. 7, No. 2, pp. 21–44.

Lot, F. (1927) *La fin du monde antique et le debut du Moyen Age* (Paris: Albin Michel).

Lu, Xiaohe (1999), 'Economic and Ethical Values', in Kirti Bunchua, L. Fangtong, Y. Xuanmeng and Y. Wujn (eds), *The Bases of Values in a Time of Change, Chinese and Western Chinese Philosophical Studies XVI* (Washington, DC: The Council for Research in Values and Philosophy), at: www.crvp.org/book/Series03/III-16/chapter_vi.htm

Lussato, B. (1972) *Introduction critique aux théories des organisation* (Paris: Dunod).

Luzzatto, G. (1960) *Storia economica dell'età moderna e contemporanea, Parte seconda: L'età contemporanea* (Padova: Cedam).

Machiavelli, N. (1969) *Discorsi sopra la prima deca di Tito Livio, 1513–1519*, in *Opere* (Roma: Editori Riuniti).

Malik, F. (2010) *Idee chiare per dirigere meglio* (Milano: Il Sole 24 Ore).

Manca, C. (1995) *Introduzione alla storia dei sistemi economici in Europa dal feudalesimo al capitalismo*, parte II (Padova: Cedam).

Manca, C. (1999) *Formazione e trasformazione dei sistemi economici in Europa, dal feudalesimo al capitalismo* (Padova: Cedam).

March J. G. and H. A. Simon (1963) *Organizations* (New York: John Wiley and Sons).

Marchand, R. (1998) *Creating the Corporate Soul: the Rise of Public Relations and Corporate Imagery in American Big Business* (Berkeley: University of California Press).

Marchi, L. and S. Marasca (2009) *Le risorse immateriali nell'economia delle aziende. Profili di management* (Bologna: Il Mulino).

Maritain, J. (1948) *The Person and the Common Good* (London: Geoffrey Bles).

Marris, R. (1963) 'A Model of the "Managerial" Enterprise', *The Quarterly Journal of Economics*, Vol. 77, No. 2, pp. 185–209.

Marris, R. (1965) 'Les théories de la croissance dans l'entreprise', *Economie Appliquée*, Tome XVIII, nn. 1–2.

Marris, R. (1972) *La teoria economica del capitalismo manageriale* (Torino: Einaudi), original edition (1964), *The Economic Theory of 'Managerial' Capitalism* (London: Macmillan).

Maslow, A. H. (1943) 'A Theory of Human Motivation', *Psychological Review*, July.

Maslow, A. H. (1954) *Motivation and Personality* (New York: Harper & Row).

Mason, E. S. (1970) *La grande impresa nella società moderna* (Milano: Angeli).

Massaroni, E. and F. Ricotta (2009) 'Dal sistema impresa ai sistemi di imprese. Suggestioni e limiti delle reti d'impresa', *Rivista Sinergie*, n. 80, September–December.

Mathias, P. and M. M. Postan (1954) *The Cambridge Economic History of Europe*; Italian edition, V. Castronovo (ed., 1976) *Storia economica di Cambridge* (Torino: Einaudi).

Mayo, E. (1933) *The Human Problems of an Industrial Civilization* (New York: Macmillan).

Mayo, E. (1945) *The Social Problems of an Industrial Civilization* (Boston: Harvard University Press).

Mayo, E. (1947) *The Political Problems of an Industrial Civilization* (Boston: Harvard University Press).

Mayo, E. and G. F. Lombard (1944) *Teamwork and Labor Turnover in the Aircraft Industry of Southern California* (Boston: Harvard University Press).

Mazzarino, S. (1959) *La fine del mondo antico* (Milano: Garzanti).

McGregor, D. (1960) *The Human Side of Enterprise* (New York: McGraw-Hill Book Company).

McGregor, D. (1966) *Leadership and Motivation* (Cambridge, MA: MIT Press).

McGuire, J. W. (1964) *Theories of Business Behavior* (Englewood Cliffs: Prentice Hall).

McKernan, J. F. and P. O'Donnell (1998) 'Financial Accounting: Crisis and the Commodity Fetish', *Critical Perspectives on Accounting*, Vol. 9, No. 5, pp. 567–99.

Melé, D. (2002) 'Not Only Stakeholder Interests. The Firm Oriented toward the Common Good', in S. A. Cortright and M. J. Naughton (eds), *Rethinking the Purpose of Business* (Notre Dame: University of Notre Dame Press).

Melis, F. (1948) *La ragioneria nella civiltà minoica* (Roma: Casa Editrice della Rivista Italiana di Ragioneria).

Melis, G. (1993) *Introduzione all'economia aziendale. Impresa e sistema delle rilevazioni amministrative* (Torino: Giappichelli).

Mintzberg, H. (2009), 'Rebuilding Companies as Communities', *Harvard Business Review online*, July–August.

Mitchell, L. E. (2002) *Corporate Irresponsibility: American's Newest Export* (New Haven: Yale University Press).

Moller Gilbreth, L. (1914) *The Psychology of Management* (New York: Harper & Brothers).

Monsen, R. J., B. O. Saxberg and R. A. Sutermeister (1964) 'Les motivations sociologiques de l'entrepreneur dans l'entreprise moderne', *Economie Appliquée*, Tome XVII, n. 4.

Moscarini, F. (2007) 'Stakeholder management e responsabilità sociale d'impresa: quale legame?', *Dirigenza Bancaria*, Luglio-Agosto.

Moscarini, F. (2008a) *Impresa e responsabilità sociale. Un'analisi economico aziendale* (Roma: Edizioni Kappa).

Moscarini, F. (2008b) 'Testimonianza di caso: una ricerca internazionale sulla Responsabilità Sociale', *Le vie della buona impresa e della buona economia*, Quaderno n. 8, Convention of the Summer School Fondazione Ispirazione, Conegliano Veneto, 2–3 October.

Moscarini, F. (2008c) *Il management delle relazioni umane nell'economia dell'impresa moderna*, in L. Leuzzi, *Percorsi culturali per costruire la civiltà dell'amore* (Roma: Edizioni OCD).

Murru, F. (2009) *Responsabilità sociale d'impresa* (Milano: Angeli).

Nelson, J. (2005) 'Interpersonal Relations and Economics: Comments from a Feminist Perspective', in B. Gui and S. Robert (eds), *Economics and Social Interaction: Accounting for Interpersonal Relations* (Cambridge: Cambridge University Press).

Nye, J. S. Jr (2008) *The Powers to Lead* (New York: Oxford University Press).

Ogilvey, J. (1990) 'This Postmodern Business', *Marketing and Research Today*, 18 February.

Onida, P. (1971) *Economia d'azienda* (Torino: Utet).

Oricchio, G. (2010) *Mercati finanziari e valenza informativa del bilancio d'esercizio: una analisi fenomenologica* (Torino: Giappichelli).

O'Shaughnessy, J. (1968) *L'organisation des enterprises* (Paris: Dunod).

Paoloni, M. (1990) *Obiettivi d'impresa, motivazioni imprenditoriali e sistema decisionale* (Torino: Giappichelli).

Papandreou, A. (1952) 'Some Basic Problems in the Theory of the Firm', in B. F. Haley (ed.) *A Survey of Contemporary Economics* (Homewood: R. D. Irwin).

Penrose, E. (1959) *The Theory of the Growth of the Firm* (Oxford: Basil Blackwell).

Peppers, D. and M. Rogers (1993) *The One to One Future: Building Relationships One Customer at Time* (New York: Doubleday).

Pfiffner, J. M. and F. P. Sherwood (1960) *Administrative Organization* (Englewood Cliffs: Prentice Hall).

Pirenne, H. (1927) *Les villes du Moyen Age. Essai d'histoire économique et sociale* (Bruxelles: Lamertin).

Pirenne, H. (1973) *Mahomet et Charle Magne* (Paris: F. Alcan).

Porter, M. E. (1979) 'How Competitive Forces Shape Strategy', *Harvard Business Review*, March–April.

Prahalad, C. K. (2010) 'The Responsible Manager', *Harvard Business Review*, January–February.

Prahalad, C. K. and G. Hamel (1990) 'The Core Competence of the Corporation', *Harvard Business Review*, May–June.

Prandstraller, G. P. (2009) *L'imprenditore quaternario* (Milano: Angeli).

Proulx, S. (2005) *Il libro nero delle multinazionali americane* (Roma: Newton & Compton Editori).

Putnam, R. (1993) *Making Democracy Work* (Princeton: Princeton University Press).

Putnam, R. (2000) *Bowling Alone* (New York: Simon & Schuster).

Putnam R., L. Feldstein and D. Cohen (2003) *Better Together: Restoring the American Community* (New York: Simon & Schuster).

Rajan R. G. and L. Zingales (2004) *Salvare il capitalismo dai capitalisti* (Torino: Einaudi).

Rapoport, A. (1966) 'Mathematical Aspects of General Systems Theory', *General Systems* (yearbook of the Society of General Systems Research), Vol. XI.

Ratzinger, J. (1990) 'Concerning the Notion of Person in Theology', *Communio*, Vol. 17, No. 3, pp. 439–54.

Reich, R. B. (2008) *Supercapitalismo. Come cambia l'economia globale e i rischi per la democrazia* (Firenze: Fazi Editori).

Riccaboni, A. (1995) *Etica ed obiettivi d'impresa* (Padova: Cedam).

Rifkin, J. (2001) *The Age of Access. The New Culture of Hypercapitalism Where all of Life Is a Paid-for Experience* (New York: Tarcher/Putman).

Roethlisberger, F. J. and W. J. Dickson (1939) *Management and the Worker* (Cambridge, MA: Harvard University Press).

Roll, E. (1966) *Storia del pensiero economico* (Torino: Boringhieri).

Rossi, G. (2008) *Il mercato d'azzardo* (Milano: Adelphi).

Rostow, W. W. (1960) *The Stages of Economic Growth* (Cambridge: Cambridge University Press).

Rostow, W. W. (1962) *Gli stadi dello sviluppo economico* (Torino: Einaudi).

Rostow W. W. (1978) *The World Economy, History and Prospect* (Austin: University of Texas Press).

Rothschild, K. W. (1947) 'Price Theory and Oligopoly', the *Economic Journal*, Vol. 57, No. 227, pp. 324–36.

Rullani, C. E. (2010) *Rischio e valore della conoscenza. La nuova impresa della produzione immateriale* (Bologna: Il Mulino).

Rusconi, G. and M. Dorigatti (2004) *La responsabilità sociale d'impresa* (Milano: Angeli).

Sacconi, L. (2006) 'Corporate Social Responsibility (CSR) as a Model of "Extended" Corporate Governance. An Explanation Based on the Economic Theories of Social Contract, Reputation and Reciprocal Conformism', Liuc Papers n. 142, Serie Etica, Diritto ed Economia 10, suppl. a febbraio 2004.

Salvati, M. (1967) *Una critica alle teorie dell'impresa* (Roma: Edizioni dell'Ateneo).

Sancetta, G. (2007) *Gli intangibles e le performance dell'impresa* (Padova: Cedam).

Saraceno, P. (1967) *La produzione industriale* (Venezia: Libreria Universitaria Editrice).

Sargant Florence, P. (1961) *Ownership, Control and Success of Large Companies* (London: Sweet and Maxwell).

Savona, P. (1998) *Inflazione, disoccupazione e crisi monetarie* (Milano: Sperling & Kupfer).

Say, J. B. (1854) *Traité d'économie politique*, in *Biblioteca dell'Economista*, Vol. VII, Prima Serie (Torino: Pomba).

Schmookler, J. (1970) *Il progresso tecnologico e la moderna impresa americana*, in E. S. Mason (ed.), *La grande impresa nella società moderna* (Milano: F. Angeli).

Schumpeter, J. A. (1954) *History of Economic Analysis* (New York: Oxford University Press).

Sexton, W. P. (1970) *Organization Theories* (Columbus: C. E. Merrill Publishing Company).

Sciarelli, S. (2002) 'La produzione del valore allargato quale obiettivo dell'etica dell'impresa', *Finanza, Marketing e Produzione*, no. 4.

Sciarelli, S. (2007) *Etica e responsabilità sociale dell'impresa* (Padova: Cedam).

Shiller, R. J. (2008) *Finanza shock* (Milano: Egea).

Shonfield, A. (1967) *Il capitalismo moderno* (Milano: Etas Kompass).

Simon, H. A. (1952) 'Comments on the Theory of Organizations', *American Political Science Review*, Vol. 46, No. 4, pp. 1130–39.

Simon, H. A. (1958) *Administrative Behavior* (New York: The Macmillan Company).

Simon, H. A. (1965) 'The Architecture of Complexity', *Proceedings of the American Philosophical Society*, Vol. 106, No. 6, pp. 467–82.

Simon, H. A. and D. Zatta (2008) *Strategia e cultura d'impresa* (Milano: Il Sole 24Ore).

Skinner, D. and R. Sloan (2002) 'Earnings Surprises, Growth Expectations, and Stock Returns, or Don't Let an Earnings Torpedo Sink Your Portfolio', *Review of Accounting Studies*, Vol. 7, No. 3, pp. 289–312.

Smith, A. (1776) *An Inquiry into the Nature and Causes of the Wealth of Nations*, Italian translation (1975), *La ricchezza delle nazioni* (Torino: Utet).

Smith, T. (1995) *Contabilitá creativa* (Milano: Il Sole 24 Ore Libri).

Sombart, W. (1978) *Il borghese* (Milano: Longanesi).

Sparkes, R. (2004) 'From Mortmain to Adam Smith: Historical Insights on the Problem of Corporate Social Responsibility', unpublished paper.

Stampacchia, P. (2007) *Il governo dei processi di impresa. Principi e scelte* (Milano: McGraw-Hill Book Company).

Stiglitz, J. E. (2002) *Globalization and its Discontents* (London: Allen Lane).

Sulmasy, D. P. (2001) 'Four Basic Notions of the Common Good', *St John's Law Review*, Vol. 75, No. 2, p. 303–10.

Tabacco, G. (1974) *La storia politica e sociale. Dal tramonto dell'impero alle prime formazioni di Stati regionali*, in *Storia d'Italia, dalla caduta dell'impero romano al XVIII secolo*, Vol. II (Torino: Einaudi).

Tabb, W. K. (2002) *L'elefante amorale: la lotta per la giustizia sociale nell'era della globalizzazione* (Milano: Baldini e Castoldi).

Taleb, N. N. (2009) *Il cigno nero. Come l'improbabile governa la nostra vita* (Milano: Il Saggiatore).

Tannenbaum, R., I. R Weschler and F. Massarik (1961) *Leadership and Organization: a Behavioral Science Approach* (New York: McGraw-Hill Book Company).

Tannenbaum, R., I. R. Weschler and F. Massarik (1977) *La direzione degli uomini* (Milano: Angeli).

Taylor, F. W. (1911a) *The Principles of Scientific Management* (New York: Harper & Brothers).

Taylor, F. W. (1911b) *Shop Management* (New York: Harper & Brothers).

Taylor, F. W. (1947) *Scientific Management* (New York: Harper & Brothers).

Taylor, F. W. (1952) *L'organizzazione scientifica del lavoro* (Milano: Edizioni di Comunità). Includes: *Direzione di officina* (1903), *Principi di organizzazione scientifica del lavoro* (1911), *Deposizione di Taylor davanti alla Commissione Speciale della Camera dei Deputati* (1912).

Terry, G. (1955) *Principles of Management* (Homewood: R. D. Irwin).

Thurow, L. C. (2000) *Building Wealth. The New Rules for Individuals, Companies, and Nations in a Knowledge-Based Economy* (New York: HarperCollins).

Trequattrini, R. (2008) *Conoscenza ed economia aziendale. Elementi di teoria* (Napoli: Edizioni Scientifiche Italiane).

Vauchez, A. (2001) *Storia di Roma dall'antichità ad oggi. Roma medievale* (Bari: Laterza, special edition for Banca di Roma).

Verrecchia, R. (2001) 'Essays on Disclosure', *Journal of Accounting and Economics*, Vol. 32, Nos. 1–3.

Viganò, E. (1997) *Azienda. Primi contributi di una ricerca sistematica per un rinnovato concetto generale* (Padova: Cedam).

von Bertalanffy, L. (1971) *Teoria generale dei sistemi* (Milano: Istituto Librario Internazionale).

von Bertalanffy, L. and A. Rapoport (1959) 'Contributions to Organization Theory', *General Systems*, vol. IV (Ann Arbor: The University of Michigan).

Vroom, V. H. (1964) *Work and Motivation* (New York: John Wiley and Sons).

Watts, R. and J. L. Zimmerman (1990) *Positive Accounting Theory: a Ten Year Perspective, The Accounting Review*, Vol. 65, No. 1, pp. 131–56.

Wells, C. (1993) *Corporations and Criminal Responsibility* (Oxford: Oxford University Press).

Wiener, N. (1948) *Cybernetics* (New York: John Wiley and Sons).

Wiener, N. (1950) *The Human Use of Human Beings* (Boston: The Houghton Mifflin Company).

Williamson, O. E. (1964) *The Economics of Discretionary Behavior: Managerial Objectives in a Theory of the Firm* (Englewood Cliffs: Prentice Hall).

Wojtyla, K. (1979) *The Acting Person*, Analecta Husserliana, Vol. 10 (Dordrecht: D. Reidel Publishing Company).

Yunus, M. (2008) *Un mondo senza povertà* (Milano: Feltrinelli).

Zamagni, S. (2005) 'La critica delle critiche alla CSR e il suo ancoraggio etico', in L. Sacconi (ed.), *Guida Critica alla Responsabilità sociale e al governo dell'impresa* (Roma: Bancaria Editrice).

Zamagni, S. (2006) *L'economia come se la persona contasse: verso una teoria economica relazionale*, Working Paper no. 32, Facoltà di economia, Università di Bologna, Sede di Forlì.

Zanda, G. (1968) *La funzione direzionale di controllo* (Cagliari: STEF).

Zanda, G. (1974) *La grande impresa. Caratteristiche strutturali e di comportamento* (Milano: Giuffrè).

Zanda, G. (1979) *Nuovi modelli di organizzazione* (Padova: Cedam).

Zanda, G. (1984) *La valutazione dei dirigenti* (Padova: Cedam).

Zanda, G. (1984) *Direzione per obiettivi e razionalizzazione del governo d'impresa*, in *Scritti in onore del Prof. Domenico Amodeo* (Napoli: Liguori).

Zanda, G. (2006) *Lineamenti di economia aziendale*, 3rd edition (Roma: Kappa).

Zanda, S. (2009) *Evoluzione della qualità aziendale nell'ottica dell'eccellenza e della certificazione. Analisi delle strategie, dei metodi di gestione e dei costi* (Roma: Aracne).

Zander, A. (1950) 'Resistance to Change: Its Analysis and Prevention', *Advanced Management*, Vol. 15, No. 2.

Index

American property bubble   138
American Revolution   41

balance between total supply and
    demand   67–70

collapse of the stock market   69–70
collateralized debt obligations
    139–140, 159
company management: its historical
    evolution   1
consumers' organizations   119
control of the real functioning of the
    corporate system   74
coordination of the prices of
    international trade   116
corporate self-regulation   131
creation of value   174, 180, 183, 233
credit crunch   142
credit default swap   140
Christian Social Thought   189–211
    Aristotelian-Thomistic tradition   202
    business ethics   190–2
    civic economy   207
    common good   194–6, 200–3
    Corporate Social Responsibility
        (CSR)   190–211
    individualism   191
    personal projects enterprise strategy
        (PPES)   191
    personalist approach to business
        194, 207–9
    social contract   191
cultural capitalism   175
cyberspace   172, 175, 179

democratic capitalism   134
deregulation   113, 118–120, 132,
    138–144
development of counter-powers   131,
    143
dispersion or atomization of share
    ownership   76, 137

dollar, non-convertible   117
dollar, exchange standard is
    abandoned   116

economic and financial crisis
    135–145
    accepting increasing risks   138
    bank failures   141
    behaviour without ethics   138
    capacity to repay loans   139
    financialization of the
        economy   142
    rating agencies   140–1
    remuneration of top
        managers   137
    speculative superstructure   141
    split-up credit risk   139
    structured financial products
        144
    toxic products   140–1
efficient-market hypothesis and
    financial crisis   155–168
    accounting standards
        Financial Accounting Standards
            Board   159
        International Accounting
            Standards Board   160
    accounting theory
        positive accounting behaviour
            157
        income-smoothing hypothesis
            162
    banking business models
        originate-to-distribute   156
        originate-and-hold   157
        originate-and-manage   157
    finance theory
        adaptive market hypothesis   157,
            161
        efficient-market hypothesis   155,
            157–158
    valuation principles
        mark–to–market   155, 159

mark–to–model   159
ethical integrity   112
experience industry   175–8

fall in profits   113–19, 125
financialization of the economy
      124–6
financial shareholding managerial
      capitalism, defined
      111–154
   maximization of profits and of the
      value of the company
      119–123
   financialization of business
      124–145
   financial incentives   123
   short-term point of view   122–3
   speculative intention   123–4
   value of stock options   123
firm, defined   2
First Industrial Revolution   41–51
   application of the scientific
      method   41–3
   development of the London
      financial market   47
   Encyclopédie   43
   factories directed by capitalist-
      entrepreneurs   43–4
   financial middle class   48
   inventions in cotton industry   45
   organization of industrial
      production   44–9
   the 18th century defined as the
      century of 'enlightenment'   41
   the establishment of the capitalist
      spirit   41, 47
   the middle class   47
   use of fixed and circulating
      capital   44
   water power   44–5
   wool sector   46
first mover   181–2
fixed exchange rates   117
French Revolution   41
full employment   68, 69, 119, 122

Great Crash of 1929   67–70
Great Depression   53, 67–70
Great Economic Crisis   67–71

Great War   53, 67–70
growth, corporate as a goal of
      corporation   89–98, 111

hollow corporation   173

innovative services   173, 175, 178,
      181
innovative technologies   173
institutional investors   121, 124, 136,
      142
institutional theory   138
insurance companies   124, 136, 137,
      139, 141
intangible resources to manage
      enterprises: the market and
      the production of cultural
      goods   169–188
intellectual managerial capitalism
      7–8, 240–2
internal and external crises of
      economic systems   113–19
investment banks   135, 159, 238
investment vehicles   139, 144
irresponsible behaviour of global
      finance   135–145, 238
joint-stock company   32, 129
irresponsible corporation, the
      124–145
   defined   126–9
   links between financial
      shareholding managerial
      capitalism and appearance of
      the irresponsible corporation
      135–145
   maximization of income and share
      value   119–123
   transfer to stakeholders of
      costs   127
   opportunistic behaviour in the field
      of politics   127
   language and logic of business
      does not draw inspiration from
      ethics   127
   lobbying activities   127, 133
      illegal behaviour   128
   main provisions to adopt
      to face irresponsible
      corporations   129–135

irresponsible corporation,
the – *continued*
the present economic-financial
crisis 135–145
irresponsible behaviour of global
finance 135–145
'invisible hand' 71, 112, 117

Keynesian school, adoption of
theoretical precepts of 70

lasting commercial relationships
179
leasing 173, 178, 182, 239
leverage ratio 90–1, 98
light company 173–4

management studies
decision-making processes and
human resources management
81–95
basic research carried out on
human motivation 86
during managerial capitalism
89–97
effectiveness and efficiency of
firms in complex and dynamic
situations 82
psycho-social investigations 85
routine problems 81
the humanistic school 84
managerial motivations and the goals
of the great corporation
89–95, 98–103
the motivational system 90, 101
safety needs 87, 181
normal and usual dividends 97–8
financing indispensable
investments 91, 97–8
growing rates of return,
increasing rate of size,
development and objectives of
social responsibility 92
the utility function of professional
managers 98–103
managerial revolution 65–111
defined 71
decisional structure 74–5
economic subject 74

mature corporation 75, 78–81,
99, 103
oligopolies and market dynamism
71
pluralistic decisional structure
73
power of non-owner managers in
large corporations 76, 77–81
separation between ownership
and control 77–81
strategic decisions 71, 74
technological progress 72
the techno-structure 73–74, 78
professionalization of the
function of management 75
the capitalistic system
(managerial capitalism)
and progress of the world
economy 80–1
the so-called 'great compression'
80
management process 86–94
managers, awakening of conscience of
129–135
market economy 55, 132, 144, 243
maximization of profit and normal
profit 71, 100, 132, 138,
212
minimum viable size of a firm 57,
72
multimedia network 171–3, 240–1
mutual funds 136

new marketing 180, 240
new types of knowledge: the
knowledge revolution
111–154

OPEC cartel 116
organizational inertia 239
Ottoman Empire, decline 29
owner-entrepreneur 75–6

patterns of management 212–36
a new theory, and a good theory of
management 234
effective leadership model 225–34
fusion process 225
hard management style 221, 233

hierarchical organizational
  structures 213
hierarchy of ends and means 216
hierarchy of functions 216
hierarchy of objectives 216
intrinsic compensation 227
leader as force of attraction 217–18,
  228, 230
new models of management 224–8
positive entropy 215
revision of management
  philosophy 221
self-control 213–226
self-direction 227
self-discipline 227–8
soft management style 222
'speak softly and carry a big
  stick' 222
'Theory X' 221, 223, 226, 231
'Theory Y' 226
political system which influences
  the objectives, values and
  organization of society 1–2
power in society and in firms by
  landowners 8–40
power associated with land
  ownership 8–17
Aegean–European civilization 9
ancient Greek civilization 9
hedonism and private
  property 10
slavery 11, 22
Roman world 8–21
crisis of the Empire 14
first phase of feudalism, the 17–21
medieval civilization 22–4, 26
commendatio 18
Roman barbarian kingdoms 16–
  18
Merovingians and Carolingians
  19
beneficium 18–19, 25
pars dominica and *pars
  massaricia* 20
second phase of feudalism, the 21–6
change in the development of
  European feudalism 21
progress in agricultural
  techniques 21

medieval cities 23
the activity of the merchant-
  entrepreneur 23–26
colonial expansion, Dutch republic/
  Netherlands and England 30
the large merchant bankers 30
mercantile capitalism 26–33
the physiocrats 33
private equity funds 136, 137
propensity to liquidity (of savers) 68
public company 78, 111

rating agencies 140
real economy 141, 142
reawakening of shareholders 118,
  123–137
policies to increase operational
  efficiency 121
participation of shareholders in
  strategic management 121
tight control over decisions 121
choice of the members of the
  techno-structure 122
a new model of corporate
  behaviour 122
reduction of interest rates permits the
  absorption of any quantity of
  savings 68
relational marketing 239–243
relationship capital 179–180
relationship between profitability and
  increase in company size 95–7
relationship between objectives of
  social responsibility and rate of
  profitability and company size
  development 97–8
reliability of clients 143
remuneration of top managers 137
resistance to change 169, 230–1
rigidity of the amount of
  investments 58, 62, 68

Say's law of markets 69
Second Industrial Revolution 52–64
growing use of capital 52, 57–8
institutionalization of pure
  and applied research
  and development within
  companies 55–7

Second Industrial Revolution –
continued
  motivation of personnel 52, 58
  new technologies 52, 58
  oligopoly and high
    profitability 54–5
  the use of electricity 52, 53–4
  role of joint-stock companies 58
  shift in power in favour of
    capital 52
self-financing 79
social empathy 133
social legitimization 133, 242
social state 113
sovereign funds 136
speculative (activities) 111–112, 123,
  136–144
strategic alliances 174
strategic management 174, 182–4
structured investments 139
student protest movement 119
studies and practices in the field of
  management 58–62
sub-prime loans 139–141
style of leadership 124, 247
system of evaluation of the system of
  floating exchange rates 117

task management 59–60, 219
tax on international speculative
  transactions 144
technological maturity 52, 54, 58,
  65, 72
theatre companies 176
theory of systems 84
Third Industrial Revolution 169,
  238
'too big to fail' 138
trust funds 136

utility function (preference function)
  71, 89–90, 94, 181–184
  in proprietor-managed companies
    75
  in managerial capitalism 98–103
  in financial shareholding
    managerial capitalism 122–6
  in intellectual capitalism 81, 184

valuation ratio 90–1, 97–8, 240
value of stock options 123
virtual world 170, 175–6, 240
'visible hand', the 71, 112–7

workers' protest movement 115